WHAT EVERYBODY SHOULD KNOW ABOUT PATENTS, TRADEMARKS AND COPYRIGHTS

WHAT EVERYBODY SHOULD KNOW ABOUT PATENTS, TRADEMARKS AND COPYRIGHTS

INCLUDES FULL TEXT
AND SUMMARY
OF THE
NEW COPYRIGHT LAW

Edited by
Donald M. Dible

The Entrepreneur Press

Published in 1978 by

The Entrepreneur Press
3422 Astoria Circle
Fairfield, California 94533

Printed in The United States of America

TABLE OF CONTENTS

PART ONE

WHAT EVERYBODY SHOULD KNOW ABOUT PATENTS

PART TWO

WHAT EVERYBODY SHOULD KNOW ABOUT TRADEMARKS

PART THREE

WHAT EVERYBODY SHOULD KNOW ABOUT COPYRIGHTS

APPENDIX

FULL TEXT OF THE NEW COPYRIGHT LAW

INTRODUCTION

PATENTS, TRADEMARKS, AND COPYRIGHTS

Let's talk about creativity and its rewards. Imagine that you have designed a product, authored a book, composed a song, written a play, invented a process, or marketed a product or service under a unique brand name you have conceived. In so doing, you have manifested a form of creativity. In particular, you have manifested a form of creativity that probably should entitle you to economic reward. Without a system of protective measures, however, the results of your creative efforts could be exploited by anybody—without your receiving just compensation. Deprived of economic incentive—it seems reasonable to suggest—many individuals would be reluctant or unwilling to labor the long hours and risk the capital necessary to bring their creative ideas to fruition.

Recognizing the need to nurture and reward creativity so that our society may continue to enjoy the benefits of new products, services, and works of art, federal and state agencies have seen fit to provide for periods of monopoly for those who serve society through their creativity. In particular, the U.S. Patent Office (an agency of the U.S. Department of Commerce) regulates patents and trademarks while the Copyright Office (an agency of the Library of Congress) regulates copyrights. These agencies monitor, and provide or deny, statutory protection for creative works.

This book represents a distillation and compilation of the latest information available covering trademarks, patents, and copyrights. Each topic is presented in a manner so as to stand alone. Furthermore, each topic is covered in a simple style designed to communicate all of the essential points with a minimum of legalistic jargon.

While most of the material presented is clear and unambiguous, you must recognize that rarely is the law simple in its interpretation. That's why this country has such a phenomenal number of lawyers (twenty times as many per capita as Japan). While reading this book, remember the admonition of Thomas Alva Edison, this nation's most famous inventor: "A patent is a license for a lawsuit." The same may also be said of trademarks and copyrights. Infringement of patents, trademarks, and copyrights usually constitutes a civil matter. As a holder of a patent, trademark, or copyright that has been infringed, you have much in common with a landlord whose tenants have failed to pay the rent. Beyond pleading and threatening, your only recourse to collect what is rightly yours is to go to court. Normally, this means you go to the expense of hiring an attorney. No government agency will go in and help you collect the rent (analogous to extracting royalties) or evict your tenants (analogous to making your infringer stop and desist) without your securing a directive from the courts. You must initiate the action, initially, and you must pay the court costs out of your own pocket. Of course, if you win your infringement case, the courts may rule that you receive compensation for your actual losses, reimbursement for court costs, and—if you can prove malicious intent on the part of the infringer—punitive damages.

Once again, let me emphasize: infringement is a civil, not a criminal, matter. The cops will not arrest your infringer just because you dial 911, the almost universal police emergency telephone number, and holler, "I'm being had."

There! You have been warned. If you still have an uncontrollable urge to create (and I sincerely hope you do), go do it with your eyes open, a pencil in one hand, and a sword in the other.

Donald M. Dible
Fairfield, California

PART ONE

What Everybody
Should Know About

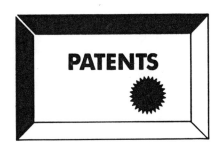

FUNCTIONS OF THE PATENT AND TRADEMARK OFFICE

The Patent and Trademark Office is an agency of the U.S. Department of Commerce, the Department of the Federal Government primarily concerned with assisting and encouraging the development of the business and industry of the United States.

The role of the Patent and Trademark Office in carrying out this mission is to provide patent protection for inventions and the registration of trademarks to serve the interests of inventors and businesses with respect to their inventions and corporate and product identifications, to advise and assist other bureaus and offices of the Department of commerce and other agencies of the Government

other bureaus and offices of the Department of Commerce and other agencies

other bureaus and offices of the Department of Commerce and other agencies of the Government in matters involving patents and inventions and the transfer of technology, and, through the preservation, classification, and dissemination of patent information, to aid and encourage innovation and the scientific and technical advancement of the Nation.

In discharging its duties, the Patent and Trademark Office examines applications and grants patents on inventions when applicants are entitled to them; it publishes and disseminates patent information, records assignments of patents, maintains search files of U.S. and foreign patents and a search room for public use in examining issued patents and records, and supplies copies of patents and official records to the public. Similar functions are performed relating to trademarks.

PURPOSE OF THIS INFORMATION

The purpose of this information is to give the reader some general information about patents and the operations of the Patent and Trademark Office. It attempts to answ

The purpose of this information is to give the reader some general information about patents and the operations of the Patent and Trademark Office. It attempts to answer many of the questions commonly asked of the Patent and Trademark Office but is not intended to be a comprehensive textbook on patent law or a guide for the patent lawyer. Consequently, many details are omitted and complications have been avoided as much as possible. It is hoped that this information will be useful to inventors and prospective applicants for patents, to students, and to others who may be interested in patents by giving them a brief general introduction to the subject.

Additional information may be obtained from the Patent and Trademark Office publications *Patent Laws and Title 37, CFR.* The Patent and Trademark Office does not publish any textbooks on patent law.

WHAT IS A PATENT?

A patent for an invention is a grant by the Government to an inventor of certain rights.

A patent is granted by the Government acting through the Patent and Trademark Office.

The subject matter of the patent is an invention.

The person entitled to receive the patent grant is the inventor (or his heirs or assigns).

The duration of the patent grant is 17 years.

The right conferred by the patent grant extends throughout the United States and its territories and possessions.

The right conferred by the patent grant is, in the language of the statute and of the grant itself, "the right to exclude others from making, using, or selling" the invention. What is granted is not the right to make, use, or sell, but the right to exclude others from making, using, or selling the invention.

Most of the statements in the preceding paragraphs will be explained in greater detail in later sections.

Some persons occasionally confuse patents, copyrights, and trademarks. Although there may be some resemblance in the rights of these three kinds of intangible property, they are completely different and serve different purposes.

Copyrights

Copyright protects the writings of an author against copying. Literary, dramatic, musical and artistic works are included within the protection of the copyright law, which in some instances also confers performing and recording rights. The copyright goes to the form of expression rather than to the subject matter of the writing. A description of a machine could be copyrighted as a writing, but this would only prevent others from copying the description—it would not prevent others from writing a description of their own or from making and using the machine. Copyrights are registered in the Copyright Office in the Library of Congress and the Patent and Trademark Office has nothing whatever to do with copyrights. Information concerning copyrights may be obtained by addressing: Register of Copyrights, Library of Congress, Washington, D.C. 20540.

Trademarks

A trademark relates to any word, name, symbol or device which is used in trade with goods to indicate the source or origin of the goods and to distinguish them from the goods of others. Trademark rights may be used to prevent others from using a confusingly similar mark, but not to prevent others from making the same goods or from selling them under a non-confusing mark. Similar rights may be acquired in marks used in the sale or advertising of services (service marks). Trademarks and service marks which are used in interstate or foreign commerce may be registered in the Patent and Trademark Office.

PATENT LAWS

The Constitution of the United States gives Congress the power to enact laws relating to patents, in Article 1, section 8, which reads "Congress shall have power . . . to promote the progress of science and useful arts, by securing for limited times to authors and inventors the exclusive right to their respective writings and discoveries." Under this power Congress has from time to time enacted various laws relating to patents. The first patent law was enacted in 1790. The law now in effect is a general revision which was enacted July 19, 1952, and which came into effect January 1, 1953. This law is reprinted in a pamphlet entitled *Patent Laws,* which is sold by the Superintendent of Documents, U.S. Government Printing Office, Washington, D.C. 20402.

The patent law specifies the subject matter for which a patent may be obtained and the conditions for patentability. The law establishes the Patent and Trademark Office for administering the law relating to the granting of patents, and contains various other provisions relating to patents.

WHAT CAN BE PATENTED

The patent law specifies the general field of subject matter that can be patented, and the conditions under which a patent may be obtained.

In the language of the statute, any person who "invents or discovers any new and useful process, machine, manufacture, or composition of matter, or any new and useful improvements thereof, may obtain a patent," subject to the conditions and requirements of the law. By the word "process" is meant a process or method, and new processes, primarily industrial or technical processes, may be patented. The term "machine" used in the statute needs no explanation. The term "manufacture" refers to articles which are made, and includes all manufactured articles. The term "composition of matter" relates to chemical compositions and may include mixtures of ingredients as well as new chemical compounds. These classes of subject matter taken together include practically everything which is made by man and the processes for making them.

The Atomic Energy Act of 1954 excludes the patenting of inventions useful solely in the utilization of special nuclear material or atomic energy for atomic weapons.

The statute specifies that the subject matter must be "useful." The term "useful" in this connection refers to the condition that the subject matter has a useful purpose and also includes operativeness, that is, a machine which will not operate to perform the intended purpose would not be called useful. Alleged inventions of perpetual motion machines are refused patents.

Interpretations of the statute by the courts have defined the limits of the field of subject matter which can be patented, thus it has been held that methods of doing business and printed matter cannot be patented. In the case of mixtures of ingredients, such as medicines, a patent cannot be granted unless there is more to the mixture than the effect of its components. (So-called patent medicines are ordinarily not patented; the phrase "patent medicine" in this connection does not have the meaning that the medicine is patented.) It is often said that a patent cannot be obtained upon a mere idea or suggestion. The patent is granted upon the new machine, manufacture, etc., as has been said, and not upon the idea or suggestion of the new machine. As will be stated later, a complete description of the actual machine or other subject matter sought to be patented is required.

NOVELTY AND OTHER CONDITIONS FOR OBTAINING A PATENT

In order for an invention to be patentable it must be new as defined in the statute. The statute provides that an invention cannot be patented if—

"(a) The invention was known or used by others in this country, or patented or described in a printed publication in this or a foreign country, before the invention thereof by the applicant for patent, or

"(b) The invention was patented or described in a printed publication in this or a foreign country or in public use or on sale in this country more than one year prior to the date of the application for patent in the United States. . . .

If the invention has been described in a printed publication anywhere in the world, or if it has been in public use or on sale in this country before the date that the applicant made his invention, a patent cannot be obtained. If the invention has been described in a printed publication anywhere, or has been in public use or on sale in this country more than one year before the date on which an application for patent is filed in this country, a valid patent cannot be obtained. In this connection it is immaterial when the invention was made, or whether the printed publication or public use was by the inventor himself or by someone else. If the inventor describes the invention in a printed publication or uses the invention publicly, or places it on sale, he must apply for a patent before one year has gone by, otherwise any right to a patent will be lost.

Even if the subject matter sought to be patented is not exactly shown by the prior art, and involves one or more differences over the most nearly similar thing already known, a patent may still be refused if the differences would be obvious. The subject matter sought to be patented must be sufficiently different from what has been used or described before so that it may be said to amount to invention over the prior art. Small advances that would be obvious to a person having ordinary skill in the art are not considered inventions capable of being patented. For example, the substitution of one material for another, or changes in size, are ordinarily not patentable.

THE UNITED STATES PATENT AND TRADEMARK OFFICE

Congress has established the United States Patent and Trademark Office to perform the function of issuing patents on behalf of the Government. The

Patent and Trademark Office as a distinct bureau may be said to date from the year 1802 when a separate official in the Department of State who became known as "Superintendent of Patents" was placed in charge of patents. The revision of the patent laws enacted in 1836 reorganized the Patent and Trademark Office and designated the official in charge as Commissioner of Patents and Trademarks. The Patent and Trademark Office remained in the Department of State until 1849 when it was transferred to the Department of the Interior and in 1925 it was transferred to the Department of Commerce, in which Department it is today.

The chief functions of the Patent and Trademark Office are to administer the patent laws as they relate to the granting of letters patent for inventions, and to perform other duties relating to patents. It examines applications for patents to ascertain if the applicants are entitled to patents under the law, and grants the patents when they are so entitled; it publishes issued patents and various publications concerning patents and patent laws, records assignments of patents, maintains a search room for the use of the public to examine issued patents and records, supplies copies of records and other papers, and the like. Analogous and similar functions are performed with respect to the registration of trademarks. The Patent and Trademark Office has no jurisdiction over questions of infringement and the enforcement of patents, nor over matters relating to the promotion or utilization of patents or inventions.

The head of the Office is the Commissioner of Patents and Trademarks and his staff includes several assistant commissioners of patents and other officials. As head of the Office, the Commissioner superintends or performs all duties respecting the granting and issuing of patents and the registration of trademarks; exercises general supervision over the entire work of the Patent and Trademark Office; prescribes the rules, subject to the approval of the Secretary of Commerce, for the conduct of proceedings in the Patent and Trademark Office and for recognition of attorneys and agents; decides various questions brought before him by petition as prescribed by the rules, and performs other duties necessary and required for the administration of the Patent and Trademark Office and the performance of its functions.

The examination of applications for patents is the largest and most important function of the Patent and Trademark Office. The work is divided among a number of examining groups, each group having jurisdiction over certain assigned fields of invention. Each group is headed by a group director and staffed by a number of examiners. The examiners perform the work of examining applications for patents and determine whether patents can be granted. An appeal can be taken to the Board of Appeals from their decisions refusing patents and a review by the Commissioner of Patents and Trademarks may be had on other matters by petition. The examiners also determine when an interference exists between pending applications, or a pending application and a patent, institute interference proceedings in such cases and hear and decide certain preliminary questions raised by contestants.

In addition to the examining groups, the Patent and Trademark Office has a number of sections, divisions, and branches which perform various other services, such as receiving and distributing mail, receiving new applications, handling sales of printed copies of patents, making copies of records, inspecting drawings, recording assignments, and so on.

At the present time the Patent and Trademark Office has about 2,700 employees, of whom about half are examiners and others with technical and legal training. Patent applications are received at the rate of over 90,000 per year. The Patent and Trademark Office receives over three million pieces of mail each year.

PUBLICATIONS OF THE PATENT AND TRADEMARK OFFICE

Patents.—The specification and accompanying drawings of all patents are published on the day they are granted and printed copies are sold to the public by the Patent and Trademark Office. Over 4 million patents have been issued.

Printed copies of any patent identified by its patent number, may be purchased from the Patent and Trademark Office at a cost of 50 cents each, postage free, except plant patents which are $1.00 each and design patents which are 20 cents each.

Official Gazette of the United States Patent and Trademark Office.—The *Official Gazette* of the United States Patent and Trademark Office is the official journal relating to patents and trademarks. It has been published weekly since January 1872 (replacing the old "Patent Office Reports"), and is now issued each Tuesday, simultaneously with the weekly issue of the patents. It contains an abstract and a selected figure of the drawings of each patent granted on that day; notices of patent and trademark suits; indexes of patents and patentees; list of patents available for license or sale; and much general information such as orders, notices, changes in rules, changes in classification, etc. The *Official Gazette* is sold on subscription and by single copies by the Superintendent of Documents, U.S. Government Printing Office, Washington, D.C. 20402.

Since July, 1952, the illustrations and claims of the patents have been arranged in the *Official Gazette* according to the Patent and Trademark Office classification of subject matter, permitting ready reference to patents in any particular field. Street addresses of patentees have been published since May 24, 1960, and a geographical index of residents of inventors has been included since May 18, 1965. Copies of the *Official Gazette* may be found in public libraries of larger cities.

Index of Patents.—This annual index to the *Official Gazette* is currently issued in two volumes, one an index of patentees and the other an index by subject matter of the patents. Sold by Superintendent of Documents.

Index of Trademarks.—An annual index of registrants of trademarks. Sold by Superintendent of Documents.

Manual of Classification.—A looseleaf book containing a list of all the classes and subclasses of inventions in the Patent and Trademark Office classification system, a subject matter index, and other information relating to classification. Substitute pages are issued from time to time. Annual subscription includes the basic manual and substitute pages. Sold by Superintendent of Documents.

Classification Definitions.—Contain the changes in classification of patents as well as definitions of new and revised classes and subclasses. Sold by Patent and Trademark Office.

Weekly Class Sheets.—Lists showing classification of each patent in the weekly issue of the *Official Gazette.* Sold on annual subscription by Patent and Trademark Office.

Patent Laws.—A compilation of patent laws in force. Sold by Superintendent of Documents.

37 Code of Federal Regulations.—Includes rules of Practice for Patents, Trademarks and Copyrights. Available from the Superintendent of Documents.

Trademark Rules of Practice of the Patent and Trademark Office With Forms and Statutes.—Rules governing the procedures in the Patent and Trademark Office in Trademark matters and a compilation of trademark laws in force. Sold by Superintendent of Documents.

Directory of Registered Patent Attorneys and Agents Arranged by States and Countries.—A geographical listing of patent attorneys and agents registered to practice before the U.S. Patent and Trademark Office. Sold by Superintendent of Documents.

Manual of Patent Examining Procedure.—A loose-leaf manual which serves primarily as a detailed reference work on patent examining practice and procedure for the Patent and Trademark Office's Examining Corps. Subscription service includes basic manual, quarterly revisions, and change notices. Sold by Superintendent of Documents.

Guide for Patent Draftsmen.—Patent and Trademark Office requirements for patent drawings. Illustrated. Sold by Superintendent of Documents.

The Story of the United States Patent Office.—A chronological account of the development of the U.S. Patent and Trademark Office and patent system and of inventions which had unusual impact on the American economy and society. Sold by Superintendent of Documents.

GENERAL INFORMATION AND CORRESPONDENCE

All business with the Patent and Trademark Office should be transacted in writing. The personal attendance of applicants at the Office is unnecessary. Mail should be addressed to *"COMMISSIONER OF PATENTS AND TRADEMARKS, WASHINGTON, D.C.* 20231." The physical location of the Office is Crystal Plaza, 2021 Jefferson Davis Highway, Arlington, Va.

Applicants and attorneys are required to conduct their business with the Office with decorum and courtesy. Papers presented in violation of this requirement will be returned.

A separate letter (but not necessarily in a separate envelope) should be written in relation to each distinct subject of inquiry such as assignments for recording, payment of issue fees, orders for printed copies of patents, orders for photographic copies of records, and requests for other services. None of these should be included with letters responding to Office actions in applications (p. 19).

When a letter concerns a patent, it should state the name of the patentee, the invention, and the patent number and date.

In making inquiry concerning the status of his application, the inventor should be sure to give its serial number and filing date and the Group Art unit number.

The zip code should be included as part of the address in all correspondence.

An order for a copy of an assignment must give the book and page or reel and frame of the record, as well as the name of the inventor; otherwise, an additional charge is made for the time consumed in making a search for the assignment.

Applications for patents are not open to the public, and no information concerning them is released except on written authority of the applicant, his assignee, or his attorney, or when necessary to the conduct of the business of the Office. Patents and related records, including records of any decisions, the records of assignments other than those relating to assignments of patent applications, books, and other records and papers in the Office are open to the public. They may be inspected in the Patent and Trademark Office Search Room or copies may be ordered.

The Office cannot respond to inquiries concerning the novelty and patentability of an invention in advance of the filing of an application; give advice as to possible infringement of a patent; advise of the propriety of filing an application; respond to inquiries as to whether or to whom any alleged invention has been patented; act as an expounder of the patent law or as counselor for individuals, except in deciding questions arising before it in regularly filed cases. Information of a general nature may be furnished either directly or by supplying or calling attention to an appropriate publication.

LIBRARY, SEARCH ROOM SEARCHES

The Scientific Library of the Patent and Trademark Office at Crystal Plaza, 2021 Jefferson Davis Highway, Arlington, Va., has available for public use over 120,000 volumes of scientific and technical books in various languages, about 90,000 bound volumes of periodicals devoted to science and technology, the official journals of foreign patent offices, and over 8 million foreign patents in bound volumes. (In many cases there are two sets of foreign patents, one set arranged in numerical order and another set arranged according to the subject classification system of the country of origin of the patents.)

A Search Room is provided where the public may search and examine United States patents granted since 1836. Patents are arranged according to the Patent and Trademark Office classification system of over 300 subject classes and 64,000 subclasses. By searching in these classified patents, it is possible to determine, before actually filing an application, whether an invention has been anticipated by a United States patent, and it is also possible to obtain the information contained in patents relating to any field of endeavor. The Search Room contains a set of United States patents arranged in numerical order and a complete set of the *Official Gazette*.

A Record Room also is maintained where the public may inspect the records and files of issued patents and other open records.

Applicants and their attorneys or agents may examine their own cases in the Record Room, and public records may be examined in the Scientific Library, Search Room, or Record Room, as the case may be. Applicants, their attorneys or agents, and the general public are not entitled to use the records and files in the examiners' rooms.

The Search Room is open from 8 a.m. to 8 p.m. Monday through Friday except on legal holidays.

Since a patent is not always granted when an application is filed, many inventors attempt to make their own investigation before applying for a patent. This may be done in the Search Room of the Patent and Trademark Office, and to a limited extent in some public libraries. Patent attorneys or agents may be employed to make a so-called preliminary search through the prior United States patents to discover if the particular device or one similar to it has been shown in some prior patent. This search is not always as complete as that made by the Patent and Trademark Office during the examination of an application, but only serves, as its name indicates, a preliminary purpose. For this reason, the Patent and Trademark Office examiner may, and often does, reject claims in an application on the basis of prior patents or publications not found in the preliminary search.

Those who cannot come to the Search Room may order from the Patent and Trademark Office copies of lists of original patents or of cross-referenced patents contained in the subclasses comprising the field of search, and inspect printed copies of the patents in a library which has a numerically arranged set of patents. These libraries and their locations are: Albany, N.Y., University of State of New York; Atlanta, Ga., Georgia Tech Library; Boston, Mass., Public Library; Buffalo, N.Y., Buffalo and Erie County Public Library; Chicago, Ill., Public Library; Cincinnati, Ohio, Public Library; Cleveland, Ohio, Public Library; Columbus, Ohio, Ohio State University Library; Detroit, Mich., Public Library; Kansas City, Mo., Linda Hall Library; Los Angeles, Calif., Public Library; Madison, Wis., State Historical Society of Wisconsin; Milwaukee, Wis., Public Library; Newark, N.J., Public Library; New York, N.Y., Public Library; Philadelphia, Pa., Franklin Institute; Pittsburgh, Pa., Carnegie Library; Providence, R.I., Public Library; St. Louis, Mo., Public Library; Stillwater, Okla., Oklahoma Agricultural and Mechanical College; Sunnyvale, Calif., Public Library[1]; Toledo, Ohio, Public Library.

The Patent and Trademark Office has also prepared on microfilm lists of the numbers of the patents issued in each of its subclasses, and many libraries have purchased copies of these lists. In libraries which have the lists and a copy of the Manual of Classification, and also a set of patent copies or the *Official Gazette,* it will be unnecessary for the searcher to communicate with the Patent and Trademark Office before commencing his search, as he can learn from the Manual of Classification the subclasses which his search should include, then identify the numbers of the patents in these subclasses from the microfilm lists, and examine the patent copies so identified, or the disclosures of these patents in the *Official Gazette* volumes.

While the classification printed on any patent is correct at the time the patent is issued, it should be noted that the constantly expanding arts often require reclassification. As a result, the classification indicated on the patent may be incorrect at a later date.

ATTORNEYS AND AGENTS

The preparation of an application for patent and the conducting of the proceedings in the Patent and Trademark Office to obtain the patent is an undertaking requiring the knowledge of patent law and Patent and Trademark Office practice as well as knowledge of the scientific or technical matters involved in the particular invention.

The inventor may prepare his own application and file it in the Patent and Trademark Office and conduct the proceedings himself, but unless he is familiar with these matters or studies them in detail, he may get into considerable difficulty. While a patent may be obtained in many cases by persons not skilled in this work, there would be no assurance that the patent obtained would adequately protect the particular invention.

Most inventors employ the services of persons known as patent attorneys or patent agents. The statute gives the Patent and Trademark Office the power to make rules and regulations governing the recognition of patent attorneys and agents to practice before the Patent and Trademark Office, and persons who are not recognized by the Patent and Trademark Office for this practice are not permitted by law to represent inventors. The Patent and Trademark Office maintains a register of attorneys and agents. To be admitted to this register, a person must comply with the regulations prescribed by the Office, which now require a showing that the person is of good moral character and of good repute and that he has the legal and scientific and technical qualifications necessary to enable him to render applicants for patents valuable service. Certain of these qualifications must be demonstrated by the passing of an examination. Those admitted to the examination must have a college degree in engineering or science or the equivalent of such a degree. The Patent and Trademark Office registers both attorneys at law and persons who are not attorneys at law. The former persons are now referred to as "patent attorneys" and the latter persons are referred to as "patent agents." Insofar as the work of preparing an application for

---

[1] Arranged by subject matter, collection dates from Jan. 2, 1962.

patent and conducting the prosecution in the Patent and Trademark Office is concerned, patent agents are usually just as well qualified as patent attorneys, although patent agents cannot conduct patent litigation in the courts or perform various services which the local jurisdiction considers as practicing law. For example, a patent agent could not draw up a contract relating to a patent, such as an assignment or a license, if the State in which he resides considers drawing contracts as practicing law.

By regulation, registered patent attorneys and agents are forbidden to advertise for patent business. Some individuals and organizations that are not registered advertise their services in the fields of patent searching and patent promotion. Such individuals and organizations cannot represent inventors before the Patent and Trademark Office. They are not subject to Patent and Trademark Office discipline, and the Office cannot assist inventors in dealing with them.

The Patent and Trademark Office cannot recommend any particular attorney or agent, or aid in the selection of an attorney or agent, as by stating, in response to inquiry that a named patent attorney, agent, or firm, is "reliable" or "capable." The Patent and Trademark Office publishes a Directory of all registered patent attorneys and agents who have indicated their availability to accept new clients, arranged by states, cities, and foreign countries.

The telephone directories of most large cities have, in the classified section, a heading for patent attorneys under which those in that area are listed. Many large cities have associations of patent attorneys.

In employing a patent attorney or agent, the inventor executes a power of attorney or authorization of agent which must be filed in the Patent and Trademark Office and is usually a part of the application papers. When an attorney has been appointed, the Office does not communicate with the inventor directly but conducts the correspondence with the attorney since he is acting for the inventor thereafter, although the inventor is free to contact the Patent and Trademark Office concerning the status of his application. The inventor may remove the attorney or agent by revoking the power of authorization. See form 8, page 39.

The Patent and Trademark Office has the power to disbar, or suspend from practicing before it, persons guilty of gross misconduct, etc., but this can only be done after a full hearing with the presentation of evidence concerning the misconduct. The Patent and Trademark Office will receive and, in appropriate cases, act upon complaints against attorneys and agents. The fees charged to inventors by patent attorneys and agents for their professional services are not subject to regulation by the Patent and Trademark Office. Definite evidence of overcharging may afford basis for Patent and Trademark Office action, but the Office rarely intervenes in disputes concerning fees.

WHO MAY APPLY FOR A PATENT

According to the statute, only the inventor may apply for a patent, with certain exceptions. If a person who is not the inventor should apply for a patent, the patent, if it were obtained, would be void. The person applying in such a case who falsely states that he is the inventor would also be subject to criminal penalties. If the inventor is dead, the application may be made by his legal representatives, that is, the administrator or executor of his estate, in his place. If the inventor is insane, the application for patent may be made by his guardian, in his place. If an inventor refuses to apply for a patent or cannot be found, a joint inventor or a person having a proprietary interest in the invention may apply on behalf of the missing inventor.

If two or more persons make an invention jointly, they apply for a patent as joint inventors. A person who makes a financial contribution is not a joint inventor and cannot be joined in the application as an inventor. It is possible to correct a innocent mistake in omitting a joint inventor or in erroneously joining a person as an inventor.

Officers and employees of the Patent and Trademark Office are prohibited by law from applying for a patent or acquiring, directly or indirectly, except by inheritance or bequest, any patent or any right or interest in any patent.

APPLICATION FOR PATENT

The application for patent is made to the Commissioner of Patents and Trademarks and includes:

(1) A written document which comprises a specification (description and claims), and an oath or declaration;

(2) A drawing in those cases in which a drawing is possible; and

(3) The filing fee. See subheading "Filing Fee."

The specification and oath or declaration must be in the English language and must be legibly written or printed in permanent ink on one side of the paper. The Office prefers typewriting on legal size paper, 8 to 8½ by 10½ to 13 inches, double spaced, with margins of 1½ inches on the left-hand side and at the top. If the papers filed are not correctly, legibly, and clearly written, the Patent and Trademark Office may require typewritten or printed papers.

The application for patent is not accepted and placed in the files for examination until all its required parts, complying with the rules relating thereto, are received, except that certain minor informalities are waived subject to correction when required.

If the papers and parts are incomplete, or so defective that they cannot be accepted as a complete application for examination, the applicant will be notified; the papers will be held for six months for completion and, if not by then completed, will thereafter be returned or otherwise disposed of. The filing fee may be refunded when an application is refused acceptance as incomplete.

It is desirable that all parts of the complete application be deposited in the Office together; otherwise each part must be signed and a letter must accompany each part, accurately and clearly connecting it with the other parts of the application.

All applications are numbered in regular order, and the applicant is informed of the serial number and filing date of the complete application by filing receipt. The filing date of the application is the date on which a complete and acceptable application is received in the Patent and Trademark Office; or the date on which the last part completing such application is received in the case of a previously incomplete or defective application.

Oath or Declaration, Signature

The oath or declaration of the applicant is required by statute. The inventor must make an oath or declaration that he believes himself to be the original and first inventor of the subject matter of the application, and he must make various other allegations required by the statute and various allegations required by the Patent and Trademark Office rules. The form of oath in the usual case is given in the list of forms. The oath must be sworn to by the inventor before a notary public or other officer authorized to administer oaths. A declaration may be used in lieu of an oath as part of the original application for a patent involving designs, plants, and other patentable inventions; for reissue patents; when claiming matter originally shown or described but not originally claimed; or when filing a divisional or continuing application. An illustrative form (11), page 41, to use in the original application is given in the list of forms. Illustrative declaration forms for other uses are found in Title 37 of the Code of Federal Regulations.

The application must be signed by the inventor in person, or by the person entitled by law to make application on the inventor's behalf. A full first or middle name of each inventor without abbreviation and a middle or first initial, if any, is required. The post-office address of the inventor is also required.

Blank forms for applications or certain other papers are not supplied by the Patent and Trademark Office. Some specimen forms for application papers are given at the end of this pamphlet.

The papers in a complete application will not be returned for any purpose whatever, nor will the filing fee be returned. If applicants have not preserved copies of the papers, the Office will furnish copies at the usual cost.

Filing Fees

The filing fee of an application for an original patent, except in design cases, consists of a basic fee and additional fees. The basic fee is $65 and entitles applicant to present ten (10) claims, including not more than one (1) in independent form. An additional fee of $10 is required for each claim in independent form which is in excess of one (1) and an additional fee of $2 is required for each claim (whether independent or dependent) which is in excess of a total of ten (10) claims.

The following formula may be used in the calculation of the filing fee:

Basic Fee. $65.00
Additional Fees: .
    Total number of claims in excess of 10, times $2. _____
    Number of independent claims in excess of 1, times $10. . . . . _____
      Total Filing Fee. . . . . _____

To avoid errors in the payment of fees it is suggested that a table such as given above be included in the letter of transmittal.

In calculating fees, a claim is in dependent form if it incorporates by reference a single preceding claim which may be an independent or a dependent claim, and includes all the limitations of the claim incorporated by reference.

13

The law also provides for the payment of additional fees on presentation of claims after the application is filed.

When an amendment is filed which presents additional claims over the total number already paid for, or additional independent claims over the number of independent claims already accounted for, it must be accompanied by any additional fees due.

SPECIFICATION (DESCRIPTION AND CLAIMS)

The specification must include a written description of the invention and of the manner and process of making and using it, and is required to be in such full, clear, concise, and exact terms as to enable any person skilled in the art to which the invention pertains, or with which it is most nearly connected, to make and use the same.

The specification must set forth the precise invention for which a patent is solicited, in such manner as to distinguish it from other inventions and from what is old. It must describe completely a specific embodiment of the process, machine, manufacture, composition of matter or improvements invented, and must explain the mode of operation or principle whenever applicable. The best mode contemplated by the inventor of carrying out his invention must be set forth.

In the case of an improvement, the specification must particularly point out the part or parts of the process, machine, manufacture, or composition of matter to which the improvement relates, and the description should be confined to the specific improvement and to such parts as necessarily cooperate with it or as may be necessary to a complete understanding or description of it.

The title of the invention, which should be as short and specific as possible, should apepar as a heading on the first page of the specification, if it does not otherwise appear at the beginning of the application.

A brief abstract of the technical disclosure in the specification must be set forth immediately following the title and preceding the disclosure in a separate paragraph under the heading "Abstract of the Disclosure."

A brief summary of the invention indicating its nature and substance, which may include a statement of the object of the invention, commensurate with the invention as claimed and any object recited should precede the detailed description. Such summary should be that of the invention as claimed.

When there are drawings, there shall be a brief description of the several views of the drawings, and the detailed description of the invention shall refer to the different views by specifying the numbers of the figures, and to the different parts by use of reference letters or numerals (preferably the latter).

The specification must conclude with one or more claims particularly pointing out and distinctly claiming the subject matter which the applicant regards as his invention.

When more than one claim is presented, they may be placed in dependent form in which a claim may refer back to and further restrict a single preceding claim.

The claim or claims must conform to the invention as set forth in the remainder of the specification and the terms and phrases used in the claims must find clear support or antecedent basis in the description so that the meaning of the terms in the claims may be ascertainable by reference to the description.

The claims are brief descriptions of the subject matter of the invention, eliminating unnecessary details and reciting all essential features necessary to distinguish the invention from what is old. The claims are the operative part of the patent. Novelty and patentability are judged by the claims, and, when a patent is granted, questions of infringement are judged by the courts on the basis of the claims.

The following order of arrangement should be observed in framing the specification:

(*a*) Title of the invention; or a preamble stating the name, citizenship, and residence of the applicant and the title of the invention may be used.

(*b*) Abstract of the disclosure.

(*c*) Cross-references to related applications, if any.

(*d*) Brief summary of the invention.

(*e*) Brief description of the several views of the drawing, if there are drawings.

(*f*) Detailed description.

(*g*) Claim or claims.

DRAWING

The applicant for a patent is required by statute to furnish a drawing of his invention whenever the nature of the case admits of it; this drawing must be filed with the application. This includes practically all inventions except compositions of matter or processes, but a drawing may also be useful in the case of many processes.

The drawing must show every feature of the invention specified in the claims and is required by the Office rules to be in a particular form. The Office specifies the size of the sheet on which the drawing is made, the type of paper, the margins, and other details relating to the making of the drawing. The reason for specifying the standards in detail is that the drawings are printed and published in a uniform style when the patent issues, and the drawings must also be such that they can be readily understood by persons using the patent descriptions.

No names or other identification will be permitted within the "sight" of the drawing, and applicants are expected to use the space above and between the hole locations to identify each sheet of drawings. This identification may consist of the attorney's name and docket number or the inventor's name and case number and may include the sheet number and the total number of sheets filed (for example, "sheet 2 of 4").

The following rules relate to the standards for drawings:

1.84 *Standards for Drawings.*

(*a*) *Paper and Ink.* Drawings must be made upon pure white paper of a thickness corresponding to two-ply or three-ply bristolboard. The surface of the paper must be calendered and smooth and of a quality which will permit erasure and correction with India ink. India ink, or its equivalent in quality, must be used for pen drawings to secure perfectly black solid lines. The use of white pigment to cover lines is not acceptable.

(*b*) *Size of Sheet and Margins.* The size of a sheet on which a drawing is made must be exactly 8½ by 14 inches. One of the shorter sides of the sheet is regarded as its top. The drawing must include a top margin of 2 inches and bottom and side margins of one-quarter inch from the edges, thereby leaving a "sight" precisely 8×11¾ inches. Margin border lines are not permitted. All work must be included within the "sight". The sheets may be provided with two ¼ inch-diameter holes having their centerlines spaced eleven-sixteenths inch below the top edge and 2¾ inches apart, said holes being equally spaced from the respective side edges.

(*c*) *Character of Lines.* All drawings must be made with drafting instruments or by a process which will give them satisfactory reproduction characteristics. Every line and letter must be absolutely black and permanent; the weight of all lines and letters must be heavy enough to permit adequate reproduction. This direction applies to all lines however fine, to shading and to lines representing cut surfaces in sectional views. All lines must be clean, sharp, and solid, and fine or crowded lines should be avoided. Solid black should not be used for sectional or surface shading. Freehand work should be avoided wherever it is possible to do so.

(*d*) *Hatching and Shading.* (1) Hatching should be made by oblique parallel lines, which may be not less than about one-twentieth inch apart. (2) Heavy lines on the shade side of objects should be used except where they tend to thicken the work and obscure reference characters. The light should come from the upper left-hand corner at an angle of 45°. Surface delineations should be shown by proper shading, which should be open.

(*e*) *Scale.* The scale to which a drawing is made ought to be large enough to show the mechanism without crowding when the drawing is reduced in reproduction, and views of portions of the mechanism on a larger scale should be used when necessary to show details clearly; two or more sheets should be used if one does not give sufficient room to accomplish this end, but the number of sheets should not be more than is necessary.

(*f*) *Reference Characters.* The different views should be consecutively numbered figures. Reference numerals (and letters, but numerals are preferred) must be plain, legible and carefully formed, and not be encircled. They should, if possible, measure at least one-eighth of an inch in height so that they may bear reduction to one twenty-fourth of an inch; and they may be slightly larger when there is sufficient room. They must not be so placed in the close and complex parts of the drawing as to interfere with a thorough comprehension of the same, and therefore should rarely cross or mingle with the lines. When necessarily grouped around a certain part, they should be placed at a little distance, at the closest point where there is available space, and connected by lines with the parts to which they refer. They should not be placed upon hatched or shaded surfaces but when necessary, a blank space may be left in the hatching or shading where the character occurs so that it shall appear perfectly distinct and separate from the work. The same part of an invention appearing in more than one view of the drawing must always be designated by the same character, and the same character must never be used to designate different parts.

(*g*) *Symbols, Legends.* Graphical drawing symbols and other labeled representations may be used for conventional elements when appropriate, subject to approval by the Office. The elements for which such symbols and labeled representations are used must be adequately identified in the specification. While descriptive matter on drawings is not permitted, suitable legends may be used, or may be required in proper cases, as in diagrammatic views and flow sheets or to show materials or where labeled representations are employed to illustrate conventional elements. Arrows may be required in proper cases, to show direction of movement. The lettering should be as large as, or larger than, the reference characters.

(*i*) *Views.* The drawing must contain as many figures as may be necessary to show the invention; the figures should be consecutively numbered if possible, in the order in which they appear. The figures may be plain, elevation, section, or perspective views, and detail views of portions or elements, on a larger scale if necessary, may also be used. Exploded views, with the separated parts of the same figure embraced by a bracket, to show the relationship or order of assembly of various parts are permissible.

When necessary, a view of a large machine or device in its entirety may be broken and extended over several sheets if there is no loss in facility of understanding the view (the different parts should be identified by the same figure number but followed by the letters, a, b, c, etc., for each part). The plane upon which a sectional view is taken should be indicated on the general view by a broken line, the ends of which should be designated by numerals corresponding to the figure number of the sectional view and have arrows applied to indicate the direction in which the view is taken. A moved position may be shown by a broken line superimposed upon a suitable figure if this can be done without crowding, otherwise a separate figure must be used for this purpose. Modified forms of construction can only be shown in separate figures. Views should not be connected by projection lines nor should center lines be used.

(j) *Arrangement of Views.* All views on the same sheet must stand in the same direction and should if possible, stand so that they can be read with the sheet held in an upright position. If views longer than the width of the sheet are necessary for the clearest illustration of the invention, the sheet may be turned on its side so that the two-inch margin is on the right-hand side. One figure must not be placed upon another or within the outline of another.

(k) *Figure for Official Gazette.* The drawing should, as far as possible, be so planned that one of the views will be suitable for publication in the Official Gazette as the illustration of the invention.

(l) *Extraneous Matter.* An inventor's, agent's or attorney's name, signature, stamp, or address or other extraneous matter, will not be permitted upon the face of a drawing, within or without the margin, except that identifying indicia (attorney's docket number, inventor's name, number of sheets, etc.) should be placed within three-fourths inch of the top edge and between the hole locations defined in paragraph (b) of this rule. Authorized security markings may be placed on the drawings provided they be outside the illustrations and are removed when the material is declassified.

(m) *Transmission of drawings.* Drawings transmitted to the Office should be sent flat, protected by a sheet of heavy binder's board, or may be rolled for transmission in a suitable mailing tube; but must never be folded. If received creased or mutilated, new drawings will be required. (See rule 1.152 for design drawings, 1.165 for plant drawings, and 1.174 for reissue drawings.)

The requirements relating to drawings are strictly enforced, but a drawing not complying with all of the regulations is accepted for purpose of examination, and correction or a new drawing will be required later.

Applicants are advised to employ competent draftsmen to make their drawings. The Office may furnish drawings at the applicant's expense as promptly as its draftsmen can make them for applicants who cannot otherwise conveniently procure them.

MODELS, EXHIBITS, SPECIMENS

Models were once required in all cases admitting of a model, as a part of the application, and these models became a part of the record of the patent. Such models are no longer generally required since the description of the invention in the specification, and the drawings, must be sufficiently full and complete, and capable of being understood, to disclose the invention without the aid of a model. A model will not be admitted unless specifically called for.

A model, working model, or other physical exhibit, may be required by the Office if deemed necessary for any purpose on examination of the application. This is not done very often. A working model will be called for in the case of applications for patent for alleged perpetual motion devices.

When the invention relates to a composition of matter, the applicant may be required to furnish specimens of the composition, or of its ingredients or intermediates, for inspection or experiment.

EXAMINATION OF APPLICATIONS AND PROCEEDINGS IN THE PATENT AND TRADEMARK OFFICE

Applications filed in the Patent and Trademark Office and accepted as complete applications are assigned for examination to the respective examining groups having charge of the classes of inventions to which the applications relate. In the examining group applications are taken up for examination by the examiner to whom they have been assigned in the order in which they have been filed or in accordance with examining procedures established by the Commissioner.

Applications will not be advanced out of turn for examination or for further action except as provided by the rules, or upon order of the Commissioner to expedite the business of the Office, or upon a verified showing which, in the opinion of the Commissioner, will justify so advancing it.

The examination of the application consists of a study of the application for compliance with the legal requirements and a search through the prior art represented by prior United States patents, prior foreign patents which are available in the United States Patent and Trademark Office, and such prior literature as may be available, to see if the invention is new. A decision is reached by the examiner in the light of the study and the result of the search as to compliance with the statutes and rules and as to the novelty of the invention as claimed, as well as to formal matters. The examination is ordinarily complete with respect both to compliance of the application with the statute and rules and to the patentability of the invention as claimed, as well as with respect to matters of form, unless otherwise indicated.

Office Action

The applicant is notified in writing of the examiner's decision by an "action" which is mailed to the attorney or agent. The reasons for any adverse action or any objection or requirement are stated in the action and such information or references are given as may be useful in aiding the applicant to judge of the propriety of continuing the prosecution of his application.

The examiner's action will be complete as to all matters, except that in appropriate circumstances, such as misjoinder of invention, fundamental defects in the application, and the like, the action of the examiner may be limited to such matters before further action is made. However, matters of form need not be raised by the examiner until a claim is found allowable.

If the invention is not considered patentable, or not considered patentable as claimed, the claims, or those considered unpatentable, will be rejected. If the examiner finds that the invention as defined by the claims is not new, the claims are refused. The claims may also be refused if they differ somewhat from what is found to be old but the difference is not considered sufficient to justify a patent. It is not uncommon for some or all of the claims to be rejected on the first action by the examiner; relatively few applications are allowed as filed.

Terms such as "anticipation," "fully met," "lack of novelty," are used when rejecting claims under section 102 of the patent statute if the invention claimed is not new. Terms such as "unpatentable over," "obvious over" are used when rejecting claims when the invention claimed is not sufficiently different from the prior art under section 103 of the patent statute to warrant a patent.

Applicant's Response

After the Office action, if adverse in any respect, the applicant, if he persists in his application for a patent, must reply thereto within the time allowed, and may request reexamination or reconsideration, with or without amendment.

In order to be entitled to reexamination or reconsideration, the applicant must make request therefor in writing, and he must distinctly and specifically point out the supposed errors in the examiner's action; the applicant must respond to every ground of objection and rejection in the prior Office action (except that request may be made that objections or requirements as to form not necessary to further consideration of the claims be held in abeyance until allowable subject matter is indicated), and the applicant's action must appear throughout to be a bona fide attempt to advance the case to final action. The mere allegation that the examiner has erred will not be received as a proper reason for such reexamination or reconsideration.

In amending an application in response to a rejection, the applicant must clearly point out the patentable novelty which he thinks the claims present in view of the state of the art disclosed by the references cited or the objections made. He must also show how the amendments avoid such references or objections.

After response by applicant the application will be reexamined and reconsidered, and the applicant will be notified if claims are rejected, or objections or requirements made, in the same manner as after the first examination. The second Office action usually will be made final.

Final Rejection

On the second or any subsequent examination or consideration, the rejection or other action may be made final, whereupon applicant's response is limited to appeal in the case of rejection of any claim and further amendment is restricted. Petition may be taken to the Commissioner in the case of objections or requirements not involved in the rejection of any claim. Response to a final rejection or action must include cancellation of, or appeal from the rejection of, each claim so rejected and, if any claim stands allowed, compliance with any requirement or objection as to form.

In making such final rejection, the examiner repeats or states all grounds of rejection then considered applicable to the claims in the case.

Interviews with examiners may be arranged, but an interview does not remove the necessity for response to Office actions within the required time, and the action of the Office is based solely on the written record.

If two or more inventions are claimed in a single application, and are regarded by the Patent and Trademark Office to be of such a nature that a single patent may not be issued for both of them, the applicant will be required to limit the application to but one of the inventions. The other invention may be made the subject of a separate application which, if filed while the first application is still pending, will be entitled to the benefit of the filing date of the first application. A requirement to restrict the application to one invention may be made before further action by the examiner.

As a result of the examination by the Patent and Trademark Office, patents are granted in the case of about two out of every three applications for patents which are filed.

AMENDMENTS TO APPLICATION

The preceding section referred to amendments to the application. Following are some details concerning amendments:

The applicant may amend before or after the first examination and action as specified in the rules, or when and as specifically required by the examiner.

After final rejection or action amendments may be made canceling claims or complying with any requirement of form which has been made but the admission of any such amendment or its refusal, and any proceedings relative thereto, shall not operate to relieve the application from its condition as subject to appeal or to save it from abandonment.

If amendments touching the merits of the application be presented after final rejection, or after appeal has been taken, or when such amendment might not otherwise be proper, they may be admitted upon a showing of good and sufficient reasons why they are necessary and were not earlier presented.

No amendment can be made as a matter of right in appealed cases. After decision on appeal, amendments can only be made as provided in the rules.

The specifications, claims, and drawing must be amended and revised when required, to correct inaccuracies of description and definition or unnecessary words, and to secure correspondence between the claims, the description, and the drawing.

All amendments of the drawings or specifications, and all additions thereto, must conform to at least one of them as it was at the time of the filing of the application. Matter not found in either, involving a departure from or an addition to the original disclosure, cannot be added to the application even though supported by a supplemental oath or declaration, and can be shown or claimed only in a separate application.

The claims may be amended by canceling particular claims, by presenting new claims, or by amending the language of particular claims (such amended claims being in effect new claims). In presenting new or amended claims, the applicant must point out how they avoid any reference or ground of rejection of record which may be pertinent.

Erasures, additions, insertions, or alterations of the papers and records must not be made by the applicant. Amendments are made by filing a paper, directing or requesting that specified changes or additions be made. The exact word or words to be stricken out or inserted in the application must be specified and the precise point indicated where the deletion or insertion is to be made.

Amendments are "entered" by the Office by making the proposed deletions by drawing a line in red ink through the word or words canceled and by making the proposed substitutions or insertions in red ink, small insertions being written in at the designated place and larger insertions being indicated by reference.

No change in the drawing may be made except by permission of the Office. Permissible changes in the construction shown in any drawing may be made only by the Office. A sketch in permanent ink showing proposed changes, to become part of the record, must be filed. The paper requesting amendments to the drawing should be separate from other papers. The drawing may not be withdrawn from the Office.

Substitute drawings will not ordinarily be admitted in any case unless required by the Office.

If the number or nature of the amendments render it difficult to consider the case, or to arrange the papers for printing or copying, the examiner may require the entire specification or claims, or any part thereof, to be rewritten. A substitute specification will ordinarily not be accepted unless it has been required by the examiner.

The original numbering of the claims must be preserved throughout the prosecution. When claims are canceled, the remaining claims must not be renumbered. When claims are added by amendment or substituted for canceled claims, they must be numbered by the applicant consecutively beginning with the number next following the highest numbered claim previously presented. When the application is ready for allowance, the examiner, if necessary, will renumber the claims consecutively in the order in which they appear or in such order as may have been requested by applicant.

TIME FOR RESPONSE AND ABANDONMENT

The response of an applicant to an action by the Office must be made within a prescribed time limit. The maximum period for response is set at 6 months by the statute. The statute also provides that the Commissioner may shorten the time for reply to not less than 30 days. The usual period for response to an Office action is 3 months. Upon request, timely filed in the Office and for sufficient cause, a shortened time for reply may be extended up to the maximum 6 months period. If no reply is received within the time period, the application is considered as abandoned and no longer pending. However, if it can be shown that the failure to prosecute was unavoidable, the application may be revived by the Commissioner. This revival requires a petition to the Commissioner, accompanied by a verified showing of the cause of the delay and a fee for the petition, which should be filed without delay. The proper response must also accompany the petition if it has not yet been filed.

APPEAL TO THE BOARD OF APPEALS AND TO THE COURT

If the examiner persists in his rejection of any of the claims in an application, or if the rejection has been made final, the applicant may appeal to the Board of Appeals in the Patent and Trademark Office. The Board of Appeals consists of the Commissioner of Patents and Trademarks, the Assistant Commissioners, and not more than fifteen examiners-in-chief, but normally each appeal is heard by only three members. An appeal fee is required and the applicant must file a brief to support his position. He is entitled to an oral hearing if he desires one.

As an alternative to appeal, in situations where an applicant desires consideration of different claims or further evidence, a new continuation application is often filed. The new application requires a filing fee and should submit the claims and evidence for which consideration is desired. If it is filed before expiration of the period for appeal and specific reference is made therein to the earlier application, applicant will be entitled to his earlier filing date for subject matter common to both applications.

If the decision of the Board of Appeals is still adverse to the applicant, he has a choice of appealing to the Court of Customs and Patent Appeals or of filing a civil action against the Commissioner of Patents and Trademarks in the United States District Court for the District of Columbia. The court in the appeal will review the record made in the Patent and Trademark Office and may affirm or reverse the action taken by the Patent and Trademark Office. In the civil action, the applicant may present testimony in the court, and the court will make a decision holding that he either is or is not entitled to the patent.

INTERFERENCES

Occasionally two or more applications are filed by different inventors claiming substantially the same patentable invention. The patent can only be granted to one of them, and a proceeding known as an "interference" is instituted by the Patent and Trademark Office to determine who is the first inventor and entitled to the patent. About 1 percent of the applications filed become involved in an interference proceeding. Interference proceedings may also be instituted between an application and a patent already issued, provided the patent has not been issued for more than 1 year prior to the filing of the conflicting application, and provided that the conflicting application is not barred from being patentable for some other reason.

Each party to such a proceeding must submit evidence of facts proving when he made the invention. In view of the necessity of proving the various facts and circumstances concerning the making of the invention during an interference, inventors must be able to produce evidence to do this. If no evidence is submitted a party is restricted to the date of filing his application as his earliest date. The priority question is determined by a board of three interference examiners on the evidence submitted. From the decision of the Board of Patent Interferences, the losing party may appeal to the Court of Customs and Patent Appeals or file a civil action against the winning party in the appropriate United States district court.

The terms "conception of the invention" and "reduction to practice" are encountered in connection with priority questions. Conception of the invention refers to the completion of the devising of the means for accomplishing the result. Reduction to practice refers to the actual construction of the invention in physical form; in the case of a machine it includes the actual building of the machine, in the case of an article or composition it includes the actual making of the article or composition, in the case of a process it includes the actual carrying out of the steps of the process; and actual operation, demonstration, or testing for the intended use is also usually necessary. The filing of a regular application for patent completely disclosing the invention is treated as equivalent to reduction to practice. The inventor who proves to be the first to conceive the invention and the first to reduce it to practice will be held to be the prior inventor, but more complicated situations cannot be stated this simply.

ALLOWANCE AND ISSUE OF PATENT

If, on examination of the application, or at a later stage during the reexamination or reconsideration of the application, the patent application is found to be allowable, a notice of allowance will be sent to the applicant, his attorney or his agent, and a fee for issuing the patent is due within 3 months from the date of the notice.

The issue fee for each original or reissue patent, except in design cases, constitutes a basic fee of $100, and additional fees of $10 for each page (or portion thereof) of specification as printed, and $2 for each sheet of drawing.

The written notice of allowance given or mailed to each applicant entitled to a patent under the law will be accompanied by an estimate of the issue fee determined in accordance with the number of pages in the specification and the number of sheets of drawing. This issue fee is to be paid within three months thereafter and if timely payment is not made the application shall be regarded as abandoned (forfeited).

The notice of any remaining balance of the issue fee will be sent to the applicant at the time of the grant of the patent. If this remaining balance is not paid within three months therefrom the patent shall lapse.

A provision is made in the statute whereby the Commissioner may accept the fee late, up to 3 months, on a showing of unavoidable delay. When the issue fee is paid, the patent issues as soon as possible after the date of payment, dependent upon the volume of printing on hand. The patent grant then is delivered or mailed on the day of its grant, or as soon thereafter as possible, to the inventor's attorney or agent if there is one of record, otherwise directly to the inventor.

On the date of the grant, the record of the patent in the Patent and Trademark Office becomes open to the public. Printed copies of the specification and drawing are available on that same date, or shortly thereafter.

In case the publication of an invention by the granting of a patent would be detrimental to the national defense, the patent law gives the Commissioner of Patents and Trademarks the power to withhold the grant of the patent and to order the invention kept secret for such period of time as the national interest requires.

NATURE OF PATENT AND PATENT RIGHTS

The patent is issued in the name of the United States under the seal of the Patent and Trademark Office, and is either signed by the Commissioner of Patents and Trademarks or has his name written thereon and attested by an official of the Patent and Trademark Office. The patent contains a grant to the patentee and a printed copy of the specification and drawing is annexed to the patent and forms a part of it. The grant to the patentee is of "the right to exclude others from making, using or selling the invention throughout the United States" for the term of 17 years. The United States in this phrase includes Territories and Possessions.

The exact nature of the right conferred must be carefully distinguished, and the key is in the words "right to exclude" in the phrase just quoted. The patent does not grant the right to make, use, or sell the invention but only grants the exclusive nature of the right. Any person is ordinarily free to make, use, or sell anything he pleases, and a grant from the Government is not necessary. The patent only grants the right to exclude others from making, using, or selling the invention. Since the patent does not grant the right to make, use, or sell the invention, the patentee's own right to do so is dependent upon the rights of others and whatever general laws might be applicable.

A patentee, merely because he has received a patent for an invention, is not thereby authorized to make, use or sell the invention if doing so would violate any law. An inventor of a new automobile would not be entitled to use his new automobile in violation of the laws of a State requiring a license, because he has obtained a patent, nor may a patentee sell an article the sale of which may be forbidden by a law, merely because he has obtained a patent. Neither may a patentee make, use or sell his own invention if doing so would infringe the prior rights of others. A patentee may not violate the Federal antitrust laws, such as by resale price agreements of entering into combinations in restraint of trade, or the pure food and drug laws, by virtue of his having a patent. Ordinarily there is nothing which prohibits a patentee from making, using, or selling his own invention, unless he thereby infringes anothers' patent which is still in force.

Since the essence of the right granted by a patent is the right to exclude others from commercial exploitation of the invention, the patentee is the only one who may make, use, or sell his invention. Others may not do so without authorization from the patentee. The patentee may manufacture and sell the invention himself or he may license, that is, give authorization to others to do so.

The term of a patent is 17 years. After the patent has expired anyone may make, use, or sell the invention without permission of the patentee, provided that matter covered by other unexpired patents is not used. The term may not be extended except by special act of Congress. Provision was made by a law which has now expired for granting extensions of patents owned by veterans of World War II.

CORRECTION OF PATENTS

Once the patent is granted, it is outside the jurisdiction of the Patent and Trademark Office except in a few respects.

The Patent and Trademark Office may issue without charge a certificate correcting a clerical error it has made in the patent when the patent does not correspond to the record in the Patent and Trademark Office. These are mostly corrections of typographical errors made in printing.

Some minor errors of a typographical nature made by the applicant may be corrected by a certificate of correction for which a charge is made.

The patentee may disclaim one or more claims of his patent by filing in the Patent and Trademark Office a disclaimer as provided by the statute.

When the patent is defective in certain respects, the law provides that the patentee may apply for a reissue patent. This is a patent granted to replace the first one and is granted only for the balance of the unexpired term. However, the nature of the changes that can be made by means of the reissue are rather limited; new matter cannot be added.

ASSIGNMENTS AND LICENSES

A patent is personal property and may be sold to others or mortgaged; it may be bequeathed by a will, and it may pass to the heirs of a deceased patentee. The patent law provides for the transfer or sale of a patent, or of an application for patent, by an instrument in writing. Such an instrument is referred to as an assignment and may transfer the entire interest in the patent. The assignee, when the patent is assigned to him, becomes the owner of the patent and he has the same rights that the original patentee had.

The statute also provides for the assignment of a part interest, that is, a half interest, a fourth interest, etc., in a patent. There may also be a grant which conveys the same character of interest as an assignment but only for a particular specified part of the United States.

A mortgage of patent property passes ownership thereof to the mortgagee or lender until the mortgage has been satisfied and a retransfer from the mortgagee back to the mortgagor, the borrower, is made. A conditional assignment also passes ownership of the patent and is regarded as absolute until canceled by the parties or by the decree of a competent court.

An assignment, grant, or conveyance of any patent or application for patent should be acknowledged before a notary public or officer authorized to administer oaths or perform notarial acts. The certificate of such acknowledgment constitutes prima facie evidence of the execution of the assignment, grant, or conveyance.

Recording of Assignments

The Patent and Trademark Office records assignments, grants, and similar instruments sent to it for recording, and the recording serves as notice. If an assignment, grant, or conveyance of a patent or an interest in a patent (or an application for patent) is not recorded in the Patent and Trademark Office within 3 months from its date, it is void against a subsequent purchaser for a valuable consideration without notice, unless it is recorded prior to the subsequent purchase.

An instrument relating to a patent should identify the patent by number and date (the name of the inventor and title of the invention as stated in the patent should also be given). An instrument relating to an application should identify the application by its serial number and date of filing, and the name of the inventor and title of the invention as stated in the application should also be given. Sometimes an assignment of an application is executed at the same time that the application is prepared and before it has been filed in the Patent and Trademark Office. Such assignment should adequately identify the application, as by its date of execution and name of the inventor and title of the invention, so that there can be no mistake as to the application intended.

If an application has been assigned and the assignment is recorded, on or before the date the issue fee is paid, the patent will be issued to the assignee as owner. If the assignment is of a part interest only, the patent will be issued to the inventor and assignee as joint owners.

Joint Ownership

Patents may be owned jointly by two or more persons as in the case of a patent granted to joint inventors, or in the case of the assignment of a part interest in a patent. Any joint owner of a patent, no matter how small his part interest, may make, use, and sell the invention for his own profit, without regard to the other owner, and may sell his interest or any part of it, or grant licenses to others, without regard to the other joint owner, unless the joint owners have made a contract governing their relation to each other. It is accordingly dangerous to assign a part interest without a definite agreement between the parties as to the extent of their respective rights and their obligations to each other if the above result is to be avoided.

The owner of a patent may grant licenses to others. Since the patentee has the right to exclude others from making, using or selling the invention, no one else may do any of these things without his permission. A license is the permission granted by the patent owner to another to make, use, or sell the invention. No particular form of license is required; a license is a contract and may include whatever provisions the parties agree upon, including the payment of royalties, etc.

The drawing up of a license agreement (as well as assignments) is within the field of an attorney at law, although such attorney should be familiar with patent matters as well. A few States have prescribed certain formalities to be observed in connection with the sale of patent rights.

INFRINGEMENT OF PATENTS

Infringement of a patent consists in the unauthorized making, using, or selling of the patented invention within the territory of the United States, during the term of the patent. If a patent is infringed, the patentee may sue for relief in the appropriate Federal court. He may ask the court for an injunction to prevent the continuation of the infringement, and he may also ask the court for an award of damages because of the infringement. In such an infringement suit, the defendant may raise the question of the validity of the patent, which is then decided by the court. The defendant may also aver that what he is doing, does not constitute infringement. Infringement is determined primarily by the language of the claims of the patent and, if what the defendant is making does not fall within the language of any of the claims of the patent, he does not infringe.

Suits for infringement of patents follow the rules of procedure of the Federal courts. From the decision of the district court, there is an appeal to the appropriate Federal court of appeals. The Supreme Court may thereafter take a case by writ of certiorari. If the United States Government infringes a patent, the patentee has a remedy for damages in the Court of Claims of the United States. The Government may use any patented invention without permission of the patentee, but the patentee is entitled to obtain compensation for the use by or for the Government.

If the patentee notifies anyone that he is infringing his patent or threatens suit, the one charged with infringement may himself start the suit in a Federal court and get a judgment on the matter.

The Patent and Trademark Office has no jurisdiction over questions relating to infringement of patents. In examining applications for patent no determination is made as to whether the invention sought to be patented infringes any prior patent. An improvement invention may be patentable, but it might infringe a prior unexpired patent for the invention improved upon, if there is one.

PATENT MARKING AND "PATENT PENDING"

A patentee who makes or sells patented articles, or a person who does so under him, is required to mark the articles with the word "Patent" and the number of the patent. The penalty for failure to mark is that the patentee may not recover damages from an infringer unless the infringer was duly notified of the infringement and continued to infringe after the notice.

The marking of an article as patented when it is not in fact patented is against the law and subjects the offender to a penalty.

Some persons mark articles sold with the terms "Patent Applied For" or "Patent Pending." These phrases have no legal effect, but only give information that an application for patent has been filed in the Patent and Trademark Office. The protection afforded by a patent does not start until the actual grant of the patent. False use of these phrases or their equivalents is prohibited.

DESIGN PATENTS

The patent laws provide for the granting of design patents to any person who has invented any new, original and ornamental design for an article of manufacture. The design patent protects only the appearance of an article, and not its structure or utilitarian features. The proceedings relating to granting of design patents are the same as those relating to other patents with a few differences.

The filing fee on each design application is $20; the issue fee is $10 for a 3½-year term, $20 for a 7-year term, and $30 for a 14-year term. If, on examination it shall appear that an applicant is entitled to a design patent under the law, a notice of allowance will be sent to him, his attorney, or his agent, calling for the payment of an issue fee in an appropriate amount depending on the duration of the term desired by the applicant.

The drawing of the design patent conforms to the same rules as other drawings, but no reference characters are required.

The specification of a design application is short and ordinarily follows a set form. Only one claim is permitted, following a set form.

PLANT PATENTS

The law also provides for the granting of a patent to anyone who has invented or discovered and asexually reproduced any distinct and new variety of plant, including cultivated sports, mutants, hybrids, and newly found seedlings, other than a tuber-propagated plant or a plant found in an uncultivated state.

Asexually propagated plants are those that are reproduced by means other than from seeds, such as by the rooting of cuttings, by layering, budding, grafting, inarching, etc.

With reference to tuber-propagated plants, for which a plant patent cannot be obtained, the term "tuber" is used in its narrow horticultural sense as meaning a short, thickened portion of an underground branch. The only plants covered by the term "tuber-propagated" are the Irish potato and the Jerusalem artichoke.

An application for a plant patent consists of the same parts as other applications.

The application papers for a plant patent and any responsive papers pursuant to the prosecution must be filed in duplicate (to provide an original and duplicate file) but only one need be signed (in the case of the application papers the original should also be signed); the second copy may be a legible carbon copy of the original. The reason for thus providing an original and duplicate file is that the duplicate file is utilized for submission to the Agricultural Research Service, Department of Agriculture for an advisory report on the plant variety, the original file being retained in the Patent and Trademark Office at all times.

The specification should include a complete detailed description of the plant and the characteristics thereof that distinguish the same over related known varieties, and its antecedents, expressed in botanical terms in the general form followed in standard botanical text books or publications dealing with the varieties of the kind of plant involved (evergreen tree, dahlia plant, rose plant, apple tree, etc.), rather than a mere broad non-botanical characterization such as commonly found in nursery or seed catalogs. The specification should also include the origin or parentage of the plant variety sought to be patented and must particularly point out where and in what manner the variety of plant has been asexually reproduced. Where color is a distinctive feature of the plant the color should be positively identified in the specification by reference to a designated color as given by a recognized color dictionary. Where the plant variety originated as a newly found seedling, the specification must fully describe the conditions (cultivation, environment, etc.) under which the seedling was found growing to establish that it was not found in an uncultivated state.

A plant patent is granted on the entire plant. It therefore follows that only one claim is necessary and only one is permitted.

The oath or declaration required of the applicant in addition to the statements required for other applications must include the statement that the applicant has asexually reproduced the new plant variety.

Plant patent drawings are not mechanical drawings and should be artistically and competently executed. The drawing must disclose all the distinctive characteristics of the plant capable of visual representation. When color is a distinguishing characteristic of the new variety, the drawing must be in color. Two duplicate copies of color drawings must be submitted. Color drawings may be made either in permanent water color or oil, or in lieu thereof may be photographs made by color photography or properly colored on sensitized paper. The paper in any case must correspond in size, weight, and quality to the paper required for other drawings. Mounted photographs are acceptable.

Specimens of the plant variety, its flower or fruit, should not be submitted unless specifically called for by the examiner.

All inquiries relating to plant patents and pending plant patent applications should be directed to the Patent and Trademark Office and not to the Department of Agriculture.

The Plant Variety Protection Act (Public Law 91–577, approved December 24, 1970) provides for a system of protection for sexually reproduced varieties, for which protection was not previously provided, under the administration of a newly established Plant Variety Protection office within the Department of Agriculture. Requests for information regarding the protection of sexually reproduced varieties should be addressed to Commissioner, Plant Variety Protection Office, Consumer and Marketing Service, Grain Division, 6525 Bellcrest Road, Hyattsville, Maryland 20782.

TREATIES AND FOREIGN PATENTS

Since the rights granted by a United States patent extend only throughout the territory of the United States and have no effect in a foreign country, an inventor who wishes patent protection in other countries must apply for a patent in each of the other countries. Almost every country has its own patent law, and a person desiring a patent in a particular country must make an application for patent in that country, in accordance with the requirements of that country.

The laws of many countries differ in various respects from the patent law of the United States and even from each other. In most foreign countries, publication of the invention before the date of the application will bar the right to a patent. In most foreign countries, a series of fees are due after the grant of the patent. These fees are usually annual and increase in amount each year. Most foreign countries require that the patented invention must be manufactured in that country after a certain period, usually 3 years. If there is no manufacture within this period, the patent may be void in some countries, although in most countries the patent may be subject to the grant of compulsory licenses to any other person who may apply for a license.

There is a treaty relating to patents which is adhered to by 79 countries, including the United States, and is known as the Paris Convention for the Protection of Industrial Property. It provides that each country guarantees to the citizens of the other countries the same rights in patent and trademark matters that it gives to its own citizens. The treaty also provides for the right of priority in the case of patents, trademarks and industrial designs (design patents). This right means that, on the basis of a regular first application filed in one of the member countries, the applicant may, within a certain period of time, apply for protection in all the other member countries. These later applications will then be regarded as if they had been filed on the same day as the first application. Thus, these later applications will have priority over applications for the same invention which may have been filed during the said period of time by other persons. Moreover, these later applications, being based on the first application, will not be invalidated by any acts accomplished in the interval, such as, for example, publication or exploitation of the invention, the sale of copies of the design, or use of the trademark. The period of time mentioned above, within which the subsequent applications may be filed in the other countries, is 12 months in the case of applications for patent and 6 months in the case of industrial designs and trademarks.

Another treaty, known as the Patent Cooperation Treaty, was negotiated at a diplomatic conference in Washington, D.C., in June of 1970. It has been signed by 35 countries, including the United States, but has not yet come into force. When in effect, the treaty will facilitate the filing of applications for patent on the same invention in member countries by providing, among other things, for centralized filing procedures and a standardized application format.

The Patent and Trademark Office cannot assist in the filing of applications for patents in foreign countries. A number of patent attorneys specialize in obtaining patents in foreign countries. In general, an inventor should be satisfied that he could make some profit from foreign patents or that there is some particular reason for obtaining them, before he attempts to apply for foreign patents.

Under United States law it is necessary, in the case of inventions made in the United States, to obtain a license from the Commissioner of Patents and Trademarks before applying for a patent in a foreign country. Such a license is required if the foreign application is to be filed before an application is filed in the United States or before the expiration of 6 months from the filing of an application in the United States. The request for a license may be a simple letter referring to the United States application if one has already been filed. After 6 months from the United States filing, a license is not required unless the invention has been ordered to be kept secret. If the invention has been ordered to be kept secret, consent to the filing abroad must be obtained from the Commissioner of Patents and Trademarks during the period of the order of secrecy is in effect.

FOREIGN APPLICANTS FOR UNITED STATES PATENTS

The patent laws of the United States make no discrimination with respect to the citizenship of the inventor. Any inventor, regardless of his citizenship, may apply for a patent on the same basis as an American citizen. There are, however, a number of particular points of special interest to applicants located in foreign countries.

The application for patent in the United States must be made by the inventor and the inventor must sign the papers (with certain exceptions), differing from the law in many countries where the signature of the inventor and an oath of inventorship are not necessary. If the inventor is dead, the application may be made by his executor or administrator, or equivalent, and in the case of mental disability it may be made by his legal representative (guardian).

No United States patent can be obtained if the invention was patented abroad before applying in the United States by the inventor or his legal representatives or assigns on an application filed more than 12 months before filing in the United States. Six months are allowed in the case of a design patent.

An application for patent filed in the United States by any person who has previously regularly filed an application for a patent for the same invention in a foreign country which affords similar privileges to citizens of the United States shall have the same force and effect for the purpose of overcoming intervening acts of others as if filed in the United States on the date on which the application for patent for the same invention was first filed in such foreign country, provided the application in the United States is filed within 12 months (6 months in the case of a design patent) from the earliest date on which any such foreign application was filed. A copy of the foreign application certified by the patent office of the country in which it was filed is required to secure this right of priority.

If any application for patent has been filed in any foreign country by the applicant or by his legal representatives or assigns prior to his application in the United States, the applicant must, in the oath or declaration accompanying the application, state the country in which the earliest such application has been filed, giving the date of filing the application; and all applications filed more than a year before the filing in the United States must also be recited in the oath or declaration.

An oath or declaration must be made with respect to every application. When the applicant is in a foreign country the oath or affirmation may be made before any diplomatic or consular officer of the United States, or before any officer having an official seal and authorized to administer oaths in the foreign country, whose authority shall be proved by a certificate of a diplomatic or consular officer of the United States, the oath being attested in all cases by the proper official seal of the officer before whom the oath is made.

When the oath is taken before an officer in the country foreign to the United States, all the application papers (except the drawing) must be attached together and a ribbon passed one or more times through all the sheets of the application, and the ends of the ribbon brought together under the seal before the latter is affixed and impressed, or each sheet must be impressed with the official seal of the officer before whom the oath was taken.

If the application is filed by the legal representative (executor, administrator, etc.) of a deceased inventor, the legal representative must make the oath or declaration.

When a declaration is used, the ribboning procedure is not necessary, nor is it necessary to appear before an official in connection with the making of a declaration.

A foreign applicant may be represented by any patent attorney or agent who is registered to practice before the United States Patent and Trademark Office.

FEES AND PAYMENT

The following fees and charges are payable to the Patent and Trademark Office:

1. Filing fee. On filing each application for an original patent, except in design cases $65.00
   In addition:
   On filing or on presentation at any other time, for each claim in independent form which is in excess of one 10.00
   For each claim (whether independent or dependent) which is in excess of 10 . . . . 2.00
   Errors in payment of the additional fees may be rectified in accordance with regulations of the Commissioner.
2. Issue fee. For issuing each original or reissue patent, except in design cases 100.00
   In addition:
   For each page (or portion thereof) of specification as printed 10.00
   For each sheet of drawing 2.00

3. In design cases:
    a. On filing each design application............................ $20. 00
    b. On issuing each design patent:
        For 3 years and 6 months.. .... 10. 00
        For 7 years... 20. 00
        For 14 years.. 30. 00
4. Reissues. On filing each application for the reissue of patent............ 65. 00
    In addition:
        On filing or on presentation at any other time, for each claim in independent form which is in excess of the number of independent claims of the original patent................................. 10. 00
        For each claim (whether independent or dependent) which is in excess of ten and also in excess of the number of claims of the original patent...................................... 2. 00
    Errors in payment of the additional fees may be rectified in accordance with regulations of the Commissioner.
5. On filing each disclaimer... 15. 00
6. On filing each petition for the revival of an abandoned application for patent 15. 00
7. On filing each petition for the delayed payment of the issue fee.......... 15. 00
8. On appeal for the first time from the examiner to the Board of Appeals.. 50. 00
    On filing a brief in support of the appeal........................ 50. 00
9. For certification of copies of records, etc., in any case, in addition to the cost of copy certified... 1. 00
10. For certificate of correction of applicant's mistake..................... 15. 00
11. For uncertified copies of the specifications and accompanying drawings of patents, except design patents.................................... . 50
12. For uncertified copies of design patents................................ . 20
13. For recording every assignment, agreement, or other paper relating to the property in a patent or application................................ 20. 00
    For each additional item, where the document relates to more than one patent or application... 3. 00
14. For typewritten copies of records, for each page produced (double-spaced) or fraction thereof..................................... 1. 50
15. For photocopies or other reproductions of records, drawings or printed material, per page of material copied............................. . 30
16. For abstracts of title to each patent or application:
    For the search, one hour or less, and certificate...................... 3. 00
    Each additional hour or fraction thereof.............................. 1. 50
    For each brief from the digest of assignments, of 200 words or less........ 1. 00
    Each additional 100 words or fraction thereof......................... . 10
17. For translations from foreign languages into English, made only of references cited in applications or of papers filed in the Patent and Trademark Office insofar as facilities may be available:
    Written translations, for every 100 words of the original language, or fraction thereof... 5. 00
    Oral translations (dictation or assistance), for each one-half hour or fraction thereof that service is rendered............................ 4. 00
18. For making patent drawings, when facilities are available, the cost of making the same, minimum charge per sheet....................... 25. 00
19. For correcting drawings, the cost of making the correction, minimum charge 3. 00
20. For the mounting of unmounted drawings and photoprints received with patent applications, provided they are of approved permanency....... 2. 00
21. Lists of U.S. Patents:
    All patents in a subclass, per sheet (containing 100 patent numbers or less)... . 50
    Minimum charge per order.. 1. 00
    Patents in a subclass limited by date or patent number, per sheet (containing 50 numbers or less)............................... . 50
    Minimum charge per order.. 1. 00

22. Search of Patent and Trademark Office records for purposes not otherwise specified in this section, per one-half hour of search or fraction
thereof $3.00
23. For special service to expedite furnishing items or services ahead of
regular order:
On orders for copies of U.S. patents and trademark registrations, in addition to the charge for the copies, for each copy ordered.............. .50
On all other orders or requests for which special service facilities are
available, in addition to the regular charge, a special service charge
equal to the amount of regular charge; minimum special service charge
per order or request... 1.00
24. For air mail delivery:
On "special service" orders to destinations to which U.S. domestic air
mail postage rates apply, no additional charge.
On regular service orders to any destination and "special service" orders
to destinations other than those specified in the preceding subpara-
graph, an additional charge equal to the amount of air mail postage.
(Available only when the ordering party has, with the Patent and
Trademark Office, a deposit account.)
25. For items and services, that the Commissioner finds may be supplied,
for which fees are not specified by statute or by this section, such
charges as may be determined by the Commissioner with respect to
each such item or service.

The following are sold by the U.S. Department of Commerce, National
Technical Information Service, Springfield, Va. 22151, to whom all communications respecting the same should be addressed:

Microfilm Lists of Patents.—The reels containing the mechanical, electrical
and chemical patent numbers in original and cross-referenced classification
may be purchased for $70.00 or individual reels for $6.00 per reel (identified
as PB 185–900). The classification of all design patents is listed on a single
reel which may be purchased for $6.00 (PB 185–917).

The following publications are sold, and the prices for them fixed, by
the Superintendent of Documents, Government Printing Office, Washington,
D.C. 20402, to whom all communications respecting the same should be
addressed:

Official Gazette of the United States Patent Office:
    Annual subscription, domestic.................................... $342.20
    Annual subscription, foreign..................................... 427.75
    Single numbers.. 6.60
Annual Index Relating to Patents, price varies.
Manual of Classifications of Patents................................. 44.00
    Foreign 55.00
Manual of Patent Examining Procedure............................. 19.65
    Foreign 24.60
Patents and Inventions. An Information Aid for Inventors............... .40
Trademark Rules of Practice of the United States Patent Office With Forms
    and Statutes.. 5.00
    Foreign 6.25
Patent Laws 2.10
Attorneys and Agents Registered to Practice Before the U.S. Patent Office.. 3.70
Guide for Patent Draftsmen .... .65
37. Code of Federal Regulations 3.00

THE ABOVE PRICES ARE SUBJECT TO CHANGE WITHOUT NOTICE.

All payment of money required for Patent and Trademark Office fees should be made in United States specie, Treasury notes, national bank notes, post office money orders or postal notes payable to the Commissioner of Patents and Trademarks, or by certified checks. If sent in any other form, the Office may delay or cancel the credit until collection is made. Postage stamps are not acceptable. Money orders and checks must be made payable to the Commissioner of Patents and Trademarks. Remittances from foreign countries must be payable and immediately negotiable in the United States for the full amount of the fee required.

Money paid by actual mistake or in excess, such as a payment not required by law, will be refunded, but a mere change of purpose after the payment of money, as when a party desires to withdraw his application for a patent or to withdraw an appeal, will not entitle a party to demand such a return. Amounts of 50 cents or less will not be returned unless specifically demanded, within a reasonable time, nor will the payer be notified of such amount; amounts over 50 cents but less than $1 may be returned in postage stamps; and amounts of one dollar or more will be refunded by check.

FORMS

The following forms illustrate the manner of preparing parts of applications for patent and other papers (see page 12, under "application for patent" for size of paper and preferred writing). Additional forms are given in the Rules of Practice. Forms for patent specifications and drawings are not given since these vary so considerably. Specifications and drawings of patents may be inspected and studied in those libraries which maintain collections of patents (see p. 9). Particular patents of interest can be located from the *Official Gazette* (see p. 6) and copies purchased:

1. Patent Application, sole inventor; power of attorney, oath.
2. Patent Application, joint inventors; power of attorney, oath.
3. Patent Application, Administrator of estate of deceased inventor; power of attorney, oath.
4. Oath not accompanying application.
5. Design Application; specification, oath.
6. Plant patent application, power of attorney, oath.
7. Power of attorney or authorization of agent, not accompanying application.
8. Revocation of power of attorney or authorization of agent.
9. Assignment of patent.
10. Assignment of application.
11. Declaration which may be included in an application in lieu of an oath.

1. PATENT APPLICATION, SOLE INVENTOR; POWER OF ATTORNEY, OATH

To the Commissioner of Patents and Trademarks:

Your petitioner, ..., a citizen of the United States and a resident of ...., State of ...., whose post-office address is ...., prays that letters patent may be granted to him for the improvement in......................, set forth in the following specification; and he hereby appoints ...., of ...., (Registration No. ....), his attorney (or agent) to prosecute this application and to transact all business in the Patent and Trademark Office connected therewith. (If no power of attorney is to be included in the application, omit the appointment of the attorney.)

[The specification, which includes the description of the invention and the claims, is written here.]

...................., the above-named petitioner, being sworn (or affirmed), deposes and says that he is a citizen of the United States and resident of ...., State of ...., that he verily believes himself to be the original, first and sole inventor of the improvement in .... described and claimed in the foregoing specification; that he does not know and does not believe that the same was ever known or used before his invention thereof, or patented or described in any printed publication in any country before his invention thereof, or more than one year prior to this application, or in public use or on sale in the United States more than one year prior to this application; that said invention has not been patented or made the subject of an inventor's certificate in any country foreign to the United States on an application filed by him or his legal representatives or assigns more than twelve months prior to this application; that he acknowledges his duty to disclose information of which he is aware which is material to the examination of this application; and that no application for patent or inventor's certificate on said invention has been filed by him or his representatives or assigns in any country foreign to the United States, except as follows: ....

....
(Inventor's full signature)

State of.....................⎫
County of..................... ⎬ ss:
                              ⎭

Sworn to and subscribed before me this .... day of ...., 19.....

....
(Signature of notary or officer)

[SEAL]

....
(Official character)

2. PATENT APPLICATION, JOINT INVENTORS; POWER OF ATTORNEY, OATH

To the Commissioner of Patents and Trademarks:

Your petitioners, ... and ...., citizens of the United States and residents, respectively, of ...., State of ...., and of ...., State of .... whose post-office addresses are, respectively, ... and .... pray that letters patent may be granted to them, as joint inventors, for the improvements in ...., set forth in the following specifications; and they hereby appoint ...., of .... (Registration No. ....), their attorney (or agent), to prosecute this application and to transact all business in the Patent and Trademark Office connected therewith. (If no power of attorney is to be included in the application, omit the appointment of the attorney.)

[The specification, which includes the description of the invention and the claims, is written here.]

.... and ...., the above-named petitioners, being sworn (or affirmed), depose and say that they are citizens of the United States and rsidents of ...., State of ...., that they verily believe themselves to be the original, first and joint inventors of the improvement in .... described and claimed in the foregoing specification; that they do not know and do not believe that the same was ever known or used before their invention thereof, or patented or described in any printed publication in any country before their invention thereof, or more than one year prior to this application, or in public use or on sale in the United States for more than one year prior to this application; that said invention has not been patented or made the subject of an inventor's certificate in any country foreign to the United States on an application filed by them or their legal representatives or assigns more than 12 months prior to this application; that they acknowledge their duty to disclose information of which they are aware which is material to the examination of this application, and that no application for patent or inventor's certificate on said invention has been filed by them or their representatives or assigns in any country foreign to the United States, except as follows: ....

....
(Inventor's full signature)

STATE OF........................ } ss:
County of........................

Sworn to and subscribed before me this .... day of ...., 19.....

....
(Signature of notary or officer)

[SEAL]

....
(Official character)

3. PATENT APPLICATION, ADMINISTRATOR OF ESTATE OF DECEASED INVENTOR; POWER OF ATTORNEY, OATH

To the Commissioner of Patents and Trademarks:

Your petitioner, A .... B ...., a citizen of the United States and a resident of ...., State of ...., whose post-office address is ...., administrator of the estate of C .... D ...., late a citizen of the United States and a resident of ...., State of ...., deceased (as by reference to the duly certified copy of letters of administration, hereto annexed, will more fully appear), prays that letters patent may be granted to him for the invention of the said C .... D .... for an improvement in .... set forth in the following specification; and he hereby appoints ...., of .... (Registration No. ....), his attorney (or agent), to prosecute this application and to transact all business in the Patent and Trademark Office connected therewith.

(If no power of attorney is to be included in the application, omit the appointment of the attorney.)

[The specification, which includes the description of the invention and the claims, is written here.]

A .... B ...., the above-named petitioner, being sworn (or affirmed), deposes and says that he is a citizen of the United States of America and a resident of ...., that he is the administrator of the estate (or executor of the last will and testament) of C .... D ...., deceased, late a citizen of the United States and resident of ...., that he verily believes the said C .... D .... to be the original,

36

first and sole inventor of the improvement in .... described and claimed in the foregoing specification; that he does not know and does not believe that the same was ever known or used before the invention thereof by the said C .... D ...., or patented or described in any printed publication in any country before the said invention thereof, or more than one year prior to this application, or in public use or on sale in the United States for more than one year prior to this application; that said invention has not been patented or make the subject of an inventor's certificate in any country foreign to the United States on an application filed by the said C .... D .... or his legal representatives or assigns more than 12 months prior to this application; that he acknowledges his duty to disclose information of which he is aware which is material to the examination of this application, and that no application for patent or inventor's certificate on said invention has been filed by the said C .... D .... or his representatives or assigns in any country foreign to the United State, except as follows: ....

A .... B ....
(Signature)
ADMINISTRATOR, ETC.

STATE OF....................⎤
County of....................⎦ ss:

Sworn to and subscribed before me this .... day of ...., 19....
[SEAL]

....
(Signature of notary or officer)
....
(Official character)

4. OATH NOT ACCOMPANYING APPLICATION

STATE OF....................⎤
County of....................⎦ ss:

...................., being sworn (or affirmed), deposes and says that he is a citizen of the United States of America and resident of ...., that on ...., 19..., he filed application for patent Serial No. .... in the United States Patent and Trademark Office, that he verily believes himself to be the original, first and sole inventor of the improvement in .... described and claimed in the specification of said application for patent; that he does not know and does not believe that the same was ever known or used before his invention thereof, or patented or described in any printed publication in any country before his invention thereof, or more than one year prior to the date of said application, or in public use or on sale in the United States for more than one year prior to the date of said application; that said invention has not been patented or made the subject of an inventor's certificate before the date of said application in any country foreign to the United States on an application filed by him or his legal representatives or assigns more than twelve months prior to the date of said application; that he acknowledges his duty to disclose information of which he is aware which is material to the examination of this application, and that no application for patent or inventor's certificate on said invention has been filed by him or his representatives or assigns in any country foreign to the United States, except as follows: ....

....
(Inventor's full signature)
Sworn to and subscribed before me this .... day of ...., 19...
....
(Signature of notary or officer)

[SEAL]

....
(Official character)

5. DESIGN APPLICATION, SPECIFICATION, OATH

To the Commissioner of Patents and Trademarks:

Your petitioner, ..., a citizen of the United States and a resident of .... in the county of .... and State of ...., whose post-office address is ...., city of ...., State of ...., prays that letters patent may be granted to him for the new and original design for ...., set forth in the following specification; and he hereby appoints, ..., of ...., (Registration No. ....), his attorney (or agents), to prosecute this application and to transact all business in the Patent and Trademark Office connected therewith.

Be it known that I have invented a new, original, and ornamental design for .... of which the following is a specification, reference being had to the accompanying drawing, forming a part hereof.

The figure is a plan view of a ...., showing my new design.
I claim:

The ornamental design for a ...., as shown.

................, the above-named petitioner being sworn (or affirmed), deposes and says that he is a citizen of the United States and resident of county of ...., State of ...., that he verily believes himself to be the original, first, and sole inventor of the design for .... described and claimed in the foregoing specification; that he does not know and does not believe that the same was ever known or used before his invention thereof, or patented or described in any printed publication in any country before his invention thereof, or more than one year prior to this application, or in public use or on sale in the United States for more than one year prior to this application; that said design has not been patented or made the subject of an inventor's certificate in any country foreign to the United States on an application filed by him or his legal representatives or assigns more than 6 months prior to this application; that he acknowledges his duty to disclose information of which he is aware which is material to the examination of this application, and that no application for patent or inventor's certificate on said design has been filed by him or his representatives or assigns in any country foreign to the United States, except as follows: ....
....

....
(Inventor's full signature)

State of...................... ⎫
County of..................... ⎬ ss:
⎭

Sworn to and subscribed before me this .... day of ...., 19.....
[SEAL]   ....
(Signature of notary or officer)
....
(Official character)

6. PLANT PATENT APPLICATION; POWER OF ATTORNEY, OATH

To the Commissioner of Patents and Trademarks:

Your petitioner, ..., a citizen of the United States and a resident of ...., in the State of ...., whose post-office address is ...., prays that letters patent may be granted to him for the new and distinct variety of .... , set forth in the following specification; and he hereby appoints .... of .... (Registration No. ....), his attorney (or agent), to prosecute this application and to transact all business in the Patent and Trademark Office connected therewith.

(If no power of attorney is to be included in the application, omit the appointment of the attorney.)

[The specification, which includes the description of the invention and the claims, is written here.]

.................., the above-named petitioner, being sworn (or affirmed), deposes and says that he is a citizen of the United States of America and resident of ...., that he verily believes himself to be the original, first, and sole inventor of the new and distinct variety of .... described and claimed in the foregoing specification; that he has asexually reproduced the said new and distinct variety; that he does not know and does not believe that the same was ever known or used before his invention thereof, or patented or described in any printed publication in any country before his invention thereof, or more than one year prior to this application, or in public use or on sale in the United States for more than one year prior to this application; that said invention has not been patented or made the subject of an inventor's certificate in any country foreign to the United States on an application filed by him or his legal representatives or assigns more than 12 months prior to this application; that he acknowledges his duty to disclose information of which he is aware which is material to the examination of this application, and that no application for patent or inventor's certificate on said new and distinct variety of plant has been filed by him or his representatives or assigns in any country foreign to the United States, except as follow: ....

....
(Inventor's full signature)

STATE OF......................⎫
County of......................⎬ ss:
Sworn to and subscribed before me this .. .. day of ...., 19.....

....
(Signature of notary or officer)

[SEAL]

.. ..
(Official character)

7. POWER OF ATTORNEY OR AUTHORIZATION OF AGENT, NOT ACCOMPANYING APPLICATION

To the Commissioner of Patents and Trademarks:

The undersigned having, on or about the .... day of .. .... , 19...., made application for letters patent for an improvement in ...., Serial Number ...., hereby appoints .... of ...., State of ...., Registration No. ...., his attorney (or agent), to prosecute said application, and to transact all business in the Patent and Trademark Office connected therewith.

....
(Signature)

8. REVOCATION OF POWER OF ATTORNEY OR AUTHORIZATION OF AGENT

To the Commissioner of Patents and Trademarks:

The undersigned having, on or about the .... day of ...., 19...., appointed ...., of ...., State of ...., his attorney (or agent) to prosecute an application for letters patent which application was filed on or about the .... day of ...., 19 ...., for an improvement in ...., Serial Number ...., hereby revokes the power of attorney (or authorization of agent) then given.

....
(Signature)

9. ASSIGNMENT OF PATENT

(No special form is prescribed for assignments, which may contain various provisions depending upon the agreement of the parties. The following two forms are specimens of assignments which have been used in some cases.)

Whereas, I, ..., of ...., did obtain Letters Patent of the United States for an improvement in ....

No. ...., dated ....; and whereas, I am now the sole owner of said patent; and,

WHEREAS, ..., of ...., whose post-office address is ...., City of ...., and State of ...., is desirous of acquiring the entire interest in the same;

Now, THEREFORE, in consideration of the sum of .... dollars ($.......), the receipt of which is hereby acknowledged, and other good and valuable considerations, I, ..., by these presents do sell, assign, and transfer unto the said ...., the entire right, title, and interest in and to the said Letters Patent aforesaid; the same to be held and enjoyed by the said ...., for his own used and behoof, and for his legal representatives and assigns, to the full end of the term for which said Letters Patent are granted, as fully and entirely as the same would have been held by me had this assignment and sale not been made.

Executed, this .... day of ...., 19...., at ....

STATE OF....................⎫
                           ⎬ ss:
County of....................⎭

Before me personally appeared said .... and acknowledged the foregoing instruments to be his free act and deed this .... day of ....,

....
(Notary Public)

[SEAL]

10. ASSIGNMENT OF APPLICATION

WHEREAS, I, ..., of .... have invented certain new and useful Improvements in ...., for which an application for United States Letters Patent was filed on ...., Serial No. ...., [if the application has been prepared but not yet filed, state "for which an application for United States Letters Patent was executed on ...." instead] and

WHEREAS, ..., of ...., whose post-office address is ...., is desirous of acquiring the entire right, title and interest in the same;

Now, THEREFORE, in consideration of the sum of .... dollars ($......), the receipt whereof is hereby acknowledged, and other good and valuable consideration, I, the said ...., by these presents do sell, assign and transfer unto said ...., the full and exclusive right to the said invention in the United States and the entire right, title, and interest in and to any and all Letters Patent which may be granted, therefore in the United States.

I hereby authorize and request the Commissioner of Patents and Trademarks to issue said Letters Patent to said ...., as the assignee of the entire right, title, and interest in and to the same, for his sole use and behoof; and for the use and behoof of his legal representatives, to the full end of the term for which said Letters Patent may be granted, as fully and entirely as the same would have been held by me had this assignment and sale not been made.

Executed this .... day of ...., 19...., at ....

....

STATE OF....................⎫
                           ⎬ ss:
County of....................⎭

Before me personally appeared said .... and acknowledged the foregoing instrument to be his free act and deed this ...... day of ...., 19.....

....
(Notary Public)

[SEAL]

40

11. DECLARATION WHICH MAY BL INCLUDED IN AN APPLICATION IN LIEU OF AN OATH

(Rules 65 and 68 of the Rules of Practice provide for a declaration in lieu of an oath in ceitain instances. The petition and specification precede the declaration.)
..............., the above-named petitioner .... declares that he is a citizen of the United States and resident of .... that he verily believes himself to be the original, first, and sole inventor of the improvement in .... described and claimed in the annexed specification; that he does not know and does not believe that the same was ever known or used before .... invention thereof, or patented or described in any printed publication in any country before his invention thereof, or more than one year prior to this application, or in public use or on sale in the United States more than one year prior to this application; that said invention has not been patented in any country foreign to the United States on an application filed by him or his legal representatives or assigns more than twelve months prior to this application; that he acknowledges his duty to disclose information of which he is aware which is material to the examination of this application, and that no application for patent on said invention has been filed by him or his representatives or assigns in any country foreign to the United States, except as follows: ....

The undersigned petitioner .... declare .... further that all statements made herein of .... own knowledge are true and that all statements made on information and belief are believed to be true; and further that these statements were made with the knowledge that willful false statements and the like so made are punishable by fine or imprisonment, or both, under section 1001 of Title 18 of the United States Ccde and that such willful false statements may jeopardize the validity of the application or any patent issuing thereon.

Inventor's full name or names ....
....
(Signature)
Date ....

The Independent Inventor

A great deal of the progress of the United States has resulted from inventions made by inventors working independently of any large organization. It is believed that such people will make many important inventions in the future, as they have in the past. These inventors are often puzzled by such problems as whether to seek patent protection and what steps to take to obtain the benefit of the patent law. In the following discussion we will therefore assume that you have made an invention and that you need a practical guide to help you solve these problems.

You should seek professional advice at a very early stage in connection with any invention, and this pamphlet is provided as an outline of the basic facts you should know in cooperating with your patent practitioner. It cannot possibly serve as a substitute for the detailed professional advice you will need in relation to your particular problems.

Summary of Basic Steps

The questions uppermost in the minds of most inventors are these:
1. Should I try to obtain a patent?
2. If I decide to try to obtain a patent, what steps can I take to secure the best possible patent protection?
3. What steps can I take to improve my chances of developing and marketing my invention successfully?

It is important that you realize there is no way to get assurance in advance that you will be granted a patent, or that you will be able to profit if you obtain one. However, you may improve your chances greatly by following the suggestions made in this pamphlet if your invention is useful and new. If on the other hand the features you consider important are not new or are not useful, these suggestions will help you to discover this early enough to avoid needless expense. The steps you should take are these:

1. Study your invention in relation to other available ways of doing the job, and decide whether the invention provides advantages that make it salable.

2. Get a trustworthy friend to sign his name as witness on a dated drawing or description of the invention, and keep careful records of the steps you take and their dates. Note also, Disclosure Document Program Offered by the Patent and Trademark Office.

3. Make a search to find the most closely related prior patents. This can be done for you by any patent practitioner.

4. Compare the patents found in the search with your invention. Your decision whether to seek patent protection should be based on your own comparison of these patents with the features of your invention which you believe to be new and valuable, and on the advice of your practitioner.

5. If you find that your invention includes valuable features not shown in the patents found in the search, instruct your practitioner to prepare an application for patent and to file it in the Patent and Trademark Office. Help him prepare a good application by giving him all the useful information you can provide.

6. Keep in close touch with the progress of your application in the Patent and Trademark Office. Tell your practitioner promptly of any changes you may make in your invention and of the steps you take to develop and market it. Study the patents which the Patent and Trademark Office may cite against your application. Help your practitioner to overcome rejections by pointing out in what way your invention differs from those described in earlier patents.

Each of these points is explained in some detail in the following sections.

FIRST STEP

Make Certain It is Practical

Many persons believe they can profit from their inventions merely by patenting them. This is a mistake. No one can profit from a patent unless it covers some feature which provides an improvement for which people are willing to pay. You should therefore try to make sure that your invention will provide this kind of advantage before you spend money in trying to patent it.

SECOND STEP

Witnesses, Records and Diligence

Importance of Witnesses. It may become important for you later to be able to prove the date when you first conceived the idea of your invention. If you made a written description or drawings or built and tested it, you may also need to prove these facts and dates, and your diligence in completing and testing it. You will not be able to prove any of these things to the satisfaction of the Patent and Trademark Office or a United States court unless your own testimony is supported by one or more other persons who have knowledge of these facts from first-hand observation, so that at least one other person can testify in your behalf as your corroborating witness.

Make and Keep Good Records. You should prepare a record in the form of a sketch or drawing or written description promptly after you first get the idea of your invention, and ask one or more of your trustworthy friends to read and understand and sign and date this record as witnesses. You should also keep a carefully dated record of other steps you take in working on the invention, and get one or more friends to witness these steps and sign their names as witnesses to your records. You should keep correspondence about the invention, sales slips of materials you buy for use in working on it, and any models or drawings, so that these will be on hand if needed to help you prove the facts and dates of the steps you have taken.

Letter to Yourself Will Not Protect You. Many persons believe that they can protect their inventions against later inventors merely by mailing to themselves a registered letter describing the invention. This is not true. Your priority right against anyone else who makes the same invention independently cannot be sustained except by testimony of someone else who corroborates your own testimony as to all important facts, such as conception of the invention, diligence, and the success of any tests you may have made. It is therefore important that some trustworthy friend witness these things. The invention will not be full protected until patented.

Disclosure Document Program. The Patent and Trademark Office provides a service of storing, for two years, papers disclosing an invention. This service does not diminish the value of the conventional witnessed and notorized records, but does provide a creditable form of evidence. A free brochure detailing the procedures of this program is available on request. Address: Commissioner of Patents and Trademarks, Washington, D.C. 20231.

THIRD STEP

The Search

Why the Search Is Important. You cannot obtain a valid patent if your invention is anticipated by any earlier printed publication or patent in any country, or by commercial use in the United States. If you decide that your invention is valuable enough to patent, your next step should be to make a careful search through patents already issued to find out if it is new as compared to these patents. This is important for a number of reasons:

First, making a search involves less expense than trying to obtain a patent. If you learn through the search that the invention cannot be patented you will save the cost of preparing and filing a patent application.

Second, even if none of the earlier patents shows all the details of your invention, they may show the only *important* features or they may show other ways of doing the job that are as good or better than yours. If this is the case, you will not want to try to get patent protection on an invention that cannot be commercialized.

Third, even if nothing is found in the search which comes very close to your invention, you will still find it helpful to consider the closest patents of others in taking steps to obtain a strong patent on your own invention.

Search in Patent and Trademark Office Search Room. The search should be made in the Search Room of the Patent and Trademark Office in Crystal Plaza, 2021 Jefferson Davis Highway, Arlington, Virginia. You may make this search yourself if you wish; the staff of the Patent and Trademark Office Search Room will assist you in deciding which classes and subclasses should be searched but they cannot make the search for you. Many inventors have done this and have found it helpful and stimulating. With somewhat more difficulty, a search can be made in any one of 22 libraries located throughout the country which keep a numerical file of United States Patents. The book, "General Information Concerning Patents" contains a list of these libraries. However, making a proper search requires both skill and experience. Most inventors hire practitioners to make their searches, both for this reason and in order to save the time and expense of a trip to the Patent and Trademark Office. Patent practitioners having offices in any part of the country can make the searches, either personally on one of their trips to the Pattent and Trademark Office, or through an associate located near the Patent and Trademark Office.

Get Help From Patent and Trademark Office Roster. The Patent and Trademark Office has a roster of all registered practitioners who are available to prepare and prosecute patent applications for inventors and you may employ someone from this roster to make your search. You can buy a copy of this roster from the Superintendent of Documents, U.S. Government Printing Office, Washington, D.C. 20402 (see the list of publications in the front of this pamphlet for price), or see one at any of the district office of the U.S. Department of Commerce or the Small Business Administration, at your State Department of Commerce and Industry, or at a public library designated as a depository for Government publications. The Patent and Trademark Office can send a list of those practitioners with offices in your own region to you without charge. Address your request to Commissioner of Patents and Trademarks, Washington, D.C. 20231.

Your Searcher Will Furnish Estimate. The search to determine whether your invention is new is called a *Preliminary Search*, as it is preliminary to the possible preparation and filing of a patent application. You may ask the practitioner you have chosen to furnish an advance estimate of the cost of making such a search, and also an estimate of his further fees in case you should later decide to file a patent application. The search fee will depend somewhat on whether you decide to have the search cover both the United States patents and readily available foreign patents, or only the United States patents.

Explain Invention to Searcher. You should explain to your searcher the features which you believe are new and important, and how they work to provide improved results. This explanation may be made through drawings or sketches, models, written description, oral discussion, or a combination of these.

Keep Correspondence for Evidence. Correspondence about the search should be kept in a safe place, as it may be needed later to prove dates and other facts about the invention.

FOURTH STEP

Studying Patents Found in the Search

Study Search Results. Your decision whether to try to get a patent is primarily a business decision. It should be based on your own consideration of the practical advantages of your invention over the closest patents found in the search. Your searcher will send you copies of these patents. If any of them is exactly like your invention you will have no chance to obtain a patent. On the other hand one or more patents may describe inventions which are intended for the some purpose as yours, but are different in various ways. You should study these and decide whether it is worthwhile to go ahead.

46

Are Your Important Features New? If the features which make your invention different from prior inventions provide important advantages, you should discuss the situation with your practitioner to determine whether, in his judgment, there is a fair chance for you to obtain a patent covering these features.

No Patent Can Cover Old Features. There is one point which you should especially bear in mind. You cannot obtain a patent which will prevent others from using inventions shown in prior patents, *and any patent which you may be able to obtain will cover features which make your invention different from these prior patents.*

FIFTH STEP

Preparing the Patent Application

Patent Application Includes Written Description. If you decide to try to get a patent, it will be necessary for you to send to the Patent and Trademark Office a formal written application describing your invention. This is called *Filing* the patent application.

Employ Registered Attorney or Agent. Every inventor has the right to prepare his own patent application and *Prosecute* [2] it in the Patent and Trademark Office without the help of any attorney or agent. However, the task of prosecuting a patent application to obtain strong protection requires a great deal of professional knowledge and skill based on training and experience. An inventor who prepares and prosecutes his own application is therefore almost certain to endanger his chances of obtaining a good patent, unless he has a great deal of experience in these matters. The following discussion of Patent and Trademark Office procedure is therefore provided to help you cooperate with a registered patent practitioner and not with the thought that you should prepare and prosecute your own application.

Only Registered Persons May Legally Represent You. If your search has been made by a registered patent attorney or agent, you will probably want to have this same person prepare and prosecute your patent application. In any case, in selecting someone for this purpose you should realize that only registered persons are permitted to represent you. It is illegal for anyone to hold himself out as a practitioner qualified to prepare and prosecute patent applica-

[2] The word "Prosecute" means the writing of letters and legal amendments to the Patent and Trademark Office to convince the Patent and Trademark Office examiner that a patent should be granted, and to fix the legal scope of the patent protection.

tions unless he is so registered before the Patent & Trademark Office. All of the ottorneys and agents available to represent private clients and who have been examined by the Patent and Trademark Office and found qualified are listed in the roster. This roster is for your protection against unqualified or unscrupulous persons claiming competence to represent you.

An Application Consists of These Parts. The patent application will include an oath or declaration, a description of the invention, called the *Specification*, which ends with definitions of the invention called *Claims* and filing fee. There will also be a drawing if the invention is one that can be illustrated. If a practitioner is used, a power of attorney is also included.

Importance of Care. A great deal depends upon the care and skill with which the specification and claims are written. If you fail to supply your practitioner with enough information to help him write a good specification and claims, the patent which you obtain may be so restricted that it has little value, or you may even lose your right to obtain a patent. While your practitioner will doubtless ask you questions to bring out the important points, it should be helpful to you in answering these questions to understand some of the basic principles of patent law and Patent and Trademark Office practice.

Patent Specification Must Describe Invention. The patent law requires that the patent specification must provide a description of the invention which is sufficiently full and clear to teach a person skilled in the field of the invention to make and use it. The patent must also contain claims that distinguish your invention from others and your most important problem will be to secure the grant of claims which cover your invention fully and give your patent the best chance for commercial success. You should read the application carefully before signing it.

Do Not Limit Patent Unnecessarily. If the claims of your patent are limited to unimportant incidental features, other persons may be able to use the important features without paying you merely by making simple changes. If your invention can be carried out in different ways, your practitioner will try to make this clear in the patent specification. He will try to claim the invention in language broad enough to include these different ways if this is necessary for your protection. You should therefore be careful to explain to him any other ways you may have in mind for obtaining the principal advantages of your invention, and not merely the best way.

Critical Importance of Breadth of Claims. The claims are the most important part of the patent application. They define the boundaries of your patent rights and fix the amount of protection granted to you by the patent. Even though you may have made a broad invention, it will not be protected unless your claims are also broad.

Claims Must Distinguish Invention. You will understand from the previous discussion that your claims cannot properly be allowed if their language is so broad that they describe earlier inventions. On the other hand, one or more of your claims should be written in language which is general enough to provide the proper legal protection. The difficult job that your practitioner has to accomplish is first to find the features which distinguish your invention from earlier ones, and then to prepare claims which define it in language which is broad enough to provide proper protection while still including one or another of the features which distinguish the invention from earlier ones.

Ask Practitioner to Send You Office Actions. As discussed in the next section, your patent application will be studied by a Patent and Trademark Office examiner. There will usually be an exchange of letters between your practitioner and the Patent and Trademark Office to determine whether a patent shall be granted, and the claims it shall contain. To make sure that you are informed about these developments, you should establish an understanding with your practitioner that he will furnish you promptly a copy of each letter he receives from the Patent and Trademark Office and of each patent discussed by the Patent and Trademark Office in these letters. Ask him also to send you a copy of each letter of amendment or argument which he may file in response to these Patent and Trademark Office letters. Your practitioner can obtain for you copies of the United States patents cited by the examiner at a cost of 50 cents each. You can be helpful to your practitioner by reading these patents and discussing them with him.

SIXTH STEP

Patent and Trademark Office Prosecution

The Patent and Trademark Office Examiner's Task. Every application is examined by a Patent and Trademark Office examiner who will first read your application to satisfy himself that the invention has been properly described and will then read the claims and make a search among prior patents and printed publications to find those most closely related to the features covered in these claims. This search by the examiner is similar to the preliminary search already made for you, but the examiner's search will be more far-reaching in most cases.

Patent and Trademark Office Letter of Rejection. In presenting claims broad enough to protect you fully, your practitioner may write some of them in a form so broad that the examiner will hold them to be unpatentable. The examiner will make an *Office Action* in the form of a letter in which he will reject your claims if he finds earlier patents or publications which show the features you claim. He will also reject them even though they include some new feature, if he decides that the new feature would be obvious to a person having skill in the field of the invention. The examiner almost always finds one or more earlier patents or publications close enough to some of your claims to cause him to reject them; some claims may be rejected while others may be held to be allowable. The action of the Patent and Trademark Office in rejecting claims that cannot be validly patented serves as a guide to practitioners in their efforts to secure for their clients strong and valid patents.

Avoiding or Overcoming Rejection. Every Patent and Trademark Office action must be answered within the time period required by the examiner to avoid abandonment. This answer is in the form of a letter addressed to the Commissioner of Patents and Trademarks. This letter may direct him to cancel some of the original claims, and to change the language of other claims. Such a letter is called an *Amendment*. In submitting such an amendment, your practitioner will try to avoid adding limitations which will restrict your patent unreasonably. In any case the letter must point out the reasons for believing that a patent should be granted.

Help Your Practitioner in Prosecution. While your practitioner will make a careful study of patents cited in the Office action in preparing your amendment, it will be helpful to him if you also study these patents. The information you will obtain in this way will help you to decide whether you should abandon your patent application and avoid further expense or whether you should continue with your efforts. If you decide to continue you may, by your own study and knowledge of the practical details, be able to point out features and advantages which will help your practioner in preparing the amendment.

Tell Practitioner Promptly About Changes. It is important that you tell your practitioner promptly of any changes in your invention which you have made or plan to make. The Patent and Trademark Office rules do not permit an application to be changed by adding new matter such as improvements, after the application has been filed in the Patent and Trademark Office. However, it is important that you keep your practitioner informed so that he can do everything possible to secure full coverage and properly protect your interests. If he finds he cannot fully protect your improvements in the application already on file in the Patent and Trademark Office, he may recommend that you file a new application to obtain full protection.

Reconsideration by Examiner. After the examiner receives your amendment, he will again study the application and make a second office action. This may be a notice of allowance, telling you that you will be granted a patent, a rejection of all claims, or a rejection of some claims while allowing others. This exchange of office actions and amendments may be repeated until the application is allowed by the examiner, or until the examiner states that the rejection is *final.*

Where To Get Further Information. The prosecution of your application may include an appeal from the decision of the examiner to the Board of Appeals of the Patent and Trademark Office, or other procedures not discussed in this pamphlet. *You may obtain information on these procedures from the other Patent and Trademark Office publications listed in the front of this pamphlet.* The Patent and Trademark Office cannot act as your individual counsellor; you should seek detailed counsel from your own practitioner. If you have any question of a general nature regarding patents, however, you may write to the Commissioner of Patents and Trademarks, Washington, D.C. 20231. If your question relates to commercial promotion of your invention or patent, you may write or get in touch with one of the other offices mentioned in the answers to questions 41, 42 and 44 near the end of this pamphlet.

Marketing and Developing the Invention

Importance of Development Effort

Let us assume now that you have obtained your patent and that you want to know what you may do to profit from it. You were told at the beginning of this pamphlet that you could not hope to profit unless your invention provided some result or feature having an advantage which would enable you to sell it. It is equally true that you are very unlikely to profit, even after you have received a patent, unless you either use the invention yourself or persuade others to use it by pointing out to them the advantages which it provides. Patents seldom promote themselves. It is unlikely that other people, merely by reading the patent, will recognize the advantages and come to you with an offer to purchase the patent or license rights under it.

Government Assistance

Neither the Patent and Trademark Office nor any other Government agency can help you to the extent of acting as a salesman on your behalf to encourage others to adopt the features of your patent and pay you for their use. However, the Patent and Trademark Office and other Government agencies provide services which may help in your own activities. Services which may be helpful are discussed in the answers to questions 40 to 44 in the question and answer section at the end of this pamphlet.

When May Invention be Revealed?

Many inventors ask when they may safely reveal their inventions to others in their efforts to obtain financial backing or to induce some person or business organization to buy their patent rights. No answer can be given to this question which may be applied to every individual situation; you should seek competent legal advice in regard to your particular problems. However, the following general statements may be helpful.

Precaution After Patent Issuance

After the patent is issued it is safe to reveal to others everything that is actually described or illustrated in the patent. These details are then no longer secret, for they are published in the printed copies of your patent which are available to anyone. A precautionary word should be given, however, in connection with later inventions or improvements which are related to the patent. You should be guided by legal counsel in deciding what to say to a prospective purchaser or licensee.

Added Precaution Before Patent Issuance

If you decide to try to sell the invention or license rights under it while your application is still pending in the Patent and Trademark Office you will need to consider another point. Your patent application serial number and filing date are maintained in confidence by the Patent and Trademark Office, and these and other dates may be important if any question arises as to who is the first inventor. You should avoid revealing this information prematurely or carelessly, and get legal advice on this point in connection with negotiation.

Further Precaution Before Applying for Patent

It is also possible to negotiate with a purchaser for sale of rights in your invention even before you have applied for a patent, but such a procedure involves other problems. Many people submit their inventions to prospective manufacturers, after having them witnessed, without having first applied for patent protection. The inventor may feel that this is the only course available if he has no way of determining whether his invention has merit, or if he is unable to afford the cost of a patent application. If you contemplate taking such a course, you are strongly urged to seek legal advice before doing so.

Answers to Questions Frequently Asked

Meaning of Words "Patent Pending"

1. *Q. What do the terms "patent pending" and "patent applied for" mean?*

   A. They are used by a manufacturer or seller of an article to inform the public that an application for patent on that article is on file in the Patent and Trademark Office. The law imposes a fine on those who use these terms falsely to deceive the public.

Patent Application

2. *Q. I have made some changes and improvements in my invention after my patent application was filed in the Patent and Trademark Office. May I amend my patent application by adding a description or illustration of these features?*

A. No. The law specifically provides that new matter shall not be introduced into the disclosure of a patent application. However, you should call the attention of your practitioner promptly to any such changes you may make or plan to make, so that he may take or recommend any steps that may be necessary for your protection.

3. *Q. How does one apply for a patent?*

A. By making the proper application to the Commissioner of Patents and Trademark, Washington, D.C. 20231.

4. *Q. Of what does a patent application consist?*

A. An application fee, a specification and claims describing and defining the invention, an oath or declaration, and a drawing if the invention can be illustrated.

5. *Q. What are the Patent and Trademark Office fees in connection with filing of an application for patent and issuance of the patent?*

A. A filing fee of $65 plus certain additional charges for claims depending on their number and the manner of their presentation are required when the application is filed. An issue fee of $100 plus certain printing charges is also required if the patent is to be granted. This issue fee is not required until your application is allowed by the Patent and Trademark Office.

6. *Q. Are models required as part of the application?*

A. Only in the most exceptional cases. The Patent and Trademark Office has the power to require that a model be furnished, but rarely exercises it.

7. *Q. Is it necessary to go to the Patent and Trademark Office to transact business concerning patent matters?*

A. No; most business with the Patent and Trademark Office is conducted by correspondence. Interviews regarding pending applications can be arranged with examiners if necessary, however, and are often helpful.

8. *Q. Can the Patent and Trademark Office give advice as to whether an inventor should apply for a patent?*

A. No. It can only consider the patentability of an invention when this question comes regularly before it as a patent application.

9. *Q. Is there any danger that the Patent and Trademark Office will give others information contained in my application while it is pending?*

A. No. All patent applications are maintained in the strictest secrecy until the patent is issued. After the patent is issued, however, the Patent and Trademark Office file containing the application and all correspondence leading up to issuance of the patent is made available in the Patent and Trademark Office Search Room for inspection by anyone, and copies of these files may be purchased from the Patent and Trademark Office.

10. *Q. May I write to the Patent and Trademark Office directly about my application after it is filed?*

A. The Patent and Trademark Office will answer an applicant's inquiries as to the status of the application, and inform him whether his application has been rejected, allowed, or is awaiting action by the Patent and Trademark Office. However, if you you have a practitioner the Patent and Trademark Office cannot correspond with both you and the attorney concerning the merits of your application. All comments concerning your invention should be forwarded through your practitioner.

11. *Q. What happens when two inventors apply separately for a patent for the same invention?*

A. If the effective filing dates are sufficiently close, an "interference" is declared and testimony may be submitted to the Patent and Trademark Office to determine which inventor is entitled to the patent. Your attorney or agent can give you further information if it becomes necessary.

12. *Q. Can a shortened statutory period of 3 months set by the Patent and Trademark Office for response to an office action in a pending application be extended?*

A. Yes, upon written request, but only up to the maximum period of six months, which is fixed by law, and with good reasons for the request. An application will become abandoned unless a complete response is received in the Patent and Trademark Office within the time set.

When To Apply for Patent

13. *Q. I have been making and selling my invention for the past 13 months and have not filed a patent application. Is it too late for me to apply for patent?*

A. Yes. A valid patent may not be obtained if the invention was in public use or on sale in the United States of America for more than one year prior to the filing of your patent application. Your own public use and sale of the invention for more than a year before your application is filed will bar your right to a patent just as effectively as if this use and sale had been done by someone else.

14. *Q. I published an article describing my invention in a magazine 13 months ago. Is it too late to apply for a patent?*

A. Yes. The fact that you are the author of the article would not save your patent application. The law provides that the inventor is not entitled to a patent if the invention has been described in a printed publication anywhere in the world more than a year before his patent application is filed.

Who May Obtain a Patent

15. *Q. Is there any restriction as to persons who may obtain a United States patent?*

A. No, except for Patent and Trademark Office employees, any inventor may obtain a patent regardless of age or sex, by complying with the provisions of the law. A foreign citizen may obtain a patent under exactly the same conditions as a United States citizen.

16. *Q. If two or more persons work together to make an invention, to whom will the patent be granted?*

A. If each had a share in the ideas forming the invention, they are joint inventors and a patent will be issued to them jointly on the basis of a proper patent application filed by them jointly. If on the other hand one of these persons has provided all of the ideas of the invention, and the other has only followed instructions in making it, the person who contributed the ideas is the sole inventor and the patent application and patent should be in his name alone.

17. *Q. If one person furnishes all of the ideas to make an invention and another employs him or furnishes the money for building and testing the invention, should the patent application be filed by them jointly?*

A. No. The application must be signed by the true inventor, and filed in the Patent and Trademark Office, in his name. This is the person who furnishes the ideas, not the employer or the person who furnishes the money.

18. *Q. May a patent be granted if an inventor dies before filing his application?*

A. Yes; the application may be filed by the inventor's executor or administrator.

19. *Q. While in England this summer, I found an article on sale which was very ingenious and has not been introduced into the United States or patented or described in a publication. May I obtain a United States patent on this invention?*

A. No. A United States patent may be obtained only by the true inventor, not by someone who learns of an invention of another.

Ownership and Sale of Patent Rights

20. *Q. May the inventor sell or otherwise transfer his right to his patent or patent application to someone else?*

A. Yes. He may sell all or any part of his interest in the patent application or patent to anyone by a properly worded assignment. The application must be filed in the Patent and Trademark Office as the invention of the true inventor, however, and not as the invention of the person who has purchased the invention from him.

21. *Q. If two persons own a patent jointly, what can they do to grant a license to some third person or company to make, use or sell the invention?*

A. They may grant the license jointly, or either one of them may grant such a license without obtaining the consent of the other. A joint owner does not need the consent of his co-owner either to make, use, or sell the invention of the patent independently, or to grant licenses to others. This is true even though the joint owner who grants the license owns only a very small part of the patent. Unless you want to grant this power to a person to whom you assign a part interest, you should ask your lawyer to include special language in the assignment to prevent this result.

22. *Q. As joint inventor, I wish to protect myself against the possibility that my co-inventor may, without my approval, license some third party under our joint patent. How can I accomplish this?*

A. Consult your lawyer and ask him to prepare an agreement for execution by you and your co-inventor to protect each of you against this possibility.

Duration of Patents

23. *Q. For how long a term of years is a patent granted?*

A. Seventeen years from the date of issue; except for patents on designs, which are granted for terms of $3\frac{1}{2}$, 7, or 14 years.

24. *Q. May the term of a patent be extended?*

A. Only by special act of Congress, and this occurs very rarely and only in most exceptional circumstances.

25. *Q. Does the patentee continue to have any control over use of the invention after his patent expires?*

A. No. Anyone has the free right to use an invention covered in an expired patent, so long as he does not use features covered in unexpired patents in doing so.

Patent Searching

26. *Q. Where can a search be conducted?*

A. In the Search Room of the Patent and Trademark Office in Crystal Plaza, 2021 Jefferson Davis Highway, Arlington, Virginia. Classified and numerically arranged sets of United States and foreign patents are kept there for public use. Numerical files are also kept by 22 libraries scattered throughout the United States. The booklet, "General Information Concerning Patents" contains a list of these libraries.

27. *Q. Will the Patent and Tradework Office make searches for individuals to help them decide whether to file patent applications?*

A. No. But it will assist inventors who come to the Search Room by helping them to find the proper patent classes in which to make their searches. For a reasonable fee it will furnish lists of patents in any class and subclass, and copies of these patents may be purchased for 50 cents each in most instances, although plant patents and unusually large "jumbo" patents cost one dollar.

Attorneys and Agents

28. *Q. Does the Patent and Trademark Office control the fees charged by patent attorneys and agents for their services?*

A. No. This is a matter between you and your patent attorney or agent in which the Patent and Trademark Office takes no part. In order to avoid possible misunderstanding you may wish to ask him for estimates in advance of his approximate charges for: (a) the search, described previously in steps three and four; (b) preparation of the patent application, step five, and (c) Patent and Trademark Office prosecution, step six.

29. *Q. Will the Patent and Trademark Office inform me whether the patent attorney or agent I have selected is reliable or trustworthy?*

A. All patent attorneys and agents registered to practice before the Patent and Trademark Office are expected to be reliable and trustworthy. The Patent and Trademark Office can report only that a particular individual is, or is not, in good standing on the register.

30. *Q. If I am dissatisfied with my patent attorney or agent may I change to another?*

A. Yes. There are forms for appointing attorneys and revoking their powers of attorney in the pamphlet entitled "General Information Concerning Patents." See the list of publications in the front of this pamphlet for price and sources.

31. *Q. Will the Patent and Trademark Office help me to select a patent attorney or agent to make my patent search or to prepare and prosecute my patent application?*

A. No. The Patent and Trademark Office cannot make this choice for you. However, your own friends or general attorney may help you in making a selection from among those listed as registered practitioners on the Patent and Trademark Office roster. Also, bar associations in some localities operate lawyer referral services that maintain lists of patent lawyers available to accept new clients.

32. *Q. How can I be sure that my patent attorney or agent will not reveal to others the secrets of my invention?*

A. Patent attorneys and agents earn their livelihood by the confidential services they perform for their clients, and if any attorney or agent improperly reveals an invention disclosed to him by a client, that attorney or agent is subject to disbarment from further practice before the Patent and Trademark Office and loss of his livelihood. Persons who withhold information about their inventions from their attorneys and agents make a serious mistake, for the attorney or agent cannot do a fully effective job unless he is fully informed.

Plant and Design Patents

33. *Q. Does the law provide patent protection for invention of new and ornamental designs for articles of manufacture, or for new varieties of plants?*

A. Yes. If you have made an invention in one of these fields, you should read the Patent and Trademark Office pamphlet. "General Information Concerning Patent."

Technical Knowledge Available From Patents

34. *Q. I have not made an invention but have encountered a problem. Can I obtain knowledge through patents of what has been done by others to solve the problem?*

A. The patents in the Patent and Trademark Office Search Room are arranged by subject matter and contain a vast wealth of technical information and suggestions. You may come to the Search Room and review these patents, or engage a patent practitioner to do this for you and send you copies of the patents most closely related to your problem.

Infringement of Others' Patents

35. *Q. If I obtain a patent on my invention will I be protected against the claims of others who assert that I am infringing their patents when I make, use, or sell my own invention?*

A. No. There may be a patent of a more basic nature on which your invention is an improvement. If your invention is a detailed refinement or feature of such a basically protected invention, you may not use it without the consent of the patentee, just as no one will have the right to use your patented improvement without your consent. You should seek competent legal advice before starting to make or sell or use your invention commercially, even if it is protected by a patent granted to you.

Enforcement of Patent Rights

36. *Q. Will the Patent and Trademark Office help me to prosecute others if they infringe the rights granted to me by my patent?*

A. No. The Patent and Trademark Office has no jurisdiction over questions relating to the infringement of patent rights. If your patent is infringed you may sue the infringer in the appropriate United States court at your own expense.

Patent Protection in Foreign Countries

37. *Q. Does a United States patent give protection in foreign countries?*

A. No. The United States patent protects your invention only in this country. If you wish to protect your invention in foreign countries, you must file an application in the patent office of each such country within the time permitted by law. This may be quite expensive, both because of the cost of filing and prosecuting the individual patent applications, and because of the fact that most foreign countries require payment of fees to maintain patents in force. You should inquire of your practitioner about these costs before you decide to file in foreign countries.

National Defense Inventions

38. *Q. I have developed an invention which may be of interest to the Armed Forces or other Government agencies. How shall I bring it to their attention?*

A. If you know the name of the agency that you think might have an interest in your invention submit complete descriptive information to that agency. If you do not know of a specific agency you can send the information to the Office of Innovation and Invention, National Bureau of Standards, U.S. Department of Commerce, Washington, D.C., 20234.

39. *Q. I believe that the publication of a patent on my invention would be detrimental to the national defense. For this reason, I am reluctant to file a patent application unless there is a special method of handling cases of this nature. What should I do?*

A. You need have no qualms about filing an application in the U.S. Patent and Trademark Office. If it is determined that publication of the invention by the granting of a patent would be detrimental to the national defense, the Commissioner of Patents and Trademarks will order that the invention be kept secret and will withhold the grant of a patent until a decision is made that disclosure of the invention is no longer detrimental to the national security. If an order is issued that the invention of your patent application be kept secret, you will be entitled to appy for compensation from the Government, if and when the application is held to be allowable.

Developing and Marketing Inventions and Patents

40. *Q. Will the Patent and Trademark Office advise me as to whether a certain patent promotion organization is reliable and trustworthy?*

A. No. The Patent and Trademark Office has no control over such organizations and does not supply information about them. *It is advisable, however, to check on the reputation of invention promotion firms before making any commitments.* It is suggested that you obtain this information by inquiring of the Better Business Bureau of the city in which the organization is located, or of the bureau of commerce and industry or bureau of consumer affairs of the state in which the organization has its place of business You may also undertake to make sure that you are dealing with reliable people by asking your own patent attorney or agent whether he has knowledge of them, or by inquiry of others who may know them.

41. *Q. Are there any organizations in my area which can tell me how and where I may be able to obtain assistance in developing and marketing my invention?*

A. Yes. In your own or neighboring communities you may inquire of such organizations as chambers of commerce, banks and area departments of power companies and railroads. Many communities have locally financed industrial development organizations which can help you locate manufacturers and individuals who might be interested in promoting your idea. You can also obtain assistance from one of the district offices of the U.S. Department of Commerce or of the Small Business Administration located near you. The addresses of these offices are listed in your local telephone directory.

42. *Q. Are there any state government agencies that can help me in developing and marketing of my invention?*

A. Yes. In nearly all states there are state planning and development agencies or departments of commerce and industry which seek new product and new process ideas to assist manufacturers and communities in the state. If you do not know the names or addresses of your state organizations you can obtain this information by writing to the governor of your state.

43. *Q. Can the Patent and Trademark Office assist me in the developing and marketing of my patent?*

A. Only to a very limited extent. The Patent and Trademark Office cannot act or advise concerning the business transactions or arrangements that are involved in the development and marketing of an invention. However, the Patent and Trademark Office will publish, at the request of a patent owner, a notice in the "Official Gazette" that the patent is available for licensing or sale. The fee for this service is $3.

44. *Q. Can any U.S. Government agency other than the Patent and Trademark Office assist me in the development and marketing of my invention?*

A. The Small Business Administration may be able to help you, or one of the district offices of the U.S. Department of Commerce field offices. SBA has over 60 offices in various cities in the United States, and it offers through its products assistance program information and counsel to small concerns who are interested in new products. You may wish to get in touch with one of these offices of the Small Business Administration. The addresses of the field offices of the U.S. Department of Commerce and of the Small Business Administration are listed in your local telephone directory.

DISCLOSURE DOCUMENT PROGRAM

A service is provided for inventors by the U.S. Patent Office—the acceptance and preservation for a limited time of "Disclosure Documents" as evidence of the dates of conception of inventions.

WHAT THE PROGRAM IS

A paper disclosing an invention and signed by the inventor or inventors may be forwarded to the Patent Office by the inventor (or by any one of the inventors when there are joint inventors), by the owner of the invention, or by the attorney or agent of the inventor(s) or owner. It will be retained for two years and then be destroyed unless it is referred to in a separate letter in a related patent application filed within two years.

The Disclosure Document is not a patent application, and the date of its receipt in the Patent Office will not become the effective filing date of any patent application subsequently filed. However, like patent applications, these documents will be kept in confidence by the Patent Office.

This program does not diminish the value of the conventional witnessed and notarized records as evidence of conception of an invention, but it should provide a more credible form of evidence than that provided by the popular practice of mailing a disclosure to oneself or another person by registered mail.

CONTENT OF DISCLOSURE DOCUMENT

Although there are no restrictions as to content and claims are not necessary, the benefits afforded by the Disclosure Document will depend directly upon the adequacy of the disclosure. Therefore, it is strongly urged that the document contain a clear and complete explanation of the manner and process of making and using the invention in sufficient detail to enable a person having ordinary knowledge in the field of the invention to make and use the invention. When the nature of the invention permits, a drawing or sketch should be included. The use or utility of the invention should be described, especially in chemical inventions.

PREPARATION OF THE DOCUMENT

The Disclosure Document must be limited to written matter or drawings on paper or other thin, flexible material, such as linen or plastic drafting material, having dimensions or being folded to dimensions not to exceed 8½ by 13 inches. Photographs also are acceptable. Each page should be numbered. Text and drawings should be sufficiently dark to permit reproduction with commonly used office copying machines.

OTHER ENCLOSURES

In addition to the fee described below, the Disclosure Document *must be accompanied by a stamped, self-addressed envelope and a separate paper in duplicate,* signed by the inventor, stating that he is the inventor and requesting that the material be received for processing under the Disclosure Document Program. The papers will be stamped by the Patent Office with an identifying number and date of receipt, and the duplicate request will be returned in the self-addressed envelope together with a warning notice indicating that the Disclosure Document may be relied upon only as evidence and that a patent application should be diligently filed if patent protection is desired. The inventor's request may take the following form:

"The undersigned, being the inventor of the disclosed invention, requests that the enclosed papers be accepted under the Disclosure Document Program, and that they be preserved for a period of two years."

DISPOSITION

The Disclosure Document will be preserved in the Patent Office for two years after its receipt and then will be destroyed unless it is referred to in a separate letter in a related patent application filed within the two-year period. The letter filed in the related patent application must identify not only the patent application, but also the Disclosure Document by its Title, number and date of receipt. Acknowledgement of receipt of such letters will be made in a separate letter from the Patent Office.

FEE

A fee of $10 is charged for this service. Payment must accompany the Disclosure Document when it is submitted to the Patent Office. A check or money order must be made payable to "Commissioner of Patents." Mail with the Disclosure Document to " Commissioner of Patents, Washington, D.C. 20231."

WARNING TO INVENTORS

The two year retention period should not be considered to be a "grace period" during which the inventor can wait to file his patent application without possible loss of benefits. It must be recognized that in establishing priority of invention an affidavit or testimony referring to a Disclosure Document must usually also establish diligence in completing the invention or in filing the patent application since the filing of the Disclosure Document.

Inventors are also reminded that any public use or sale in the United States or publication of the invention anywhere in the world more than one year prior to the filing of a patent application on that invention will prohibit the granting of a patent on it.

If the inventor is not familiar with what is considered to be "diligence in completing the invention" or "reduction to practice" under the patent law, or if he has other questions about patent matters, the Patent Office advises him to consult an attorney or agent registered to practice before the Patent Office. Patent Attorneys and agents may be found in the telephone directories of most major cities. Also, many large cities have associations of patent attorneys which may be consulted.

PART TWO

What Everybody
Should Know About

Trademark Statutes and Rules

These remarks are intended to serve only as a general guide in regard to trademark matters in the Patent and Trademark Office.

Applications for registration of trademarks must conform to the requirements of the Trademark Act of 1946, as amended, and the Trademark Rules of Practice. This Act, Public Law 489, Seventy-ninth Congress, Chapter 540, 60 Stat. 427, popularly known as the Lanham Act, and forming Chapter 22, Title 15 of the U.S. Code, became effective July 5, 1947, superseding the Trademark Acts of 1905 and 1920. The trademark rules form Part 2 of Title 37 of the Code of Federal Regulations, and a booklet entitled 37 C.F.R. containing the rules as well as a booklet, *Trademark Rules of Practice with Forms and Statutes* can be obtained from Superintendant of Documents, U. S. Government printing Office, Washinton, D.C. 20402.

Definition and Functions of Trademarks

Definition of Trademarks. A "trademark," as defined in section 45 of the 1946 Act, "includes any word, name, symbol, or device, or any combination thereof adopted and used by a manufacturer or merchant to identify his goods and distinguish them from those manufactured or sold by others."

Function of Trademarks. The primary function of a trademark is to indicate origin. However, trademarks also serve to guarantee the quality of the goods bearing the mark and, through advertising, serve to create and maintain a demand for the product. Rights in a trademark are acquired only by use and the use must ordinarily continue if the rights so acquired are to be preserved. Registration of a trademark in the Patent and Trademark Office does not in itself create or establish any exclusive rights, but is recognition by the Government of the right of the owner to use the mark in commerce to distinguish his goods from those of others.

Mark Must Be Used in Commerce. In order to be eligible for registration, a mark must be in use in commerce which may lawfully be regulated by Congress, for example, interstate commerce, at the time the application is filed. "Use in commerce" is defined in section 45 as follows:

For the purposes of this Act a mark shall be deemed to be used in commerce (a) on goods when it is placed in any manner on the goods or their containers or the displays associated therewith or on the tags or labels affixed thereto and the goods are sold or transported in commerce and (b) on services when it is used or displayed in the sale or advertising of services and the services are rendered in commerce, or the services are rendered in more than one State or in this and a foreign country and the person rendering the services is engaged in commerce in connection therewith.

Trade and Commercial Names. Trademarks differ from trade and commercial names which are used by manufacturers, industrialists, merchants, agriculturists, and others to identify their businesses, vocations or occupations, or the names or titles lawfully adopted by persons, firms, associations, companies, unions and other organizations. The latter are not subject to registration unless actually used as trademarks.

Registration of Trademarks

Marks Not Subject to Registration. A trademark cannot be registered if it—

(a) Consists of or comprises immoral, deceptive, or scandalous matter or matter which may disparage or falsely suggest a connection with persons, living or dead, institutions, beliefs, or national symbols, or bring them into contempt or disrepute.

(b) Consists of or comprises the flag or coat of arms or other insignia of the United States, or of any State or municipality, or of any foreign nation, or any simulation thereof.

(c) Consists of or comprises a name, portrait, or signature identifying a particular living individual except by his written consent, or the name, signature, or portrait of a deceased President of the United States during the life of his widow, if any, except by the written consent of the widow.

(d) Consists of or comprises a mark which so resembles a mark registered in the Patent and Trademark Office or a mark or trade name previously used in the United States by another and not abandoned, as to be likely when applied to the goods of another person, to cause confusion, or to cause mistake, or to deceive.

Principal and Supplemental Register Marks. The Trademark Act of 1946 provides for the establishment of two registers, designated as the Principal Register and the Supplemental Register. Coined, arbitrary, fanciful, or suggestive marks, generally referred to as "technical marks," may, if otherwise qualified, be registered on the Principal Register. Marks not qualified for registration on the principal register but which, nevertheless, are capable of distinguishing applicant's goods and have been in lawful use in commerce for at least one year, may be registered on the Supplemental Register.

Registrable Marks—Principal Register. A trademark, if otherwise eligible, may be registered on the Principal Register unless it consists of a mark which, (1) when applied to the goods/services of the applicant is merely descriptive or deceptively misdescriptive of them, or (2) when applied to the goods/services of the applicant is primarily geographically descriptive or deceptively misdescriptive of them, except as indications of regional origin, or (3) is primarily merely a surname.

Such marks, however, may be registered on the Principal Register, provided they have become distinctive as applied to the applicant's goods in commerce. The Commissioner may accept as prima facie evidence that the mark has become distinctive as applied to applicant's goods/services in commerce, proof of substantially exclusive and continuous use thereof as a mark by the applicant in commerce for the 5 years next preceding the date of filing of the application for registration.

Registrable Marks—Supplemental Register. All marks capable of distinguishing applicant's goods and not registrable on the Principal Register, which have been in lawful use in commerce for the year preceding the filing of the application for registration, may be registered on the Supplemental Register. For the purpose of registration on the Supplemental Register a mark may consist of any trademark, symbol, label, package, configuration of goods, name, word, slogan, phrase, surname, geographical name, numeral, or device, or any combination of any of the foregoing.

Application for Registration

The application for registration must be filed in the name of the owner of the mark. The owner may file and prosecute his own application for registration, or he may be represented by an attorney or other person authorized to practice in trademark cases. The Patent and Trademark Office cannot aid in the selection of an attorney or other person. Application forms for corporations, individuals, and firms are available from the Patent and Trademark Office upon request.

Parts Comprising an Application. An application comprises:

(a) A written application (see pp. 4 to 9; for suggested forms, see pp. 20 to 28);

(b) A drawing of the mark (see p. 9);

(c) Five specimens or facsimiles (see p. 11);

(d) The required filing fee (see p. 18).

Foreign Applicant. In addition to the above requirements, if the applicant is not domiciled in the United States he must designate by a written document filed in the Patent and Trademark Office the name and address of some person resident in the United States on whom may be served notices or process in proceedings affecting the mark and to whom all official communications will be addressed unless the applicant is represented by an attorney or other authorized person. If this document does not accompany or form part of the application, it will be required and registration refused unless it is supplied.

A foreign applicant using a mark in commerce which may lawfully be regulated by Congress may apply for registration in the same manner as residents of the United States.

If the mark is not being used in commerce with the United States, the application may be based upon a registration which the applicant has previously secured in his country of origin, and which is in full force and effect. The application, however, must be accompanied by a certification or a certificate of the trademark office of the foreign country showing that the mark has been registered in that country. The U.S. application may also be based upon an application for registration filed in the applicant's country of origin not more than six months prior to the filing date of the application in this country, but registration will not be granted until the application filed in the country of origin has matured into a registration. In either case the application must conform to the same requirements as for other applications except that use in commerce which may lawfully be regulated by Congress need not be alleged and the dates of first use need not be given.

Compliance With Other Laws. When the sale or transportation of any product for which registration of a trademark is sought is regulated under an Act of Congress, the Office may, before allowance, make appropriate inquiry as to compliance with such act for the sole purpose of determining lawfulness of the commerce recited in the application.

THE WRITTEN APPLICATION

The written application must be in the English language and plainly written on but one side of the paper. Legal size paper, typewritten double spaced, with at least a 1½-inch margin on the left-hand side and top of the pages is deemed preferable.

Requirements for Application. The application shall include a request for registration and must specify:

(i) The name of the applicant;

(ii) The citizenship of the applicant; if the applicant is a partnership, the names and citizenship of the general partners or, if the applicant is a corporation or association, the state or nation under the laws of which organized;

(iii) The domicile and post office address of the applicant;

(iv) That the applicant has adopted and is using the mark shown in the accompanying drawing;

(v) The particular goods on or in connection with which the mark is used;

(vi) The class of merchandise according to the official classification if known to the applicant. The official classification of goods and services appears on page 6;

(vii) The date of applicant's first use of the mark as a trademark on or in connection with goods specified in the application;

(viii) The date of applicant's first use of the mark as a trademark on or in connection with goods specified in the application in commerce which may lawfully be regulated by Congress, specifying the nature of such commerce;

(ix) The mode or manner in which the mark is used on or in connection with the particular goods specified.

If more than one item of goods is specified in the application, the dates of use required in paragraphs (vii) and (viii) of this section need be for only one of the items specified, provided the particular item to which the dates apply is designated. In combined applications, dates of use for each class are required.

The word "commerce" as used throughout this pamphlet means commerce which lawfully may be regulated by Congress as specified in section 45 of the Trademark Act. The application must also include averments to the effect that the applicant or other person making the verification believes himself or the firm, corporation, or association in whose behalf he makes the verification, to be the owner of the mark sought to be registered; that the mark is in use in commerce specifying the nature of such commerce; that no other person, firm, corporation, or association, to the best of his knowledge and belief, has the right to use such mark in commerce, either in the identical form thereof or in such near resemblance thereto as to be likely, when applied to the goods of such other person, to cause confusion, or to cause mistake, or to deceive; and that the facts set forth in the application are true.

Signature and Verification. The application must be signed and verified (sworn to) or include a declaration by the applicant or by a member of the firm or an officer of the corporation or association applying.

Use by Related Company. If the mark sought to be registered is not in fact being used by the applicant but is being used by one or more related companies whose use inures to the benefit of the applicant under section 5 of the Trademark Act, such facts must be indicated in the application.

Principal Register. All applications will be treated as requesting registration on the Principal Register unless otherwise stated in the application.

Supplemental Register. An application for registration on the Supplemental Register shall so indicate and shall specify that the mark has been in continuous use in commerce, specifying the nature of such commerce, by the applicant for the preceding year, if the application is based on such use.

Classification. An application in which a single fee is submitted must be limited to the goods or to the services comprised in a single class. An application may be filed to register the same mark on goods and services falling within a plurality of classes but a fee equaling the sum of the fees for filing an application in each class is required. The following international classification of goods and services has been adopted for convenience of administration. This classification does not limit or extend the applicant's rights.

GOODS

1. Chemical products used in industry, science, photography, agriculture, horticulture, forestry; artifical and synthetic resins; plastics in the form of powders, liquids or pastes, for industrial use; manures (natural and artificial); fire extinguishing compositions; tempering substances and chemical preparations for soldering; chemical substances for preserving foodstuffs; tanning substances; adhesive substances used in industry.

2. Paints, varnishes, lacquers; preservatives against rust and against deterioration of wood; colouring matters, dyestuffs; mordants; natural resins; metals in foil and powder form for painters and decorators.

3. Bleaching preparations and other substances for laundry use; cleaning, polishing, scouring and abrasive preparations; soaps; perfumery, essential oils, cosmetics, hair lotions; dentifrices.

4. Industrial oils and greases (other than oils and fats and essential oils); lubricants; dust laying and absorbing compositions; fuels (including motor spirit) and illuminants; candles, tapers, night lights and wicks.

5. Pharmaceutical, veterinary, and sanitary substances; infants' and invalids' foods; plasters, material for bandaging; material for stopping teeth, dental wax, disinfectants; preparations for killing weeds and destroying vermin.

6. Unwrought and partly wrought common metals and their alloys; anchors, anvils, bells, rolled and cast building materials; rails and other metallic materials for railway tracks; chains (except driving chains for vehicles); cables and wires (non-electric); locksmiths' work; metallic pipes and tubes; safes and cash boxes; steel balls; horseshoes; nails and screws; other goods in non-precious metal not included in other classes; ores.

7. Machines and machine tools; motors (except for land vehicles); machine couplings and belting (except for land vehicles); large size agricultural implements; incubators.

8. Hand tools and instruments; cutlery, forks, and spoons; side arms.

9. Scientific, nautical, surveying and electrical apparatus and instruments (including wireless), photographic, cinematographic, optical, weighing, measuring, signalling, checking (supervision), lifesaving and teaching apparatus and instruments; coin or counter-freed apparatus; talking machines; cash registers; calculating machines; fire-extinguishing apparatus.

10. Surgical, medical, dental and veterinary instruments and apparatus (including artificial limbs, eyes, and teeth).

11. Installations for lighting, heating, steam generating, cooking, refrigerating, drying, ventilating, water supply and sanitary purposes.

12. Vehicles; apparatus for locomotion by land, air or water.

13. Firearms; ammunition and projectiles; explosive substances; fireworks.

14. Precious metals and their alloys and goods in precious metals or coated therewith (except cutlery. forks and spoons); jewellery, precious stones, horological and other chronometric instruments.

15. Musical instruments (other than talking machines and wireless apparatus).

16. Paper, cardboard, articles of paper or of cardboard (not included in other classes); printed matter, newspapers and periodicals, books; book-binding material; photographs; stationery; adhesive materials (stationery); artists' materials; paint brushes; typewriters and office requisites (other than furniture); instructional and teaching material (other than apparatus); playing cards; printers' type and cliches (stereotype).

17. Gutta percha, indiarubber, balata and substitutes, articles made from these substances and not included in other classes; plastics in the form of sheets, blocks and rods, being for use in manufacture; materials for packing, stopping or insulating; asbestos, mica and their products; hose pipes (non-metallic).

18. Leather and imitations of leather, and articles made from these materials and not included in other classes; skins, hides; trunks and travelling bags; umbrellas, parasols and walking sticks; whips, harness and saddlery.

19. Building materials, natural and artificial stone, cement, lime, mortar, plaster and gravel; pipes of earthenware or cement; road-making materials; asphalt, pitch and bitumen; portable buildings; stone monuments; chimney pots.

20. Furniture, mirrors, picture frames; articles (not included in

other classes) of wood, cork, reeds, cane, wicker, horn, bone, ivory, whalebone, shell, amber, mother-of-pearl, meerschaum, celluloid, substitutes for all these materials, or of plastics.

21. Small domestic utensils and containers (not of precious metals, or coated therewith) ; combs and sponges; brushes (other than paint brushes) ; brush-making materials; instruments and material for cleaning purposes; steel wool; unworked or semi-worked glass (excluding glass used in building) ; glassware, porcelain and earthenware, not included in other classes.

22. Ropes, string, nets, tents, awnings, tarpaulins, sails, sacks; padding and stuffing materials (hair, kapok, feathers, seaweed, etc.) ; raw fibrous textile materials.

23. Yarns, threads.

24. Tissues (piece goods) ; bed and table covers; textile articles not included in other classes.

25. Clothing, including boots, shoes and slippers.

26. Lace and embroidery, ribands and braid; buttons, press buttons, hooks and eyes, pins and needles; artificial flowers.

27. Carpets, rugs, mats and matting; linoleums and other materials for covering existing floors; wall hangings (non-textile).

28. Games and playthings; gymnastic and sporting articles (except clothing) ; ornaments and decorations for Christmas trees.

29. Meats, fish, poultry and game; meat extracts; preserved, dried and cooked fruits and vegetables; jellies, jams; eggs, milk and other dairy products; edible oils and fats; preserves, pickles.

30. Coffee, tea, cocoa, sugar, rice, tapioca, sago, coffee substitutes; flour, and preparations made from cereals; bread, biscuits, cakes, pastry and confectionery, ices; honey, treacle; yeast, baking-powder; salt, mustard, pepper, vinegar, sauces, spices; ice.

31. Agricultural, horticultural and forestry products and grains not included in other classes; living animals; fresh fruits and vegetables; seeds; live plants and flowers; foodstuffs for animals, malt.

32. Beer, ale and porter; mineral and aerated waters and other non-alcoholic drinks; syrups and other preparations for making beverages.

33. Wines, spirits and liqueurs.

34. Tobacco, raw or manufactured; smokers' articles; matches.

SERVICES

35. Advertising and business.
36. Insurance and financial.
37. Construction and repair.
38. Communication.
39. Transportation and storage.
40. Material treatment.

76

41. Education and entertainment.

42. Miscellaneous.

Schedule for Certification Marks. In the case of certification marks, all goods and services are classified in two 'classes as follows:

A. Goods.

B. Services.

Schedule for Collective Membership Marks. All collective membership marks are classified as follows:

200   Collective Membership.

Note: In the Trademark Search Room the prior U.S. Classification Numbers appear on Registrations in addition to the International Classification Numbers.

DRAWING

The drawing must be a substantially exact representation of the mark as actually used in connection with the goods or services. The drawing of a service mark may be dispensed with if the mark is not capable of representation by a drawing, but in such case the written application must contain an adequate description of the mark.

If the application is for registration only of a word, letter or numeral, or any combination thereof, not depicted in special form, the drawing may be the mark typed in capital letters on paper, otherwise complying with the requirements.

Paper and Ink. The drawing must be made upon pure white durable paper, the surface of which must be calendered and smooth. A good grade of bond paper is suitable. India ink alone must be used for pen drawings to secure perfectly black solid lines. The use of white pigment to cover lines is not acceptable.

Size of Sheets and Margins. The size of the sheet on which a drawing is made must be 8 inches wide and 11 inches long. One of the shorter sides of the sheet should be regarded as its top. When the figure is longer than the width of the sheet, the sheet should be turned on its side with the top at the right. The size of the mark must be such as to leave a margin of at least one inch on the sides and bottom of the paper and at least one inch between it and the heading.

Heading. Across the top of the drawing, beginning one inch from the top edge and not exceeding one-fourth of the sheet, there should be placed a heading, listing in separate lines, applicant's name, applicant's post office address, the dates of first use, and the goods or services recited in the application (or typical items of the goods or services if a number are recited in the application). This heading may be typewritten.

Character of Lines. All drawings, except as otherwise provided, must be made with the pen or by a process which will give them satisfactory reproduction characteristics. Every line and letter, names included, must be black. This direction applies to all lines, however fine, and to shading. All lines must be clean, sharp, and solid, and they must not be too fine or crowded. Surface shading, when used, should be open. A photolithographic reproduction or printer's proof copy may be used if otherwise suitable.

Extraneous Matter. Extraneous matter must not appear upon the face of the drawing.

Linings for Color. Where color is a feature of a mark, the color or colors employed may be designated in the drawing by means of conventional linings as shown in the following color chart.

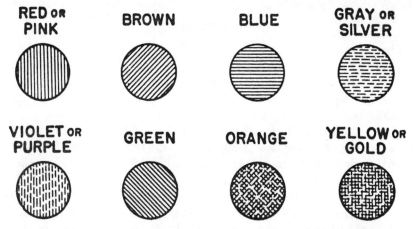

Transmission of Drawings. Drawings transmitted to the Patent and Trademark Office, other than typed drawings, should be sent flat, protected by a sheet of heavy binder's board, or should be rolled for transmission in a suitable mailing tube.

Informal Drawings. A drawing not in conformity with the foregoing requirements may be accepted for purpose of examination, but the drawing must be corrected or a new one furnished, as required, before the mark can be published or the application allowed. The necessary corrections will be made by the Patent and Trademark Office upon applicant's request and at his expense. Substitute drawings will not be accepted unless they have been required by the Examiner or correction of the original drawing would require that the mark be substantially entirely redrawn.

Patent and Trademark Office May Make Drawings. The Patent and Trademark Office, at the request of applicants and at their expense, will make drawings if facilities permit.

SPECIMENS

Trademark Specimens. A trademark may be placed in any manner on the goods, or their containers or displays associated therewith, or on tags or labels attached to the goods. The five specimens shall be duplicates of the actually used labels, tags, containers, or displays or portions thereof, when made of suitable material and capable of being arranged flat and of a size not larger than 8½ × 13". Third-dimensional or bulky material submitted as specimens cannot be accepted, and the submission of such material may result in a delay in receiving a filing date.

Trademark Facsimiles. When, due to the mode of applying or affixing the mark to the goods, or to the manner of using the mark on the goods, or to the nature of the mark, specimens as above stated cannot be furnished, five copies of a suitable photograph or other acceptable reproduction, not larger than 8½ × 13" and clearly and legibly showing the mark and all matter used in connection therewith, shall be furnished.

Service Mark Specimens or Facsimiles. In the case of a service mark, specimens or facsimiles of the mark as used in the sale or advertising of the services must be furnished unless impossible from the nature of the mark or the manner in which it is used, in which event some other representation acceptable to the Commissioner must be submitted.

In the case of service marks not used in printed or written form, three single face, unbreakable, disc recordings will be accepted. The speed at which the recordings are to be played must be specified thereon. If facilities are not available to the applicant to furnish recordings of the required type, the Patent and Trademark Office may arrange to have made, upon request and at applicant's expense, the necessary disc recordings from any type of recording the applicant submits.

Examination of Applications

Order of Examination. Applications will be docketed and examined in the order in which they are received. In the event it is found that the mark is not entitled to registration for any reason, the applicant will be notified and advised of the reasons therefor and of any formal requirements or objections.

Period for Response. The applicant has 6 months from the date of mailing of any action by the Patent and Trademark Office to respond thereto. Failure to respond within this period will result in abandonment of the application. Response may be made with or without amendment and must include such proper action by the applicant as the nature of the action and the condition of the case may require.

Reexamination or Reconsideration. After response by the applicant, the application will be reexamined or reconsidered. If on further examination or consideration, registration is refused, appeal may be taken to the Trademark Trial and Appeal Board.

Principal Register Marks Subject to Opposition. If, on examination or reexamination of an application for registration on the Principal Register, it appears that the applicant is entitled to have his mark registered, it will be published in the *Official Gazette* and will be subject to opposition. Any person who believes he would be damaged by the registration of a mark on the Principal Register may oppose the same within 30 days after publication. Oppositions are transmitted to the Trademark Trial and Appeal Board and are governed by the rules applicable to adversary proceedings.

Interference. An interference proceeding between conflicting marks in copending applications or in an application and a registration will not be instituted except upon specific authorization of the Commissioner obtained upon petition by the applicant.

Registrations or applications to register on the Supplemental Register, registrations under the 1920 Act, and registrations of marks the right to the use of which has become incontestable are not subject to interference.

Allowance of Principal Register Marks. If no notice of opposition is filed and no conflict found with other pending applications or registrations, the certificate of registration will issue in due course of business.

Allowance of Supplemental Register Marks. A Supplemental register mark, upon being found allowable, will be passed to registration, and the mark published in the *Official Gazette* when registered.

Service, Certification, and Collective Marks

The Trademark Act of 1946 also provides for the registration of service marks, certification marks, and collective marks.

Service Marks. The term "service mark" means a mark used in the sale or advertising of services to identify the services of one person and distinguish them from the services of others. Titles, character names and other distinctive features of radio or televsion programs may be registered as service marks notwithstanding that they, or the programs, may advertise the goods of the sponsor.

Certification Marks. The term "certification mark" means a mark used upon or in connection with the products or services of one or more persons other than the owner of the mark to certify regional or other origin, material, mode of manufacture, quality, accuracy or other characteristics of such goods or services or that the work or labor on the goods or services was performed by members of a union or other organization.

Collective Marks. The term "collective mark" means a trademark or service mark used by the members of a cooperative, an association, or other collective group or organization. Marks used to indicate membership in a union, an association, or other organization may be registered as Collective Membership Marks.

Registered Marks

Constructive Notice and Evidence of Ownership. Registration of a mark on the Principal Register of the 1946 Act, or under the Acts of 1881 or 1905, is constructive notice of the registrant's claim of ownership thereof, and prima facie evidence of the validity of the registration, registrant's ownership of the mark, and of registrant's exclusive right to use the mark in commerce in connection with the goods or services specified in the certificate, subject to any conditions and limitations stated therein. Such registrations give the right to sue in the United States courts and to prevent importation of goods bearing an infringing mark.

Registration on the Supplemental Register of the 1946 Act or under the Act of 1920 does not constitute constructive notice or prima facie evidence and does not give the right to prevent importation of goods bearing an infringing mark, but does give the right to sue in the United States courts.

Notice of Registration. A registrant should give notice that his mark is registered by displaying with the mark as used the words "Registered in U.S. Patent and Trademark Office," or "Reg. U.S. Pat. and Tm. Off.," or the letter R enclosed within a circle, thus ®. Use of such notice before the actual issuance of a certificate of registration for the mark is improper and may be the basis for refusal of registration.

PUBLICATION OF 1881 AND 1905 ACT REGISTRATIONS CLAIMING BENEFITS OF 1946 ACT (Sec. 12c)

Publication Requirements. A registrant of a mark registered under the provisions of the Acts of 1881 or 1905, who desires to secure the full benefits of the provisions of the Act of 1946, may at any time prior to the expiration of the period for which the registration was issued or renewed, upon the payment of the prescribed fee, file an affidavit or declaration setting forth those goods stated in the registration on which said mark is in use in commerce, specifying the nature of such commerce, and stating that the registrant claims the benefits of the Trademark Act of 1946. Publication of a mark under the provisions of section 12(c) does not extend the original term of the registration, and application for renewal must be made within the time specified in the statute. See RENEWAL (p. 15).

Publication Affidavit or Declaration. A suggested form for preparing an affidavit requesting publication of a mark registered under the Act of 1881 or 1905 appears on page 30.

AFFIDAVIT OR DECLARATION OF USE (Sec. 8)

Cancellation for Failure to File Affidavit or Declaration During Sixth Year. Any registration issued under the provisions of the Act of 1946 and any 1881 or 1905 Act registration published to secure the full benefits of the 1946 Act, as described on page 13, will be cancelled at the end of 6 years following the date of registration or the date of publication unless within 1 year next preceding the expiration of such 6 years the registrant files in the Patent and Trademark Office an affidavit or declaration showing that said mark is still in use, or showing that its nonuse is due to special circumstances which excuse such nonuse and is not due to any intention to abandon the mark.

A notice of this requirement is attached to registration certificates issued under the provisions of the 1946 Act and is included in the notices of publication under section 12(c).

The affidavit or declaration is not required in the case of 1881 and 1905 Act registrations which have not been published under section 12 (c), or 1920 Act registrations, even though such registrations have been renewed under the provisions of section 9. Such affidavits may be returned.

Requirements for Affidavit or Declaration. The affidavit or declaration must:

(1) Be executed by the registrant after expiration of the 5-year period following the date of registration or publication under section 12 (c);

(2) Identify the certificate of registration by the registration number and date of registration; and

(3) State that the registered mark is still in use, and submit a specimen, facsimile or other evidence showing the mark as currently used, or recite facts to show that nonuse of the mark is due to special circumstances which excuse such nonuse and is not due to any intention to abandon the mark.

(4) Include the required fee (see page 18).

AFFIDAVIT OR DECLARATION FOR INCONTESTABILITY
(Sec. 15)

Incontestability Under Certain Conditions of Right to Use Mark. Under certain conditions, a mark registered on the Principal Register or a mark registered under the Acts of 1881 or 1905, and published under section 12 (c), may acquire an incontestable status, upon filing an affidavit or declaration conforming to the requirements indicated in the following paragraph. Marks which have acquired such status will not be subject to interference proceedings. Such marks, however, may be cancelled upon certain grounds specified by section 14 of the 1946 Act.

Requirements for Affidavit or Declaration for Incontestability. The affidavit or declaration provided by section 15 of the Act for acquiring incontestability for a mark registered on the Principal Register or a mark registered under the Act of 1881 or 1905 and published under section 12 (c) of the Act must:

(a) Be signed by the registrant;

(b) Identify the certificate of registration by the certificate number and date of registration;

(c) Recite the goods or services stated in the registration on or in connection with which the mark has been in continuous use in commerce for a period of 5 years subsequent to the date of registration or date of publication under section 12 (c) of the Act, and is still in use in commerce specifying the nature of such commerce;

(d) Specify that there has been no final decision adverse to registrant's claim of ownership for such mark for such goods or services, or to registrant's right to register the same or to keep the same on the register;

(e) Specify that there is no proceeding involving said rights pending in the Patent and Trademark Office or in a court and not finally disposed of;

(f) Be filed within 1 year after the expiration of any such 5-year period.

RENEWAL

Term of Registrations. Registrations issued under the Act of 1946 remain in force for 20 years from the date of registration and may be renewed for periods of 20 years from the expiring period unless previously cancelled or surrendered.

Renewal Requirements. A registration may be renewed provided the mark is in use in commerce at the time the application for renewal is filed. However, if the mark is not in use in commerce, the registration will be eligible for renewal provided the nonuse is due to special circumstances which excuse the nonuse and not due to any intention to abandon the mark. Registrations issued under the Acts of 1881 and 1905 remain in force for their unexpired terms and may be renewed in the same manner as registrations under the Act of 1946.

Renewal of Registrations Issued Under Act of 1920. Registrations under the Act of 1920 which were issued on or before January 5, 1928, expired on January 5, 1948, and such registrations issued after January 5, 1928, expire 20 years from the date of issue. Such registrations cannot be renewed unless renewal is required to support a foreign registration and in such case may be renewed on the Supplemental Register in the same manner as registrations under the Act of 1946.

Requirements of Application for Renewal. (a) The application for renewal must be verified or include a declaration by the registrant and set forth the goods or services recited in the registration on or in connection with which the mark is still in use in commerce, specifying the nature of such commerce. This statement must be executed not more than 6 months before the expiration of the registration or 3 months after and be accompanied by:

(1) A specimen or facimile showing current use of the mark.

(2) The required fee, including the additional fee required in the case of a delayed application for renewal.

(b) The statement which is verified or supported by a declaration, the specimen or facsimile and the fee must be filed within the period prescribed for applying for renewal. If defective or insufficient, they cannot be completed after the period for applying for renewal has passed; if completed after the initial 6-month period has expired but before the expiration of the 3-month delay period, the application can be considered only as a delayed application for renewal.

(c) If the mark is not in use in commerce at the time of filing of the verified statement, facts must be recited to show that nonuse is due to special circumstances which excuse such nonuse and is not due to any intention to abandon the mark.

The application for renewal must also include:

(1) If the applicant is not domiciled in the United States, the designation of some person resident in the United States on whom may be served notices or process in proceedings affecting the mark.

(2) If the mark is registered under the Act of 1920, a showing which is verified or which includes a declaration by the applicant that renewal is required to support a foreign registration.

Form for Renewal Application. A suggested form for an application for renewal appears on page 28.

CORRECTION, DISCLAIMER, SURRENDER, ETC.

Provision is made in section 7 of the 1946 Act for the issuance, in case of a change of ownership of a registered mark, of a new certificate in the name of the assignee for the unexpired part of the original period; for the surrender of registrations, and for the amendment of registrations and disclaimer of registered marks, providing such amendment or disclaimer does not involve such changes as to alter materially the character of the mark. Mistakes in registrations incurred through the fault of the Office, or in good faith through fault of the applicant, may be corrected.

Request for such action must comply with rules 2.171–2.176 of the Trademark Rules of Practice. Except in the case of correction of an Office mistake, the request must be accompanied by the required fees. (See p. 18)

Cancellation. After a mark has been registered, any person who believes that he is or will be damaged by the registration may, upon payment of the required fee (see p. 18) and compliance with the provisions of the statute and rules, apply to the Commissioner of Patents and Trademarks to cancel the registration.

Assignment of Marks. A registered mark or a mark for which application to register has been filed may be assigned with the good will of the business or with that part of the good will of the business connected with the use of and symbolized by the mark. Assignments must be by instruments in writing duly executed. Acknowledgement is prima facie evidence of the execution of an assignment and when recorded in the Patent and Trademark Office the record is prima facie evidence of execution.

Registration in Foreign Countries

Owners of trademarks having business or prospective business in foreign countries who desire to protect their marks in such foreign countries should ascertain the nature of the trademark laws in those countries in order that they may take proper steps in time to protect their rights.

In many foreign countries a resident there may obtain a registration of a trademark without having actually used it in trade, and such a registration may be used to prevent the importation into that country of goods bearing the mark.

To effect registration in many foreign countries, it is essential that registration be effective in the United States. Having secured registration domestically the owner frequently may secure registration in foreign countries before actually using the mark there. Duration of certificates of registration in foreign countries varies in accordance with the domestic laws of such countries.

General Information

Correspondence With the Patent and Trademark Office. All letters should be addressed to "The Commissioner of Patents and Trademarks, Washington, D.C., 20231." When appropriate, a letter may be marked for the attention of a particular officer or individual.

Letters of Inquiry. A separate letter should, in every instance, be written in relation to each distinct subject of inquiry.

The Patent and Trademark Office cannot undertake to respond to inquiries whether certain trademarks have been registered, or, if so, to whom, or for what goods; nor can it give legal advice as to the registrability of a specified mark or the nature and extent of protection afforded by the law, except as questions may arise in connection with pending applications. Information of a general nature may be furnished either by answering the inquiry or by providing or calling attention to an appropriate publication.

Identification of Pending Applications and Registrations. A letter relating to a pending application should identify it by the name of the applicant and serial number and filing date of the application. A letter relating to a registered trademark should identify it by the name of the registrant and by the number and date of the certificate.

Business Must Be Conducted With Decorum and Courtesy. Applicants and their representatives will be required to conduct their business with the Patent and Trademark Office with decorum and courtesy. Papers presented in vialation of this requirement will be submitted to the Commissioner and will be returned by his direct order.

Fees and Payment of Money. The following is a partial schedule of fees and charges to be paid to the Patent and Trademark Office in connection with trademark matters. A complete schedule appears in the Trademark Rules of Practice.

(1) Application to register in each class _____ $35.00
(2) Renewal application in each class _____ 25.00
(3) Renewal application filed after date of expiration, in each class an additional _____ 5.00
(4) Notice of claim of benefits for a registration under prior act (sec. 12 [c]) _____ 10.00
(5) Appeal to Trademark Trial and Appeal Board from refusal of registration by an Examiner in each class _____ 25.00
(6) Opposition or cancellation filing fee in each class _____ 25.00
(7) Amendment of registration, correction of applicant's mistake, disclaimer, or new certificate in name of assignee (sec. 7) _____ 15.00
(8) Printed copy of registration with data as of date of mailing relating to renewal, cancellation, 12 (c) publication, and affidavits under sections 8 and 15

Omitting title	1.70
Showing title	3.70
(9) Certification of any paper	1.00
(10) Photocopies or other reproduction of records, drawings, or printed material, per page of material copied	.30
(11) Drawings may be made when facilities are available	
Rate per hour	12.00
Minimum charge per sheet	10.00
(12) Correction of drawings Rate per hour (including a photoprint of the uncorrected drawing)	12.00
Minimum charge	3.00
(13) For recording every assignment, agreement, or other paper relating to the property in a registration or application	20.00
(14) For indexing each additional item (where the recorded document relates to more than one application or registration)	3.00
(15) Affidavit under sec. 8 for each class	10.00

Method of Payment. All payments of money for Patent and Trademark Office fees should be made in United States specie, Treasury notes, national bank notes, post office money orders, or certified checks. If sent in any other form, the Office may delay or cancel the credit until collection is made. Money orders and certified checks must be made payable to the Commissioner of Patents and Trademarks. Remittances made from foreign countries must be payable and immediately negotiable in the United States for the full amount of the fee required. Money sent by mail to Patent and Trademark Office will be at the risk of the sender; letters containing money should be registered.

Refunds. Money paid by actual mistake or in excess, such as a payment not required by law, will be refunded, but a mere change of purpose after payment of money, as when a party desires to withdraw his application for the registration of a mark or to withdraw an appeal, will not entitle a party to demand such a return. Amounts of 10 cents or less will not be returned unless specifically demanded, nor will the payer be notified of such amount; amounts over 10 cents but less than $1 may be returned in postage stamps, and other amounts by check.

RECORDS AND PUBLICATIONS OF THE PATENT AND TRADEMARK OFFICE

Digest of Registered Marks. A digest of registered marks is maintained in the Search Room of Trademark Operations and is open to the public. This digest comprises a set of the registered word marks arranged alphabetically and a set of registrations comprising symbols, birds, animals, etc., arranged according to the classification of the goods or services with which they are used. It is advisable to search this digest before adopting a trademark so as to avoid possible conflict with previously registered marks. The Office has reference material on articles of commerce indicating their classification in the various classes of goods which have been established under the law. (See p. 6.)

Printed Copies of Registrations. Printed copies of registrations will be furnished by the Patent and Trademark Office upon payment of the fee therefor. These copies may be merely copies of the registration as issued or status copy showing all effective actions taken on the registrations, including renewal affidavits, publication under section 12 (c), cancellation, etc.

Registration Files. After a mark has been registered or published for opposition, the file of the application and all proceedings relating thereto are available for public inspection and copies of the papers may be furnished upon paying the fee therefor.

Pending Applications. A digest of pending applications with a reproduction of the mark, the name and address of the applicant, the goods or services with which the mark is used, the dates of first use, and the serial number of the application is maintained for public inspection. Access to the file of a particular pending trademark application will be permitted prior to publication upon written request. Decisions of the Trademark Trial and Appeal Board in applications and proceedings relating thereto are published or available for inspection or publication.

Assignment Records. The assignment records of the Patent and Trademark Office are open to public inspection and copies of any recorded assignment may be obtained upon payment of the fee therefor. An order for a copy of an assignment should give the liber (book) and page or the reel and frame of the record.

Official Gazette. The *Official Gazette of the Patent Office* is published weekly and the Trademark Section contains information relating to trademarks, including marks published for opposition, marks registered, amended, cancelled and renewed, and marks published under section 12 (c) of the 1946 Act.

Single copies and subscriptions of the *Official Gazette* are sold by the Superintendent of Documents, U.S. Government Printing Office, Washington, D.C., 20402. The trademark material is reprinted separately as the Trademark Section and may be purchased or subscribed to separately.

Annual Trademark Index. An annual index of registrants of trademarks is published and sold by the Superintendent of Documents.

Forms For Trademark Cases

The following forms illustrate the manner of preparing applications for registration of marks as well as various other papers to be filed in the Patent and Trademark Office in trademark cases. Applicants and other parties will find their business facilitated by following them. These forms should be used in cases to which they are applicable. A sufficient number of representative forms are given which, with the variations indicated by the notes, should take care of all the usual situations. In special situations such alterations as the circumstances render necessary may be made provided they do not depart from the requirements of the rules or of the trademark statute. Before using any forms, the pertinent requirements of the rules and the pertinent sections of the trademark statute should be studied carefully.

In using these forms, the applicant or other party filing the form may, instead of making oath or verification where such is prescribed in the forms, set forth a written declaration that all statements made of his own knowledge are true and that all statements made on information and belief are believed to be true, if declarant is warned by wording in the same paper that willful false statements and the like are punishable by fine or imprisonment, or both, under section 1001 of Title 18 of the United States Code, and may jeopardize the validity of the application or other document or any registration resulting from the application: See form 4.1a for an example.

Single copies of forms can be obtained by request addressed to the Commissioner of Patents and Trademarks, attention of the Director of the Trademark Examining Operation, Washington, D. C. 20231.

The Forms are identified by the rule numbers appearing in the Trademark Rules of Practice in 37 C.F.R.

§ 4.1 Trademark application by an individual; Principal Register with oath.

Mark `----------------------------------`
(Identify the mark)

Class No. `-----------------------------------`
(If known)

To the Commissioner of Patents and Trademarks:

`-----------------------------------------------------------------`
(Name of applicant, and trade style, if any)

`-----------------------------------------------------------------`
(Business address, including street, city and State)

`-----------------------------------------------------------------`
(Residence address, including street, city and State)

`-----------------------------------------------------------------`
(Citizenship of applicant)

The above identified applicant has adopted and is using the trademark shown in the accompanying drawing (1) for `-----------------------------------`

`-----------------------------------------------------------------`
(Common, usual or ordinary name of goods)

and requests that said mark be registered in the United States Patent and Trademark Office on the Principal Register established by the act of July 5, 1946.

The trademark was first used on the goods (2) on _____; was
                                                                    (Date)
first used in (3) _____ commerce on _____
                            (Type of commerce)
_____; and is now in use in such commerce. (4) The mark
          (Date)
is used by applying it to (5) _____ and five specimens
showing the mark as actually used are presented herewith.

   (6)
State of _____ ⎫
County of _____ ⎬ *ss.*

_____ states that: he believes himself to be the owner
         (Name of applicant)

of the trademark sought to be registered, to the best of his knowledge and belief
no other person. firm, corporation or association has the right to use said mark
in commerce, either in the identical form or in such near resemblance thereto
as to be likely, when applied to the goods of such other person, to cause confusion, or to cause mistake, or to deceive; and the facts set forth in this application are true.

(JURAT) :   _____
                                                     (Signature of applicant)

   Subscribed and sworn to before me, this _____ day of _____
_____, 19_____.

                                               _____(*)

   (*) (The person who signs the jurat must be authorized to administer oaths by the law
of the jurisdiction where executed, and the seal or stamp of the notary, or other evidence
of authority in the jurisdiction of execution, must be affixed.)

REPRESENTATION
(See form 4.2 and Note (7) below)

NOTES: (1) If registration is sought for a word or numeral mark not depicted
in any special form, the drawing may be the mark typed in capital letters on
letter-size bond paper; otherwise, the drawing shall comply with section 2.52.

   (2) If more than one item in a class is set forth and the dates given for that
class apply to only one of the items listed, insert the name of the item to which
the dates apply.

   (3) Type of commerce should be specified as "interstate," "territorial,"
"foreign," or other type of commerce which may lawfully be regulated by
Congress. Foreign applicants relying upon use must specify commerce which
Congress may regulate, using wording such as commerce with the United States
or commerce between the United States and a foreign country.

   (4) If the mark is other than a coined, arbitrary or fanciful mark, and the
mark is believed to have acquired a secondary meaning, insert whichever of the
following paragraphs is applicable:

   (a) The mark has become distinctive of applicant's goods as a result of
substantially exclusive and continuous use in _____
                                                    (Type of commerce)
commerce for the five years next preceding the date of filing of this application.

   (b) The mark has become distinctive of applicant's goods as evidence by the
showing submitted separately.

   (5) Insert the manner or method of using the mark with the goods, i.e.,
"the goods," "the containers for the goods," "displays associated with the goods,"
"tags or labels affixed to the goods," or other method which may be in use.

   (6) The required fee of $35.00 for each class must be submitted.

90

(7) If the applicant is not domiciled in the United States, a domestic representative must be designated. See form 4.4.

§ 4.1a **Trademark application by an individual; Principal Register with declaration.**

Mark _____
(Identify the mark)

Class No. _____ ____
(If known)

TO THE COMMISSIONER OF PATENTS AND TRADEMARKS:

_____
(Name of applicant, and trade style, if any)

_____
(Business address, including street, city and State)

_____
(Residence address, including street, city and State)

_____
(Citizenship of applicant)

The above identified applicant has adopted and is using the trademark shown

in the accompanying drawing (1) for _____
(Common, usual or ordinary name of good)

and requests that said mark be registered in the United States Patent and Trademark Office on the Principal Register established by the act of July 5, 1946.

The trademark was first used on the goods (2) on _____;
(Date)

was first used in (3) _____ commerce on _____;
(Type of commerce)   (Date)

and is now in use in such commerce. (4) The mark is used in applying it to (5) _____ and five specimens showing the mark as actually used are presented herewith.

(6) _____, being hereby warned
(Name of Applicant)

that willful false statements and the like so made are punishable by fine or imprisonment, or both, under Section 1001 of Title 18 of the United States Code and that such willful false statements may jeopardize the validity of the application or any registration resulting therefrom,

declares: That he believes himself to be the owner of the trademark sought to be registered; that to the best of his knowledge and belief no other person, firm, corporation, or association has the right to use said mark in commerce, either in the identical form or in such near resemblance thereto as may be likely, when applied to the goods of such other person, to cause confusion, or to cause mistake, or to deceive; that the facts set forth in this application are true; and that all statements made of his own knowledge are true and that all statements made on information and belief are believed to be true.

_____
(Signature of applicant)

_____
(Date)

REPRESENTATION

(See form 4.2 and Note (7) under form 4.1.)

NOTES: See same numbered Notes under form 4.1.

§ 4.2 Power of attorney at law (which may accompany application).

Applicant hereby appoints (8) _____,

_____, an attorney at law or attorneys
    (Address)
at law, to prosecute this application to register, to transact all business in the
Patent and Trademark Office in connection therewith, and to receive the certificate of registration.

NOTE: (8) An individual attorney at law or individual attorneys at law must
be named here. If the name of a law firm is given, it will be regarded merely as
a designation of address for correspondence.

§ 4.4 Designation of domestic representative to accompany application. (9)

_____
                        (Name of representative)
where postal address is _____,
                            (Street, city and State)
is hereby designated applicant's representative upon whom notices or process
in proceedings affecting the mark may be served.

NOTE: (9) The designation of domestic representative must be separate from
a power of attorney at law or other authorization of representation.

§ 4.5 Trademark application by a firm; Principal Register.

                         Mark _____
                                    (Identify the mark)

                         Class No. _____
                                         (If known)

TO THE COMMISSIONER OF PATENTS AND TRADEMARKS:

_____
            (Firm name and names of members comprising firm)
_____
            (Business address, including street, city and State)

_____
                    (Domicile of firm)

_____
                (Citizenship of members of firm)

(Body of application is same as in form 4.1).

State of _____⎫
County of _____⎬ 88.

_____
                    (Name of member of firm)
states that he is a member of the applicant firm; he believes said firm to be
the owner of the trademark sought to be registered; to the best of his knowledge
and belief no other person, firm, corporation or association has the right to use
said mark in commerce, either in the identical form or in such near resemblance
thereto as to be likely, when applied to the goods of such other person, to cause
confusion, or to cause mistake, or to deceive; and the facts set forth in this
application are true.

                         _____
                         (Signature of member of firm) .

(JURAT) :

Subscribed to and sworn to before me, this _____ day of
_____, 19_____.

_____(*)

(*) (The person who signs the jurat must be authorized to administer oaths by the law of the jurisdiction where executed, and the seal or stamp of the notary, or other evidence of authority in the jurisdiction of execution, must be affixed.)

REPRESENTATION

(See form 4.2 and Note (7) under form 4.1.)

§ 4.6   Trademark application by a corporation; Principal Register.

Mark _____
(Identify the mark)

Class No. _____
(If known)

To the Commissioner of Patents and Trademarks :

_____
(Corporate name and State or country of incorporation) (10)

_____
(Business address, including street, city and State)

(Body of application is same as in form 4.1.)

State of _____ }
County of _____ } 88.

(Body of application is same as in form 4.1.)

_____ states that :
(Name of corporate officer)

he is _____ of applicant corporation (10) and is
(Official title)
authorized to execute this affidavit on behalf of said corporation; he believes said corporation to be the owner of the trademark sought to be registered; to the best of his knowledge and belief no other person, firm, corporation or association has the right to use said mark in commerce, either in the identical form or in such near resemblance thereto as to be likely, when applied to the goods of such other person, to cause confusion, or to cause mistake, or to deceive; and the facts set forth in this application are true.

_____
(Corporate name)

By _____
(Signature of corporate officer
and official title.)

(JURAT) :

Subscribed to and sworn to before me, this _____ day of

_____, 19_____.

_____(*)
Notary Public

(*) (The person who signs the jurate must be authorized to administer oaths by law of the jurisdiction where executed and the seal or stamp of the notary, or other evidence of authority in the jurisdiction.)

REPRESENTATION

(See form 4.2 and Note (7) under form 4.1.)

NOTE: (10) If applicant is an association or other collective group, the word "association" or other appropriate designation should be substituted for "corporation" when referring to applicant.

§ 4.7 Service mark application; Principal Register.

Mark _____
(Identify the mark)

Class No. _____
(If known)

To the Commissioner of Patents and Trademarks:

(Insert appropriate identification of applicant in accordance with form 4.1, 4.5 or 4.6)

The above identified applicant has adopted and is using the service mark shown in the accompanying drawing (11) for _____

_____
(Common, usual or ordinary name of service)
and requests that said mark be registered in the United States Patent and Trademark Office on the Principal Register established by the act of July 5, 1946.

The service mark was first used in connection with the services (2) on _____; was first used in connection with the services
(Date)

rendered in (3) _____ commerce on
(Type of commerce)

_____; and is now in use in such commerce. (4)
(Date)

The mark is used by _____

_____
(State method of using the mark in connection with the services)
and five (12) _____ showing the mark as actually used are presented herewith.

(Insert appropriate verification or declaration from form 4.1, 4.1a, 4.5 or 4.6, changing the word "trademark" to "service mark" and the word "goods" to "services.")

REPRESENTATION

(See form 4.2 and Note (7) under form 4.1.)

NOTES: For Notes referred to in this form but not set out here, see same numbered Notes under form 4.1.

(11) See Note (1) under form 4.1, and if drawing is not practicable, insert description of the mark instead of reference to the drawing.

(12) Insert "specimens," or state the nature of the representation of the mark which is furnished.

§ 4.8 Collective mark application (including collective membership mark); Principal Register.

Mark _____
(Identify the mark)

Class No. _____
(If known)

To the Commissioner of Patents and Trademarks:

(Insert identification of applicant in accordance with form 4.6.)

The above identified applicant has adopted and is exercising legitimate control over the use of the collective mark shown in the accompanying drawing (1) for

(13) _____
(Common, usual or ordinary name of goods or services)

to indicate (14) _____ and requests that said mark be registered in the United States Patent and Trademark Office on the Principal Register established by the act of July 5, 1946.

The collective mark was first used on the (2) _____

_____
(Insert "goods" or "services") (15)

by members of applicant on _____ ; was first used by said
(Date)

members in (3) _____ commerce on
(Type of commerce)

_____, and is now in use in such commerce. (4)
(Date)
The mark is used by applying it to (5) _____
and five specimens of the mark as actually used are presented herewith.

(Insert verification from form 4.6 changing "corporation" to "association" or the like, if necessary.)

REPRESENTATION

(See form 4.2 and Note (7) under form 4.1.)

Notes: For Notes referred to in this form but not set out here, see same numbered Notes under form 4.1.

(13) If the application is for a membership mark, omit the word "for" and the space for the name of the goods or services.

(14) If the application is for a membership mark, insert "membership in applicant organization," or similar appropriate statement. If not for a membership mark, omit the words "to indicate" and the following space.

(15) If the application is for a membership mark, the phrase "on the goods or services" should be omitted.

§ 4.9 Certification mark application; Principal Register.

Mark _____
(Identify the mark)
Class No. _____
(If known)

To the Commissioner of Patents and Trademarks:

(Insert appropriate identification of applicant in accordance with form 4.1, 4.5, or 4.6.)

The above identified applicant has adopted and is exercising legitimate control over the use of the certification mark shown in the accompanying drawing (1) for _____
(Insert illustrative examples of the goods or services)

and requests that said mark be registered in the United States Patent and Trademark Office on the Principal Register established by the act of July 5, 1946.

The certification mark, as used by persons authorized by applicant, certifies (16) _____ ; said mark was first used under the authority

of applicant on _____ ; was first used in (3)_____

(Date)

_____ commerce on _____ ; and is now in

(Type of commerce)   (Date)

use in such commerce. (4)

The mark is used by applying it to (5) _____,
and five specimens showing the mark as actually used are presented herewith.

Applicant is not engaged in the production or marketing of any goods or
services to which the mark is applied.

(Insert appropriate verification or declaration from form 4.1, 4.1a, 4.5 or 4.6,
and add after the word "association" the words "other than those authorized
by applicant.")

REPRESENTATION

(See form 4.2 and Note (7) under from 4.1.)

NOTES: For Notes referred to in this form but not set out here, see same
number Notes under form 4.1.

(16) Insert an appropriate statement as to what the mark certifies, relating
to regional origin; or material, mode of manufacture, quality, accuracy or other
characteristic of the goods; or that the work or labor on the goods or in the
performance of the services was performed by members of applicant.

§ 4.10   Application based on concurrent use; Principal Register.

Mark _____

(Identify the mark)

Class No. _____

(If known)

To the Commissioner of Patents and Trademarks:

(Insert appropriate identification of applicant in accordance with form 4.1,
4.5 or 4.6.)

Use form 4.1, and add at the end of the first paragraph: "for the area comprising _____";

(List the states for which registration is sought)
and add as final paragraph of application:

The following exception(s) to applicant's right to exclusive use are:

By _____, doing business at

_____, who is using the mark

_____

(Identify mark and Reg. No. or Ser. No., if any)

for _____

(Common, usual, or ordinary name of goods or services)

in the States of _____

(Earliest known date of such use)

by applying the mark to (5) _____

from _____

(Earliest known date of such use)
to the present."

(Insert appropriate verification or declaration from form 4.1, 4.1a, 4.5 or 4.6
and add after the word "association" the words "other than specified in the
application.")

REPRESENTATION

(See form 4.2 and Note (7) under form 4.1.)

NOTES: See same numbered Notes under form 4.1.

§ 4.11 Application to register on Supplemental Register.

Mark --
(Identify the mark)

Class No. -------------------------------
(If known)

TO THE COMMISSIONER OF PATENTS AND TRADEMARKS:

(Insert appropriate identification of applicant in accordance with form 4.1, 4.5 or 4.6.)

For the body of an application trademark registration (17), use form 4.1, 4.5 or 4.6, whichever is appropriate, changing the word "Principal" to "Supplemental," and adding a final paragraph to the application as follows:

"The mark sought to be registered has been in lawful use in --------------

----
(Type of commerce)

commerce in connection with the goods for the year preceding the date of filing of this application." (18)

(Insert appropriate verification or declaration from form 4.1, 4.1a, 4.5 or 4.6.)

REPRESENTATION

(See form 4.2 and Note (7) under form 4.1.)

NOTES: (17) For the body of service mark, collective mark or certification mark applications on the Supplemental Register, use form 4.7, 4.8 or 4.9, whichever is applicable, with the change and addition indicated in this form.

(18) If the mark has not been in use for the year next preceding the filing date, and registration in the United States is required as a basis for obtaining foreign protection of the mark, substitute the following statement for the last sentence: The mark sought to be registered is not in use in ------------------

----------------------- commerce and domestic registration is required as a
(Type of commerce)

basis for foreign protection of the mark.

In this instance applicant will be required to make a showing that U.S. registration is required as a basis of foreign protection of the mark.

§ 4.13 Application for renewal.

Mark --
(Identify the mark)

Reg. No. -------------------------------

Class No. -------------------------------

TO THE COMMISSIONER OF PATENTS AND TRADEMARKS:

(Insert appropriate identification of applicant for renewal in accordance with form 4.1, 4.5 or 4.6.) (1)

The above identified applicant for renewal requests that the above identified registration, granted to ---
(Name of original registrant)

on ----------------------- which applicant for renewal now owns, as shown
(Date of Issuance)

by records in the Patent and Trademark Office, be renewed in accordance with provisions of section 9 of the act of July 5, 1946.

The mark shown in said registration is still in use in (2)------------------

----
(Type of commerce)

commerce on each of the following goods (3) recited in the registration: -------------------------, the attached specimen (or facsimile) showing the mark as currently used. (4)

(5)

State of _____ }
County of _____ } *ss.*

\-
(Name of renewal applicant or of person authorized to sign for renewal applicant)
states that to the best of his knowledge and belief the facts set forth in this application are true.

\-
(Signature of renewal applicant: if renewal applicant is a corporation or other juristic organization, give the official title of the person who signs for renewal applicant.)

(JURAT) (Use jurat from form 4.1.)

REPRESENTATION

(See form 4.2 and Note (6) below.)

NOTES: (1) Applicant for renewal must be present owner of the registration.

(2) Type of commerce should be specified as "interstate," "foreign," "territorial," or other type of commerce which may lawfully be regulated by Congress. Foreign registrants must specify commerce which Congress may regulate, using wording such as commerce with the United States or commerce between the United States and a foreign country.

(3) If a service mark registration, state "in connection with each of the following services * * *."

(4) If the mark is not in use in commerce at the time of filing the application for renewal, but there is no intention to abandon the mark, facts must be recited to show that the nonuse is due to special circumstances. A specimen (or facsimile) illustrating use, or facts as to nonuse, must be submitted for each class sought to be renewed.

(5) The required fee for renewal sought prior to expiration is $25.00 for each class; and for delayed renewal filed within three months after expiration, an additional $5.00 for each class. If renewal is sought for less than the total number of classes in the registration, the classes for which renewal is sought should be specified.

(6) If applicant for renewal is not domiciled in the United States, a domestic representative must be designated. See form 4.4. If a designation is not made, an unrevoked designation will meet the requirement if such is already in the registration file.

§ 4.14 Affidavit for publication under section 12(c).

Mark _____
(Identify the mark)

Reg. No. _____

Date of issue _____

To: _____
(Name of original registrant)

State of _____ }
County of _____ } *ss.*

\-
(Name of registrant or of person authorized to sign for a juristic registrant)
states that (1) _____ **owns the above**
(Name of registrant)

identified registration, as shown by records in the Patent and Trademark Office; that said registration is now in force; that the mark shown therein is in use in

(2) _____
(Type of commerce)
commerce on each of the following goods (3) recited in the registration
_____; and that the benefits of the act of July 5, 1946, are hereby claimed for said registration.

(4)

(Signature; if a corporation or other
juristic organization, give the official
title of the person who signs.)

(JURAT) (Use jurat from form 4.1.)

REPRESENTATION

(See form 4.2 and Note (5) below.)

NOTES: (1) The present owner of the registration must file the affidavit as registrant.

(2) Type of commerce should be specified as "interstate," "territorial," "foreign," or other type of commerce which may lawfully be regulated by Congress. Foreign registrants must specify commerce which Congress may regulate, using wording such as commerce with the United States or commerce between the United States and a foreign country.

(3) If a service mark registration, state: "in connection with each of the following services."

(4) The required fee of $10.00 must be submitted.

(5) If registrant is not domiciled in the United States, a domestic representative must be designated. See form 4.4. If a designation is not made, an unrevoked designation will meet the requirement if such is already in the registration file.

§ 4.15 Affidavit required by section 8.

Mark ------------------------------------
(Identify the mark)

Reg. No. ____ _____

Class No. ------------------------------------

County of _____⎫
State of _____⎬ ss.

(Name of registrant or of person authorized to sign for a juristic registrant)

states that (1) _____ owns the above
(Name of registrant)

identified registration issued _____ (2), as shown by records in
(Date)
the Patent and Trademark Office; and that the mark shown therein is still in use (3) as evidenced by (4) _____.

(5)

(Signature; if a corporation or other
juristic organization, give the official
title of the person who signs.)

(JURAT) (Use jurat from form 4.1.)

REPRESENTATION

(See form 4.2 and Note (6) below.)

NOTES: (1) The present owner of the registration must file the affidavit as registrant.

(2) If the registration issued under a prior act and has been published under section 12(c), add: "and published under section 12(c) on_____

_____."
(Date)

(3) If the mark is not in use at the time of filing the affidavit, but there is no intention to abandon the mark, facts must be recited to show that the nonuse is due to special circumstances.

(4) Insert "the specimen included showing the mark as currently used," or recite facts as to sales or advertising which will show that the mark is in current use. Specimen illustrating use, or facts as to use or nonuse, are required for each class for which action is sought.

(5) The required fee of $10.00 must be submitted for each class for which action is sought, and if action is sought for less than the total number of classes in the registration, the classes for which action is sought should be specified.

(6) If registrant is not domiciled in the United States, a domestic representative must be designated. See form 4.4. If a designation is not made, an unrevoked designation will meet the requirement if such is already in the registration file.

§ 4.16 Affidavit under section 15

Mark _____
(Identify the mark)

Reg. No. _____

Class No. _____

State of _____} ss.
County of _____

_____
(Name of registrant or of person authorized to sign for a juristic registrant)

states that (1) _____ owns the above
(Name of registrant)

identified registration issued _____ (2), as shown by records in the
(Date)
Patent and Trademark Office; that the mark shown therein has been in con-

tinuous use in (3) _____
(Type of commerce)

commerce for five consecutive years from (4) _____ to the present, on
(Date)

each of the following goods (5) recited in the registration: _____
(List of Goods)
_____; that such mark is still in

use in (3) _____
(Type of commerce)
commerce; that there has been no final decision adverse to registrant's claim of ownership of such mark for such goods or services, or to registrant's right to register the same tor to keep the same on the register, and that there is no

100

proceeding involving said rights pending and not disposed of either in the Patent and Trademark Office or in the courts.

```
------------------------------------
          (Signature; if a corporation or other
          juristic organization, give the official
          title of the person who signs.)
```

(JURAT) (Use jurat from form 4.1.)

REPRESENTATION

(See rule 4.2 and Note (6) below.)

NOTES: This form may be used as a combined affidavit under sections 8 and 15 provided it contains matter which will meet the requirements of section 8 as to use or nonuse and fee (see form 4.15, Notes (3), (4) and (5)).

(1) The present owner of the registration must file the affidavit as registrant.

(2) If the registration issued under a prior act and has been published under section 12(c), add: "and published under section 12(c) on _____."

(Date)

(3) Type of commerce must be specified as "interstate," "territorial," "foreign," or such other commerce as may lawfully be regulated by Congress. Foreign registrants must specify commerce which Congress may regulate, using wording such as commerce with the United States or commerce between the United States and a foreign country.

(4) The date should be the beginning of a five year period of continuous use, all of which five year period falls after the date of registration under the act of 1946 or after the date of publication under section 12(c). A date which would produce a period of continuous use which is longer than five years may be stated provided the period indicated includes five years of continuous use after registration under the act of 1946 or publication under section 12(c).

(5) If a service mark registration, state: "in connection with each of the following services."

(6) If registrant is not domiciled in the United States, a domestic representative must be designated as to the section 8 affidavit. See form 4.4. If a designation is not made, an unrevoked designation will meet the requirement if such is already in the registration file.

§ 4.17 Opposition in the United States Patent and Trademark Office.

In the matter of application Serial No. _____

Published in the OFFICIAL GAZETTE on _____.

(Date)

_____
(Name of opposer)

v.

_____
(Name of applicant)

Opposition No. _____
(To be inserted by Patent and Trademark office)

_____, a(n) (1) _____
(Name of opposer)   (Legal entity of opposer)

located and doing business at _____
(Street, city and State)

believes that he will be damaged by registration of the mark shown in the above identified application, and hereby opposes the same.

As grounds of opposition, it is alleged that:

(Numbered paragraphs should state the grounds and recite facts tending to show why opposer believes he will be damaged.)

(2)

(Signature of opposer; if opposer is a corporation or other juristic organization, give the official title of the person who signs for opposer.)

State of _____ } 88.
County of _____

(Name of opposer or of person authorized to sign for opposer)

states that he is the opposer named in the foregoing opposition, or is the person authorized to sign for the opposer named in the foregoing opposition; that he has read and signed the opposition and knows the contents thereof; and that the allegations are true, except as to the matters stated herein to be upon information and belief, and as to those matters he believes them to be true.

(Signature of opposer; if opposer is a corporation or other juristic organization, give the official title of the person who signs for opposer.)

(JURAT) (use jurat from form 4.1.)

REPRESENTATION

(See form 4.2 and Note (7) under form 4.1. For opposers who are foreigners, it is customary to regard a power of attorney as the equivalent of a domestic representative.)

NOTES: (1) If an individual, state: "an individual," or "an individual trading

as _____,"
if there is a trade style. If a partnership, state: "a partnership composed

of _____"
(Names of members)

If a corporation, association, or other organization, state "a corporation (or specify other type of organization) organized and existing under the laws

of _____"
(State or country)

(2) The required fee of $25.00 must be submitted for each class to be opposed, and if opposition is sought for less than the total number of classes, the classes sought to be opposed should be specified.

§ 4.18 Petition to cancel a registration in the United States Patent and Trademark Office.

In the matter of Registration No. _____

Date of Issue _____

(Name of petitioner)
v.

(Name of registrant)

Cancellation No. _____
(To be inserted by Patent and Trademark Office)

—————————————————————————, a(n) (1)—————————————————————————
(Name of petitioner)   (Legal entity of petitioner)

located and doing business at ——————————————————————————————————
                                  (Street, city and State)
that he is or will be damaged by the above identified registration, and hereby
petitions to cancel the same.

As grounds therefor, it is alleged that:

(Numbered paragraphs should state the grounds and recite facts tending to
show why petitioner believes that he is or will be damaged.)

(2)

————————————————————————————————
(Signature of petitioner; if petitioner
is a corporation or other juristic organization, give the official title of the
person who signs for petitioner.)

State of —————————————————— }
County of —————————————————— } ss.

——
(Name of petitioner or of person authorized to sign for petitioner)
states that he is the petitioner named in the foregoing petition to cancel, or is the
person authorized to sign for the petitioner named in the foregoing petition to
cancel; that he has read and signed the petition to cancel and knows the contents thereof; and that the allegations are true, except as to the matters stated
therein to be upon information and belief, and as to those matters he believes
them to be true.

————————————————————————————————
(Signature of petitioner to cancel; if
petitioner is a corporation or other
juristic organization, give the official
title of the person who signs for petitioner.)

(JURAT) (Use jurat from form 4.1.)

REPRESENTATION

(See form 4.2 and Note (7) under form 4.1. For petitioners who are foreigners,
it is customary to regard a power of attorney as the equivalent of a domestic
representative.)

NOTES: (1) If an individual, state: "an individual," or "an individual trading

as ——,"
if there is a trade style. If a partnership, state: " a parnership composed

of ——."
                          (Names of members)
If a corporation, association, or other organization, state "a corporation (or
specify other type of organization) organized and existing under the laws

of ——"
                          (State or country)

(2) The required fee of $25.00 must be submitted for each class sought to be
cancelled, and if cancellation is sought for less than the total number of classes,
the classes sought to be cancelled should be specified.

**§ 4.19 Ex parte appeal from Examiner of Trademarks in the United States
Patent and Trademark Office.**

——
(Name of applicant)

To the Trademark Trial and Appeal Board:

Applicant hereby appeals to the Trademark Trial and Appeal Board from the decision of the Examiner of Trademarks refusing registration.

> --
> (Signature of applicant; if applicant is a corporation or other juristic organization, give the official title of the person who signs for applicant.)

§ 4.21 Assignment of application.

Whereas _____, of
(Name of assignor)

(Street, city, and State)

has adopted and is using a mark for which he has filed application in the United States Patent and Trademark Office for registration, Serial No. _____

_____; and

Whereas _____, of
(Name of assignee)

(1) _____,
(Street, city, and State)

is desirous of acquiring said mark;

Now, therefore, for good and valuable consideration, receipt of which is

hereby acknowledged, said _____
(Name of assignor)

does hereby assign unto the said _____
(Name of applicant)

all right, title and interest in and to the said mark, together with the good will of the business symbolized by the mark, and the above identified application for registration of said mark.

(2)

The Commissioner of Patents and Trademarks is requested to issue the certificate of registration to said assignee.

State of _____⎫
County of _____⎭ *88.*

On this _____ day of _____, 19_____

before me appeared _____,
the person who signed this instrument, who acknowledged that he signed it as a free act on his own behalf (or on behalf of the identified corporation or other juristic entity with authority to do so).

> _____(*)
> (Notary Public)

(*) (The wording of the acknowledgment may vary from this illustration but should be wording acceptable under the law of the jurisdiction where executed; the person who signs the acknowledgment must be authorized to do so by the law of the jurisdiction where executed, and the seal or stamp of the notary, or other evidence of authority in the jurisdiction of execution, must be affixed.)

NOTES: (1) If the postal address of the assignee is not given either in the instrument or in an accompanying paper, registration to the assignee may be delayed.

(2) If assignee is not domiciled in the United States, a domestic representative must be designated. See Form 4.4.

§ 4.22 Assignment of registration.

Whereas _____, of

                      (Name of assignor)

_____

                 (Street, city, and State)

has adopted, used and is using a mark which is registered in the United States

Patent and Trademark Office, Registration No. _____,

dated _____, and

Whereas _____, of

                      (Name of assignee)

(1) _____,

                 (Street, city, and State)

is desirous of acquiring said mark and the rigstration thereof:

Now, therefore, for good and valuable consideration, receipt of which is hereby acknowledged, said _____

                 (Name of assignor)

does hereby assign unto the said _____

                 (Name of assignee)

all right, title and interest in and to the said mark, together with the good will of the business symbolized by the mark, and the above identified registration thereof.

(2)

_____

(Signature of assignor; if the assignor is a corporation or other juristic organization, give the official title of the person who signs for assignor.)

State of _____ }
County of _____ } 88.

On this _____ day of _____, 19_____,

before me appeared _____,

the person who signed this instrument on his own behalf, or who was authorized to sign this instrument of behalf of the identified corporation or other juristic entity, who being sworn, acknowledged that he signed this instrument as a free act.

_____(*)

(Notary Public)

(*) (The wording of the acknowledgment may vary from this illustration but should be wording acceptable under the law of the jurisdiction where executed; the person who signs the acknowledgment must be authorized to do so by the law of the jurisdiction where executed, and the seal or stamp of the notary, or other evidence of authority in the jurisdiction of execution, must be affixed.)

NOTES: (1) If the postal address of the assignee is not given either in the instrument or in an accompanying paper, recording may be delayed pending receipt of such address.

(2) If assignee is not domiciled in the United States, a domestic representative must be designated. See form 4.4, changing the word "applicant" to "assignee."

4.23 A suggested format for the certificate under 37CFR 1.8(a) to be included with the correspondence.

I hereby certify that this correspondence is being deposited with the United States Postal Service as first class mail in an envelope addressed to: Commissioner of Patents and Trademarks, Washington, D.C. 20231, on _____

Date

(Typed or Printed) Name of person signing certificate

Signature of person signing certificate

Date

NOTE: This certificate may be used for responses to Office actions, oppositions and fees therefor, requests to extend time to oppose, ex parte appeals and fees therefore. The deposit must be made in the mail within the required time period for filing the paper.

The certificate should be placed on the correspondence itself, and the certificate must be signed. The applicant, or party to the action, or the attorney for such person, should sign the certificate.

ANSWERS TO QUESTIONS FREQUENTLY ASKED

1. Q.　**What is a trademark?**

   A.　A trademark is a word, name, symbol, or device, or any combination of these, adopted and used by a manufacturer or merchant to identify his goods and distinguish them from those manufactured or sold by others. In short, it is a brand name used on goods moving in the channels of trade.

2. Q.　**What is the function of a trademark?**

   A.　The primary function of a trademark is to distinguish one person's goods from those of another; but a trademark also serves to indicate to purchasers that the quality of the goods bearing the mark remains constant, and it serves as the focal point of advertising to create and maintain a demand for the product.

3. Q.　**How are trademark rights established?**

   A.　Rights in a trademark are established by adoption and actual use of the mark on goods moving in trade, and use ordinarily must continue if the rights are to be maintained. No rights exist until there has been actual use; and a trademark may not be registered until the goods bearing the mark have been sold or shipped in interstate, foreign or Territorial commerce.

4. Q.　**Who may own a trademark?**

   A.　A trademark may be owned by an individual, a firm or partnership, a corporation, or an association or other collective group.

5. Q.　**Is any provision made for the registration of trademarks under our federal laws?**

   A.　Yes. Our first constitutional trademark registration act was passed in 1881. The present registration Act was passed on july 5, 1946, effective July 5, 1947 and is popularly known as the Lanham Act.

6. Q.　**What other types of marks may be registered?**

   A.　Service marks used in the sale or advertising of services? certification marks to certify regional origin, mode of manufacture, accuracy, quality, or other characteristics of the goods or services of someone other than the certifier; and collective marks used by cooperatives or other collective groups or organizations.

7. Q;　**What is a trade name?**

   A.　Trade or commercial names are business names used by manufacturers, merchants, and others to identify their businesses or occupations. A trademark identifies a product, and a trade name identifies a producer.

8. Q. May trade names be registered in the same manner as trade marks?

   A. No provision is made in the present trademark law for the registration of trade or commercial names used merely to identify a business entity.

9. Q. What Government agency has jurisdiction of the registration of trademarks under our federal laws?

   A. The United States Patent Office.

10. Q. Is it necessary for the trademark owner to register his mark?

    A. No. Trademark rights are protected under common law, but registration results in material advantages to the trademark owner. It constitutes notice of the registrant's claim of ownership. and it creates certain presumptions of ownership, validity and exclusive right to use the mark on the goods recited in the registration.

11. Q. Is there any time limitation within which an application should be filed?

    A. No. An application may be filed at any time after the mark has been used on the product and the product is sold or shipped in interstate, foreign or Territorial commerce.

12. Q. What has to be done by the trademark owner in order to qualify for federal registration of a trademark?

    A. The mark must be applied in some manner to goods or their containers and the goods sold or shipped in interstate, foreign or Territorial commerce.

13. Q. How may information about the filing of a trademark application be obtained?

    A. By ordering from the Patent Office a copy of the pamphlet entitled "General Information Concerning Trademarks." If more detailed information is desired, a copy of the "Trademark Rules of Practice of the Patent Office with Forms and Statutes" may be obtained from the Superintendent of Documents, Washington, D.C., 20402, for 60¢.

14. Q. Is it advisable to make a search of registered marks prior to the filing of an application?

    A. Yes. A search may be made in the public Search Room of Trademark Examining Operation of the Patent Office, located in Crystal

Plaza Building No. 2, 2011 Jefferson Davis Highway, Arlington, Virginia.

15. Q. **Will the Patent Office make a search?**

A. No. The Patent Office does not have personnel for making searches for the public.

16. Q. **How does the trademark owner apply for the registration of a trademark?**

A. By making proper application to the Commissioner of Patents.

17. Q. **Are application forms available for distribution to the public?**

A. Yes. Upon request forms for the registration of trademarks may be obtained from the Patent Office for use in filing applications in the name of (a) an individual, (b) a firm or partnership, and (c) a corporation.

18. Q. **Must the applicant be represented by an attoryney?**

A. No. The application may be filed by the applicant, or an attorney may be appointed for this purpose.

19. Q. **Are all trademarks subject to registration?**

A. No. A trademark may not be registered if it so resembles a mark previously registered in the Patent Office, or a mark or trade name previously used in the United States by another and not abandoned, as to be likely, when applied to the applicant's goods, to cause confusion, mistake or deception. Other types of marks are prohibited registration by the statute, such as those comprising immoral or deceptive matter or those including the flag or insignia of the United States.

20. Q. **Can the Patent Office give legal advice or advice as to the registrability of a specified mark prior to the filing of an application for registration?**

A. No. The Patent Office can give no assistance of this kind until a case comes regularly before it in an application duly filed.

21. Q. **What comprises a complete application for the registration of a trademark?**

A. A complete application comprises (a) a written application properly notarized, (b) a drawing of the mark, (c) five specimens or facsimilies of the mark as actually in use in commerce, and (d) the filing fee of $35.00.

22. Q. **What is the term of a registration?**

A. Twenty years from the date of issue; and the registration may be renewed at the end of each twenty-five year term so long as the mark is still in use in commerce.

23. Q. **May a trademark be assigned?**

A. Yes. A trademark may be assigned with the good will of the business with which it is used.

24. Q. **Does a U. S. registration give protection in foreign countries?**

A. No. A registration must be obtained in each country where protection is desired. A U. S. registration may, however, be used as the basis for obtaining registration in a number of foreign countries.

25. Q. **May a foreign trademark owner obtain a registration in this country?**

A. Yes. Application for registration may be based on use of the mark in commerce with this country, or on registration previously obtained in the owner's country of origin in accordance with applicable international conventions and treaties.

26. Q. **Is it necessary to go to the Patent Office to transact business concerning trademark matters?**

A. No. In general all business with the Patent Office is conducted by correspondence.

PART THREE

What Everybody
Should Know About

INTRODUCTION

The Copyright Act of 1976, Public Law 94-553 (90 Stat. 2541), is a general revision of the copyright law, Title 17, *United States Code*; it becomes fully effective on January 1, 1978. The new law supersedes the Copyright Act of 1909, as amended, and is the first extensive revision of the 1909 law.

Early in 1977 the Register of Copyrights established in the Copyright Office a Revision Coordinating Committee, chaired by the Register, to oversee the development and coordination of plans for implementation of the new law. The Committee recognized that an important part of this initial preparation was staff training and it asked Marybeth Peters, Senior Attorney-Adviser, to plan, organize, and conduct all internal training on the new law as well as to coordinate all training activities outside of the Copyright Office. As a result of her successful execution of the first part of this assignment, 260 staff members, in 15 sessions of one and one-half hours each, completed an intensive study of the new law; 125 other staff members participated in a "mini-course." Ms. Peters, who has a teaching as well as a legal background, prepared all instructional materials and designed the format for both the short- and long-term courses.

This general guide to the Copyright Act of 1976 is *not* an official summary of the law. It does *not* attempt to deal with all of the issues raised by the revision legislation nor to provide answers to legal questions. It is, however, an extensive training tool, the text of which follows the language used by Ms. Peters, with only a change in tense to avoid an appearance of obsolescence on January 1, 1978.

In developing the lectures and lesson plans, Ms. Peters relied heavily on the language of the law itself, the legislative reports, and the various statements of the Register of Copyrights to the Congress, i.e., the 1961 Report of the Register, 1965 Supplemental Report, and the 1975 Second Supplemental Report. Copies of these documents may be obtained by writing to the Copyright Office, Library of Congress, Washington, D.C. 20559. The fee for the 1961 Report of the Register is $.45 while the fee for the 1965 Supplementary Report is $1.00; there is no charge for the rest of the material.

THE VIEWS EXPRESSED IN THIS DOCUMENT ARE THOSE OF MS. PETERS AND DO NOT NECESSARILY REFLECT THE OFFICIAL VIEWS OF EITHER THE COPYRIGHT OFFICE OR THE LIBRARY OF CONGRESS.

HISTORICAL BACKGROUND

Copyright in the United States stems from a 1710 English statute known as the Statute of Anne. Following the American Revolution, most of the states enacted copyright laws generally patterned after this English act. The need for federal legislation, however, was soon recognized, and when the U.S. Constitution was drafted the principle of copyright was written into it. Article I, section 8 grants Congress the power "to promote the progress of science and useful arts by securing for limited times to authors and inventors the exclusive right to their respective writings and discoveries." Thus, the primary purpose of copyright legislation is to foster the creation and dissemination of intellectual works for the public welfare; an important secondary purpose is to give creators the reward due them for their contribution to society.

The first federal copyright statute was enacted in 1790 and covered maps, charts and books. This statute granted to authors and proprietors a term of 14 years with the privilege of renewal for a second term of 14 years. There were general revisions of the copyright law in 1831, 1870 and 1909.

The law under which we have been operating for the past 68 years is the Act of March 4, 1909. This act is based on the printing press as the prime disseminator of information. Significant changes in technology have resulted in a wide range of new communications techniques that were unknown in 1909—for example, radio, television, communications satellites, cable television, computers, photocopying machines, videotape recorders, etc., and there are promises of even greater changes in the future. This growth in technology made revision of the Act of 1909 imperative.

There were a number of unsuccessful attempts to revise the 1909 Act. The present revision effort began in 1955 when Congress appropriated the funds for a comprehensive program of research which produced a series of 35 studies analyzing what were then considered to be the major problems. In addition, the Register of Copyrights issued a report on the "General Revision of the U.S. Copyright Law," in 1961.

Comments raised both by the studies and the Register's Report led to a series of meetings with a panel of consultants drawn from the copyright bar, representatives of the interested parties, and the Copyright Office. These meetings spanned three years and provided an opportunity to thrash out many of the problems.

Statutory drafts with deliberate alternatives included were circulated for comment and Congressional consideration; then an extraordinary process of compromise and negotiation began. This process went on continuously for nearly fifteen years, down to the very day the bill was finally passed by both Houses of Congress.

In 1967, after extensive hearings, the House of Representatives passed a revision bill—H.R. 2512. It was hoped that the Senate would take quick action on S. 597, the companion bill, but the cable television issue appeared to be irresolvable at that time. There then followed a long period of relative inaction. In 1974, however, the revision effort again showed signs of life, and on September 9, 1974, by a vote of 70-1, the Senate passed S. 1361. It was, however, too late for consideration of the bill by the House in that session of Congress.

In 1976 Senator McClellan again introduced a copyright revision bill, S. 22. On February 19, 1976, by a vote of 97-0, the Senate passed it. On September 22, 1976, the House of Representatives passed a revision bill which differed in part from the Senate version, thus necessitating a Conference Committee. The Conference Report was adopted by both houses on September 30, 1976, and on October 19, 1976, President Ford signed the revision bill into law. The new copyright law, Public Law 94-553, with certain exceptions, took effect on January 1, 1978.

The Register of Copyrights, Barbara Ringer, speaking on the revision bill, made the following comment:

> *"Except for the most prescriptive and technical of its provisions, practically everything in the bill is the product of at least one compromise, and many provisions have evolved from a long series of compromises reflecting constantly changing technology, commercial and financial interests, political and social conditions, judicial and administrative developments and—not least by any means—individual personalities. The bill as a whole bespeaks concern for literally hundreds of contending and overlapping special interests from every conceivable segment of our pluralistic society. It was not enough to reach compromise on a particular point; all of the compromises had to be kept in equilibrium so that one agreement did not tip another over."*

She went on to conclude that *"It is a source of wonder that somehow all of this succeeded in the end."* But succeed it did, and we now have a new law which makes fundamental and pervasive changes in the U.S. copyright system. Some of the changes are so profound that they may mark a shift in direction for the very philosophy of copyright itself.

FEDERAL PREEMPTION AND DURATION OF COPYRIGHT

[Chapter 3, Sections 301 to 305]

SINGLE NATIONAL SYSTEM (Section 301)

Federal preemption represents the most basic change in the U.S. copyright system since its inception. Instead of the present dual system of protection of works under the common law before they are published and under the federal statute after publication, the new law would, under section 301, establish a single system of statutory protection for all works fixed in a copy or phonorecord. The common law would continue to protect works (such as live choreography and improvisations) up to the time they are fixed in tangible form, but upon fixation they would be subject to exclusive federal protection under the statute, even though they are never published or registered.

Some of the primary advantages of a single federal system are:

1. *Promote national uniformity.* One of the fundamental purposes behind the copyright clause in the U.S. Constitution was to avoid the difficulties of determining and enforcing an author's rights under different state laws. Today national uniformity is more essential than ever because of the advanced methods of disseminating an author's work.

2. *Reduce the legal significance of "publication."* The concept of "publication" is outdated; undue reliance on this concept has been one of the most serious defects with the Act of 1909. A single federal system will clear up what has become a chaotic situation.

3. *Implement the "limited times" provision in the Constitution.* Common law protection in unpublished works is now perpetual, no matter how widely they may be disseminated by means other than "publication." Section 301 will place a time limit on the duration of exclusive rights in this type of work and thus will aid scholarship by making unpublished, undisseminated manuscripts available after a reasonable time.

4. *Improve international dealings in copyrighted material.* No other country has anything like our present dual system. In an era when copyrighted works can be disseminated instantaneously to every country, the need for effective international copyright relations, and the concomitant need for national uniformity assume even greater importance.

Exclusive Federal Jurisdiction (Section 301(a))

The intent of this subsection is to preempt and abolish any rights under the common law or statutes of a state that are equivalent to copyright and that extend to works coming within the scope of the federal copyright law. Under section 301(a) all rights in the nature of copyright (which are specified as "copyright, literary property rights, or any equivalent legal or equitable right") are governed exclusively by the federal copyright statute if the work is of a kind covered by the statute. With the exception of sound recordings fixed before February 15, 1972, states cannot offer a work protection equivalent to copyright and it doesn't matter when the work was created, or whether it is published or unpublished, in the public domain, or copyrighted under the federal statute.

Section 1338 of Title 28, United States Code, also makes clear that any action involving rights under the federal copyright law would come within the exclusive jurisdiction of the federal courts.

Rights Preserved by States (Section 301(b))

Any rights which a state may claim, which are not equivalent to copyright, are preserved. Subsection (b) explicitly lists three general areas left unaffected by the preemption: (1) subject matter outside sections 102 and 103; (2) causes of action arising under state law before the effective date of the statute; and (3) violations of rights that are not equivalent to any of the exclusive rights under copyright.

Sound Recordings (Section 301(c))

This subsection provides an exception for sound recordings fixed before February 15, 1972 (the effective date of the law extending federal copyright protection to this type of work). If this provision were not included there would probably have been a resurgence of piracy of sound recordings. States may, however, only protect sound recordings fixed prior to February 15, 1972 and then may only protect them until February 15, 2047.

DURATION OF COPYRIGHT WORKS CREATED AFTER THE EFFECTIVE DATE OF NEW LAW, JANUARY 1, 1978
(Section 302)

This section specifies the duration of copyright protection under the new act.

> *Basic term.* Life of the author plus fifty years after his or her death is the term for works created after January 1, 1978.

> *Joint works.* In the case of joint works by two or more authors who did not work for hire, the fifty year period is measured from the date of the death of the last surviving author.

118

Anonymous and pseudonymous works. In the case of these works, the term lasts for 75 years from the year of first publication or 100 years from the year of its creation, whichever expires first. If the identity of the anonymous or pseudonymous author is revealed in the records of the Copyright Office, the term will be based on the life of the identified author plus fifty years.

Works made for hire. Term is 75 years from first publication or 100 years from creation, whichever is shorter. (Work made for hire is defined in section 101.) Since, under 201(b) the employer is considered the "author," it would not be appropriate to base the term on the author's life.

Presumption of author's death. Subsection (e) provides that, after a period of 75 years after first publication or 100 years after creation of a work, whichever expires first, users are entitled to rely on a presumption if they have no knowledge of whether or when a particular author died. Any person who obtains from the Copyright Office the proper document ("a certified report"), indicating that the records disclose nothing to show that a particular author is still living or died less than fifty years before, is entitled to the presumption that the author has been dead for at least fifty years. Reliance in good faith will be a complete defense in an infringement action.

Subsection (d) provides that any "interested" person may record a statement of the death of an author or a statement that the author is still living on a particular date.

There are a number of reasons for changing the term of copyright protection from a set number of years to one based upon the life of the author. Among those listed in the legislative reports are:

1. 56 years is not long enough to insure an author and his or her dependents the fair economic benefits of the work. Also, life expectancy has increased substantially.

2. Tremendous growth in the communications media has substantially lengthened the commercial life of many works. A short term discriminates against serious works whose value may not be recognized until many years after its creation.

3. There is no particular benefit to the public of a short term. The price of public domain works is usually no less than that of copyrighted works. In some cases the lack of copyright protection restrains dissemination since publishers cannot risk investing unless they are assured of exclusive rights.

4. The year of death is a simpler and clearer method of computing the term. All of a particular author's works will fall into the public domain at the same time.

5. The renewal device, one of the worst features of the 1909 Act will eventually be eliminated. [NOTE: For works in their first term of statutory protection on December 31, 1977, renewal in the last (28th) year will still be necessary in order to obtain the additional 47 years' protection. See the discussion of section 304 below.]

6. It places the United States in conformity with most of the international copyright community. It eliminates a major barrier to U.S. adherence to the Berne Copyright Union.

DURATION OF COPYRIGHT IN PRE-EXISTING WORKS UNDER COMMON LAW PROTECTION ON THE EFFECTIVE DATE OF THE NEW LAW
(Section 303)

For unpublished works already in existence on January 1, 1978, but not protected by statutory copyright and not yet in the public domain, the new act generally provides automatic federal copyright for the same life plus 50 or 75/100 year terms provided for new works. All works in this category, however, are guaranteed at least 25 years of statutory protection; the law specifies that in no case will copyright in a work of this sort expire before December 31, 2002, and if the work is published before that date the term is extended by another 25 years, through the end of 2027.

DURATION OF SUBSISTING COPYRIGHTS
(Section 304)

This section is a transitional provision, but an important one. Subsection (a) deals with copyrights that are in their first term on January 1, 1978. It provides for a first term of 28 years from the date it was originally secured, with a right to a renewal term of 47 years—extending the total potential term of copyright protection to 75 years. The application for renewal term must be submitted within one year before the expiration of the original term by the same specified renewal claimants as under the 1909 Act. The reason for retaining the renewal provision is that many of the present expectancies in these works are the subject of existing contracts, and it would be unfair and confusing to cut off or alter these interests. [NOTE: Although section 304(a) reenacts and preserves the renewal provision the definition of "posthumous" adopted in *Bartok v. Boosey & Hawkes, Inc.*, 523 F. 2d 941 (2d Cir. 1975) has been included in both the House and Senate reports. The House report defines it as "one to which no copyright assignment or other contract for exploitation of the work has occurred during the author's lifetime, rather

120

than one which is simply first published after the author's death." The Senate report states "The reference to a 'posthumous work' in this section means one as to which no assignment has occurred during an author's lifetime, rather than one which is simply first published after the author's death."]

Subsection (b), which went into effect on October 19, 1976, extends the renewal term automatically to a total of 75 years.

The last 19 years of the copyright term are subject to a right of termination.

EXPIRATION DATE
(Section 305)

The new law provides that all terms of copyright will run through the end of the calendar year in which they would otherwise expire. This will not only affect the duration of copyrights, but also the time limits for renewal registrations.

EXAMPLES OF DURATION AND RENEWAL UNDER SECTIONS 304 AND 305:

1. A book was first published with the required notice of copyright on July 1, 1950. The claim was subsequently registered in the Copyright Office.

   Under the 1909 Act the term would run from July 1, 1950 to July 1, 1978, and renewal registration was required to be made between July 1, 1977, and July 1, 1978.

   Under the new law there are two possibilities:

   a. If renewal is made before the effective date of the new law— (renewed between July 1, 1977, and December 31, 1977,) section 304(b) is applicable and the work is protected to December 31, 2025.

   b. If renewal is not made before January 1, 1978, section 304(a) is applicable. Under 304(a) a renewal application must be made "within one year prior to the expiration of the original term." While the normal expiration of the original term would be July 1, 1978, section 305 extends it to December 31, 1978. Thus, an application received before or on December 31, 1978, will be accepted. The renewal term is for 47 years and the work is protected until December 31, 2025.

2. A musical composition is registered in unpublished form on January 7, 1955.

   Under the 1909 Act the term would run from January 7, 1955 to

January 7, 1983. A renewal application must be received between January 7, 1982, and January 7, 1983. An application received after January 7, 1983, would not be accepted.

Under the new law:

a. Must renew between December 31, 1982, and December 31, 1983.

b. Renewal applications received between January 7, 1982 and December 31, 1982, will not be accepted.

c. Renewal application received after December 31, 1983, will not be accepted.

Section 304(a) provides that renewal application and registration must be made "within one year prior to the expiration of the original term." Normal expiration would be January 7, 1983, (28 years from the date the copyright was secured [here the date of the unpublished registration]) but section 305 extends this to the end of the year in which it would normally expire, in this case, December 31, 1983.

SUBJECT MATTER OF COPYRIGHT
(INCLUDING STANDARDS OF COPYRIGHTABILITY)

[Chapter I, Section 102, 103 and 105]

The copyright clause of the U.S. Constitution empowers Congress to grant to authors the exclusive rights in their "writings." The Act of 1909 repeats the constitutional phrase in Section 4 and grants copyright to "all the writings of an author." Although the broad sweep of this phrase may imply that the statutory copyright grant is co-extensive with the constitutional power, it is clear that Congress has not exhausted the scope of "writings of an author" in the 1909 law.

It is well established, by a long line of court decisions, that in order to be copyrightable under the statute the work must meet the following requirements:

1. The work must be in the form of a "writing," i.e., it must be fixed in some tangible form from which the work can be reproduced.

2. The work must be a product of original creative authorship. Two interrelated elements are required: originality and creativity.

a. The work must be original in the sense that the author produced it by his own intellectual effort, as distinguished from merely copying a preexisting work. There is no requirement of novelty, ingenuity or esthetic merit.

b. The work must represent an appreciable amount of creative authorship.

The requirement of fixation is retained in the new law and serves as the dividing line between common law and statutory copyright. Under the definitions in section 101, a work is "fixed" in a tangible medium of expression when its embodiment in a copy or phonorecord, by or under the authority of the author, is sufficiently permanent or stable to permit it to be perceived, reproduced, or otherwise communicated for a period of more than transitory duration.

The new copyright law substitutes the phrase "original works of authorship" for "writings of an author" to clarify that the Constitutional power has not been exhausted in the copyright legislation. Also, this new phrase more accurately reflects the variety of authorship covered by the copyright law. Moreover, it seems that the phrase "original works of authorship" will permit protection for new forms of expression without allowing unlimited expansion into areas completely outside the present congressional intent.

The standard of original, creative authorship is not changed by the new law. All of the 14 classes mentioned in section 5 of the 1909 law are covered by the new law as well. For the first time, however, pantomimes and choreography are specifically recognized as copyrightable works.

The new law continues and clarifies the principle of existing law that copyright in new versions covers only the new material and does not enlarge the scope or duration of protection in preexisting works. The new law specifically provides protection for compilations. The term "new versions" is changed to "derivative works." The intent is that the terms "compilations" and "derivative works" include every copyrightable work that employs preexisting material or data of any kind. A difference is that the new law does not condition copyright in such works upon securing the consent of the copyright owner of the previous material. Instead the new law provides that protection does not extend to any part of the work in which such material has been used unlawfully.

SUBJECT MATTER OF COPYRIGHT: IN GENERAL
(Section 102)

Section 102 provides that copyright protection subsists in "original works of authorship" fixed in tangible form. Seven broad categories are listed:

(1) literary works;
(2) musical works, including any accompanying words;

(3) dramatic works, including any accompanying music;
(4) pantomimes and choreographic works;
(5) pictorial, graphic, and sculptural works;
(6) motion pictures and other audiovisual works; and
(7) sound recordings.

These categories are illustrative and are not meant to be limitative. The 1965 Supplementary Report of the Register of Copyrights states the categories are overlapping and not mutually exclusive. "It is quite conceivable, for example, that within itself a motion picture might encompass copyrightable works falling into all of the other six categories."

"Literary works," "pictorial, graphic, or sculptural works," "motion pictures," "audiovisual works" and "sound recordings" are defined in section 101. These definitions make clear the distinction between "works" and "material objects." Thus, under the new law a "book" is not a work of authorship but a particular kind of "copy." Instead, as the legislative reports make clear, the author may write a "literary work," which in turn can be embodied in a wide range of "copies" and "phonorecords," including books, periodicals, computer punch cards, microfilm, tape recordings, etc.

It is Congress' intent (according to these reports) that the standards of originality and creativity developed by the courts under existing law should remain unchanged under the new law. Thus, "deminimis" works, common or standard works, blank forms, etc. will not be registrable.

Pantomimes and Choreographic Works. The old law had no specific provision for copyright in choreographic works, although they could be registered as a "dramatic work." The same is true of pantomimes. To resolve any doubt as to the necessity for dramatic content as a condition for protecting these recognized art forms, the new law specifically mentions them. Choreographic works are not defined in section 101 because the meaning is presumably clear. The 1961 Report of The Register states, "For purposes of copyright at least, the term 'choreographic works' is understood to mean dance works created for presentation to an audience, thus excluding ballroom and other social dance steps designed merely for the personal enjoyment of the dancers." The legislative reports state that "choreographic works" do not include social dance steps and simple routines.

Computer Programs. Although they are not mentioned as copyrightable subject matter in section 102(a) and they are not referred to explicitly in the definition of "literary works" in Section 101, a careful reading of the new law with the legislative reports makes it clear that computer programs or "software" is within the subject matter of copyright. The definition of "literary works" refers to works expressed in "words, numbers, or other verbal or numerical symbols or indicia."

Section 102(b) states a fundamental principle: copyright protection does not extend to ideas, systems, or methods, processes, principles, etc., no matter how unique the concept. This proviso was added as a result of the debate over the copyrightability of computer programs, and is intended to make clear that, although the programmer's "literary" expression, as embodied in a program, would be copyrightable, his ideas, system and methodology would not.

Typeface designs. House Report 94-1476 states that the House Judiciary Committee wants to study whether typeface designs should be included in a possible law to protect original designs embodied in useful articles. (Page 50.) On page 55 of the same report the following appears: "The Committee has considered, but chosen to defer, the possibility of protecting the design of typefaces ... The Committee does not regard the design of typeface ... to be copyrightable 'pictorial, graphic, or sculptural work' within the meaning of this bill and the application of the dividing line in section 101." [NOTE: In *Eltra Corp.* v. *Ringer,* E.D. Va. Oct. 26, 1976 No. 76-264-A, the court found a typeface design to be a "work of art" but refused to compel registration on the ground that Congress had acquiesced in the "long standing" practice of the Copyright Office of refusing to register such claims. 37 CFR section 202.10(c). This case has been appealed.]

Works of Art and Ornamental Designs. The definition of "pictorial, graphic, and sculptural works" in section 101 seeks to draw as clear a line as possible between copyrightable works of fine and applied art and uncopyrightable works of industrial design.

Section 101 defines "pictorial, graphic and sculptural works" as including "two-dimensional and three-dimensional works of fine, graphic, and applied art, photographs, prints and art reproductions, maps, globes, charts, technical drawings, diagrams, and models. Such works shall include works of artistic craftsmanship insofar as their form but not their mechanical or utilitarian aspects are concerned; the design of a useful article, as defined in this section, shall be considered a pictorial, graphic, or sculptural work only if, and only to the extent that, such design incorporates pictorial, graphic, or sculptural features that can be identified separately from, and are capable of existing independently of, the utilitarian aspects of the article." The second sentence in this definition is classic language and is drawn from Copyright Office regulations promulgated in the 1940's and expressly endorsed by the Supreme Court in *Mazer* v. *Stein,* 347 U.S. 201 (1954).

The copyright revision bill had a Title II which in origin and content was essentially a separate though related piece of legislation entitled "Protection of Ornamental Designs of Useful Articles." This was to provide a limited form of copyright protection to the ornamental design elements of useful articles. The House deleted Title II as did the Conference Committee. The House Report states that it will be necessary for the Committee to reconsider the question of design protection in new legislation during the 95th Congress.

Sound Recordings. A sound recording is a work "that results from the fixation of a series of musical, spoken, or other sounds, but not including the sounds accompanying a motion picture or other audiovisual work, regardless of the nature of the mater.al objects, such as disks, tapes, or other phonorecords" in which it may be embodied. Protection extends only to the particular sounds of which the recording consists, and would not prevent a separate recording or another performance in which these sounds are imitated. Thus, mere imitation of a recorded performance would not constitute a copyright infringement even where one performer deliberately sets out to simulate another's performance as exactly as possible.

SUBJECT MATTER OF COPYRIGHT: COMPILATIONS AND DERIVATIVE WORKS (Section 103)

Section 103 complements section 102; it provides that a compilation or derivative work is copyrightable if it represents an "original work of authorship" and falls within one or more of the categories listed in section 102(a). The standards of copyrightability that apply to entirely original works also apply to those containing preexisting works.

The legislative reports state that section 103(b) is intended to define, more sharply and more clearly than does section 7 of the Act of 1909, the important interrelationship and correlation between protection of preexisting material and of "new" material in a particular work. The most important point is that copyright covers only the material added by the later author, and has no effect one way or the other on the copyright or public domain status of the preexisting material.

Section 101 states that a "compilation" results from the process of selecting, bringing together, organizing and arranging previously existing material of all kinds, regardless of whether the individual items in the material have been or ever could have been subject to copyright. Thus, it would be possible to have a copyright in a compilation of blank forms.

A "derivative" work requires a process of recasting, transforming, or adapting "one or more preexisting works"; the "preexisting work" must come within the general subject matter of copyright set forth in section 102, regardless of whether it is currently, or was ever, copyrighted.

Copyright is not conditioned upon the consent of the copyright owner of the preexisting material. The new law provides that protection does not extend to "any part of the work in which such material has been used unlawfully." Thus, for example, an unauthorized translation of a novel could not be copyrighted at all. However, the owner of copyright in an anthology of poetry could sue someone who infringed the whole anthology, even though the infringer proves that publication of one of the poems was unauthorized. The legislative reports indicate that the purpose of this ·is to prevent an infringer from benefiting, through copyright protection, from his unlawful act, but preserves protection for those parts of the work that do not *employ* the preexisting work.

MATERIAL DENIED COPYRIGHT PROTECTION

The following are examples of types of works which are denied U.S. copyright protection:

Works in the public domain. Section 103 of the Transitional and Supplementary Provisions provides: This Act does not provide copyright protection for any work that goes into the public domain before January 1, 1978.

A work falls into the public domain, and is available to everyone for use without payment or permission, when the copyright owner has authorized publication of the work without the notice of copyright required by the Act of 1909. It also enters the public domain when the first 28th year term of copyright expires without renewal.

Once a work has fallen into the public domain, copyright is lost permanently. The new law will not restore the copyright.

Ideas, methods, systems, principles. One of the fundamental principles of both the old and new laws is that copyright does not protect ideas, methods, systems, principles, etc. but rather protects the particular manner in which they are expressed or described. Section 102(b) contains this basic principle; it provides "[i]n no case does copyright protection for an original work of authorship extend to any idea, procedure, process, system, method of operation, concept, principle, or discovery, regardless of the form in which it is described, explained, illustrated, or embodied in such work."

Common or standard works. Works consisting of information that is common property containing no original authorship, such as standard calendars, height and weight charts, tape measures and rulers, and lists of tables taken from public documents or other common sources are not subject to copyright protection.

Devices and blank forms. Devices for measuring, computing, or use in conjunction with a machine are not subject to copyright protection. Common examples are slide rules, wheel dials, and nomograms. Ideas, methods, systems, mathematical principles, formulas, and equations are not copyrightable, and the same is true of devices based on them. The printed material of which a device usually consists (lines, numbers, symbols, calibrations) likewise cannot be the subject of copyright because this material is necessarily dictated by the idea, principle, formula or standard of measurement involved. Blank forms and similar works, designed to record rather than convey information, are not subject to copyright protection either.

Deminimis works. There are certain works to which the legal maxim of "*de minimis non curat lex*" (the law does not concern itself with trifles) applies. These are works in which the creative authorship is too slight to be worthy of protection. Examples include names, titles, slogans, mere variations of typographic ornamentation, lettering or coloring, translation of a work from aural to printed form, transliteration of existing harmonies in a musical work from piano to guitar tablature or ukelele diagrams.

Works of the United States Government (Section 105). This section states a basic premise of the Act of 1909—that works produced for the U.S. Government by its officers and employees as part of their official duties are not subject to U.S. copyright protection. The new law makes it clear that this prohibition applies to unpublished works as well as published ones. The National Technical Information Service sought a limited exception to the prohibition in section 105. The House version included such a provision which was deleted by the Conference Committee. The Conference Report states that a hearing on this issue should be scheduled for early in the 95th Congress.

There is no mention of works prepared under a U.S. Government contract or grant. The intent is to allow an agency to determine whether or not an independent contractor or grantee is to be allowed to have a copyright in works prepared in whole or in part with the use of Government funds.

Section 105 allows the U.S. Government to hold copyrights that have been transferred to it by "assignment, bequest, or otherwise."

ELIGIBILITY FOR COPYRIGHT PROTECTION IN THE UNITED STATES

[Chapter I, Section 104]

Section 104 of the new law sets forth the basic criteria under which works of foreign origin can be protected under the United States copyright law. This section divides all works into two categories—unpublished and published. There are no qualifications of nationality and domicile with respect to unpublished works.

Published works are subject to protection if one of the following four conditions is met:

1. On the date of first publication, one or more of the authors is a national or domiciliary of the U.S., *or* is a domiciliary or national, or sovereign authority of a foreign nation that is a party to a copyright treaty of which the U.S. is also a party, *or* is a stateless person.

2. The work is first published in the U.S. or in a foreign nation that, on the date of first publication, is a party to the U.C.C.

3. The work is first published by the United Nations or any of its special-

ized agencies, or by the Organization of American States. (This represents a treaty obligation of the U.S. [Second Protocol of the U.C.C.])

4. The work comes within the scope of a Presidential Proclamation. Thus, protection is available to an alien author whose country is "proclaimed" by the President as granting to U.S. citizens and domiciliaries and to works first published in the U.S. substantially the same rights it grants to its own citizens. Section 104 of the Transitional and Supplemental Provisions provides that all proclamations issued by the President under 1(e) or 9(b) of Title 17 as it existed on December 31, 1977, or under previous copyright statutes, shall continue in force until terminated, suspended, or revised by the President.

The new law specifically recognizes stateless authors as eligible for protection. Also, it broadens eligibility conditions in three important ways:

First— it protects an author who is domiciled in a foreign country with which the U.S. has copyright relations through an international treaty. Thus, even though the U.S. has no relations with Iraq, an Iraqi author domiciled in the United Kingdom, (a U.C.C. country) would be eligible for protection here even if he or she publishes in Iraq.

Second— the new law makes eligible works first published *either* in the U.S. or another country that is a party to the U.C.C., regardless of the citizenship of the author.

Third— all unpublished works, regardless of the citizenship or domicile of the author are eligible for U.S. copyright protection.

Finally, it is now clear that a work is subject to protection in the U.S. even if only one of several authors is eligible.

OWNERSHIP AND TRANSFERS OF OWNERSHIP

[Chapter 2, Sections 201, 202, 204 and 205]

Chapter 2 of the new law deals with ownership and transfer of rights. The chapter begins with a reconfirmation that the fountainhead of copyright is the author, and that copyright ownership belongs to him or her in the first instance. As under the 1909 Act, an exception is made for works made for hire.

BASIC PRINCIPLES OF OWNERSHIP (Section 201(a))

Two basic and well established principles of copyright are restated in this section: 1) that the source of copyright ownership is the author of the work and 2) in the case of a "joint work" the coauthors are coowners.

Section 101 makes it clear that a work is "joint" when the authors collaborate with each other or if each of the authors prepared his or her contribution with the knowledge and intention that it would be merged with the contributions of other authors as "inseparable or interdependent parts of a unitary whole."

The House Report indicates that the touchstone is intention at the time the writing is done.

The definition in section 101 is the first legislative definition of a joint work. Section 201 establishes the validity of joint ownership. The respective rights of the coowners, however, are not spelled out. The legislative reports state that the new law adopts the courtmade law on this point; that is, the coowners shall have the right to free use of the jointly owned property, subject only to the duty to account to one another for the profits.

[Note: the definition in section 101 overrules the decisions in the "Melancholy Baby" (*Shapiro Bernstein & Co., Inc.* v. *Jerry Vogel Music Co., Inc.*, 161 F. 2d 406 (2d Cir. 1946) and "12th Street Rag" (*Shapiro Bernstein & Co.*, v. *Jerry Vogel Music Co.*, 221 F. 2d 569 (2d Cir. 1955) *modified on rehearing*, 223 F. 2d 252 (2d Cir. 1955)) cases. The test in these cases was "fusion of effort" rather than intent at the time of the writing.]

OWNERSHIP-WORKS MADE FOR HIRE (Section 201(b))

In this subsection another principle of the 1909 Act is adopted—that in the case of a work made for hire the employer is considered the author and is regarded as the initial owner of copyright unless there has been an agreement to the contrary. The definition of a "work made for hire" in section 101, however, appears narrower than the present case law.

A basic principle of American copyright law is that all rights to a work produced by an employee within the scope of his or her employment vest in the employer. This has been well established by the courts and in section 26 of the 1909 law. The rationale for this rule is that the work is produced under the employer's direction and expense; also the employer bears the risks and should be entitled to reap the benefits.

Works made on commission are those produced as the result of a special order, rather than in the normal course of employment. They are not mentioned in the 1909 law. In the cases concerning these works, courts have generally recognized copyright ownership in the party commissioning the work and not in the creator of the work.

This subsection vests all copyright interests in the employer in a work made for hire. It goes beyond the old law by codifying the idea that the parties may agree otherwise as to copyright ownership. Such an agreement must be in writing and must be signed by the parties. [NOTE: This section refers to "the employer or other person for whom the work was prepared." "Other person" apparently was included to make it clear that the person who commissions a work which fits within the definition in section 101 of a work made for hire shall be regarded as the author.

In section 101 of the new law, the definition of a "work made for hire" is divided into two sections. First, it says that it is a "work prepared by an employee within the scope of his or her employment." The second part is somewhat of a departure from previous interpretations. As the House Report notes on page 121, the status of works prepared on special order or commission was a major issue in revision. This definition represents a carefully balanced compromise. It spells out those specific categories of commissioned works that can be considered "works made for hire" under certain circumstances. The categories are:

1. a contribution to a collective work

2. part of a motion picture or other audiovisual work

3. a translation

4. a supplementary work (which is defined as prepared for publication as a secondary adjunct to a work by another for purposes of illustrating, introducing, concluding, etc., or assisting in the use of the other work, such as forewards, afterwords, answer material for tests, maps, musical arrangements, bibliographies, etc.)

5. a compilation

6. an instructional text, which is defined as "a literary, pictorial, or graphic work prepared for publication with the purpose of use in systematic instructional activities." (Thus, books used in teaching.)

7. a test

8. answer material for a test

9. an atlas.

HOWEVER, this is conditioned upon an express agreement in writing signed by the parties. This agreement must state that the work "shall be considered a work made for hire."

CONTRIBUTIONS TO COLLECTIVE WORKS (Section 201(c))

This subsection seeks to clarify one of the most difficult questions under the existing law—the ownership of contributions to periodicals and other collective works. It states that copyright in a contribution is separate and distinct from copyright in the collective work as a whole, and that, in absence of an express transfer, the owner of the collective work obtains only certain limited rights with respect to each contribution.

The first sentence in this subsection provides that "Copyright in each separate contribution to a collective work is distinct from copyright in the collective work as a whole, and vests initially in the author of the contribution." This is intended to establish that the copyright in a contribution and the copyright in the collective work in which it appears are two different things, and that the usual role with respect to initial ownership applies to the contribution.

Section 101 defines a "collective work" as "a work, such as a periodical issue, anthology, or encyclopedia, in which a number of contributions, constituting separate and independent works in themselves, are assembled into a collective whole."

The second sentence in 201(c), in conjunction with section 404, preserves the author's copyright in his contribution without requiring a separate notice in his name or an unqualified transfer of all his rights to the publisher.

The new law establishes a presumption that, in the absence of an express transfer, the author retains all rights except, "the privilege of reproducing and distributing the contribution as part of that particular collective work, any revision of that collective work, and any later collective work in the same series."

Under this presumption, for example, an encyclopedia publisher would be entitled to reprint an article in a revised edition of an encyclopedia, and a magazine publisher would be entitled to reprint a story in a later issue of the same periodical. The privileges extended under the presumption, however, do not permit revisions in the contribution itself or allow inclusion of the contribution in anthologies or other entirely different collective works.

DIVISIBILITY OF COPYRIGHTS (Section 201(d))

In theory, under the 1909 law, a copyright was considered a single, indivisible bundle of exclusive rights. Thus, the old law regarded copyright as a single, indivisible entity; this means that a transfer of less than the entire rights to a work was merely a license which allowed the holder to use the work in a specified way but did not permit him to exercise any right of ownership.

This theory in practice is unworkable, and copyright proprietory, with the sanction of the courts, have developed customs and usages on the basis that copyright is divisible. Various subsidiary rights have been created and marketed separately—e.g., magazine rights, paperback rights, book club rights, motion picture rights, foreign rights, etc. The copyright has also been licensed for a period of time and/or for a particular territory.

Tension between theory and practice under the present law has produced some strange and unjust results in those cases where courts have not been able to accommodate copyright theory to commercial reality.

Section 201(d)(2) contains the first explicit statutory recognition of the principle of divisibility of copyright in U.S. law. This provision was long sought by authors. It means that any of the exclusive rights that go to make up a copyright, including those listed in section 106 and any subdivision of them, can be transferred and separately owned. The definition of "transfer of copyright ownership" in section 101 makes it clear that the principle of divisibility applies whether or not the transfer is "limited in time or place of effect."

Note, too, that section 101 provides that the term "copyright owner" refers to the owner of a particular right.

The granting of a non-exclusive license, however, does *not* constitute a transfer of ownership, but only a right of usage.

132

The second sentence of 201(d)(2) provides that "The owner of any particular right is entitled, to the extent of that right, to all of the protection and remedies accorded to the copyright owner by this title." Thus, an exclusive licensee would be given standing to sue to protect that interest. This provision caused some concern; some felt that if ownership rights were split, a user might then be liable to a multiplicity of suits. The Justice Department raised this issue in 1967. This problem is solved in section 501(b), however, by setting certain limitations on the right to sue. It gives the court discretion to require a notice to all interested parties, and to order the joinder of any party whose interest might be affected by an infringement proceeding.

TRANSFERABILITY

(Section 201(d)(1)) states the fundamental rule that ownership of all or any part of a copyright is fully transferable from one owner to another by any form of assignment or conveyance or by operation of law, and that, upon the death of an owner is to be treated as personal property.

The statement of this principle is supplemented by the definition of transfer of ownership in section 101. The definition is intended, among other things, to dispel any doubts as to whether mortgages or other hypothecations, discharges of mortgages and exclusive licenses come within the meaning of a "transfer of copyright ownership."

INVOLUNTARY TRANSFERS (Section 201(e))

The legislative reports state that the purpose of this section is to reaffirm the basic principle that the U.S. copyright of an individual author shall be secured to that author, and cannot be taken away by involuntary transfer. The intent is that the author is entitled, despite any purported expropriation or involuntary transfer, to continue to exercise all rights under the U.S. law, and specifically that the governmental body or organization may not enforce or exercise any rights in that situation.

DISTINCTION BETWEEN COPYRIGHTS AND MATERIAL OBJECTS (Section 202)

The language in this section makes it clear that, unless an author expressly transferred the rights in a particular work, the sale of a material object (e.g., a manuscript or a painting) does not carry with it the copyright in the work.

All this section really says is that copyright is one thing and the material object in which the work is embodied is another; that ownership of one is distinct from ownership of the other; that the transfer of ownership of one does not, in and of itself, transfer ownership of the other.

EXECUTION OF TRANSFERS OF COPYRIGHT OWNERSHIP (Section 204)

This section retains the requirement that transfers of copyright ownership be in writing and signed by the owner. The new law allows the transfer to be signed either "by the owner of the rights conveyed" or "by such owner's duly authorized agent."

Section 204 could have considerable impact since in the new law unpublished works are placed under the federal statute and thus subject to the above requirement, i.e., that all transfers be in writing.

Subsection (b) broadens and liberalizes the provision in the 1909 law regarding certificates of acknowledgment. It provides that these certificates would be *prima facie* evidence of the execution of any domestic or foreign transfer (although they would not affect the validity of a transfer).

RECORDATION OF TRANSFERS AND OTHER DOCUMENTS
(Section 205)

The House Report states that section 205 is intended to clear up a number of uncertainties arising from sections 30 and 31 of the 1909 law and to make the recording and priority provisions more effective and practical.

Any "document pertaining to a copyright" may be recorded if it bears the actual signature of the person who executed it or is accompanied by a sworn or official certification that it is a true copy. The House Report suggests rather strongly that the Copyright Office will record self-serving or colorable documents (page 128) and the Register is told to take care that their nature is not concealed from the public in the office's indexing and search reports.

Subsection (c) provides that recordation of a document constitutes constructive notice (this is a conclusion of law that cannot be contradicted) of the facts it states only if it meets two requirements:

1. it specifically identifies the work to which it pertains so that after the document is indexed by the Copyright Office, it would be revealed by a "reasonable search" under the title or registration number; and

2. registration for the work has been made.

Subsection (d) requires a transferee to record his or her instrument of transfer as a condition to bringing an infringement suit, and thereby to place on public record the basis on which ownership is claimed. This subsection also makes it clear that a delay in making recordation until after an infringement has occurred will not affect the transferee's rights or remedies against the infringer.

Subsection (e) resolves the priorities between conflicting transfers, by retaining the current policy in favor of the initial transfer, if properly recorded. It also retains the concept of a grace period but shortens it to one month for documents executed in the U.S. and 2 months for those executed abroad. This section also makes a binding promise to pay royalties, a form of valuable consideration and therefore repudiates the decision in *Rossiter* v. *Vogel*, 134 F. 2d 908 (2d Cir. 1943).

Subsection (f) provides that whether recorded or not, a nonexclusive license taken without notice of a prior unrecorded transfer would be valid against the transferee, and an unrecorded nonexclusive license would be valid as against a subsequent transfer.

TERMINATION OF TRANSFERS AND LICENSES

[Chapter 2, Section 203 and Chapter 3, Section 304(c)]

Section 24 of the old law embodies what is known as the renewal provision. This section provided that copyright would generally revert to the author, if living, or if the author were living, to other specified beneficiaries if a renewal claim were registered in the 28th year of the original term. This provision was included in the 1909 Act to give authors a "second chance" to reap the benefits of their creative efforts. In practice, however, the second chance did not materialize because the author assigned the contingent rights in the renewal term well before his or her rights vested, and the assignee reaped the benefits of the renewal term if the author survived until the renewal vested. Moreover, failure to comply with the registration formality led to many forfeitures.

It is generally acknowledged that during the early stages of the revision effort, "the most explosive and difficult issue" concerned a provision for protecting authors against unfair copyright transfers. The aim was to protect authors against unremunerative transfers and to get rid of the complexity, awkwardness, and unfairness of the renewal provision. As both the House and Senate reports note, the problem stems from the unequal bargaining position of authors and from the impossibility of determining a work's value until it has been exploited.

In 1965 representatives of publishers and authors met and agreed on a proposal which became, in essence, section 203 of the new law. This agreement essentially ended debate on the subject.

The sections covering termination rights are complex; the majority of material is presented in a question and answer format to make it more understandable.

WHAT MAY BE TERMINATED AND BY WHOM UNDER SECTION 203

What grants are covered?

Grants by the author (other than by will) of exclusive or nonexclusive rights arising under the new law, but not including works made for hire, may be terminated. This applies only to grants made on or after January 1, 1978—there is no retroactive effect. [Note that transfers made by an author's successors in interest are not covered.]

Who may terminate?

The author or, if he is deceased, a majority of owners of his termination interest—i.e., widow or widower and children or grandchildren may terminate. The key is that those who own a total of more than one half of the interest may exercise the right of termination. In works of joint authorship, where the grant was signed by two or more authors, a majority of those who signed it must join to terminate.

TERMINATION AFTER AUTHOR'S DEATH (Section 203(a)(2))
In the case of an author who is dead, his or her termination interest is owned and may be exercised by the following:

1. Where author dies and only a widow or widower survives and there are no children, then the widow or widower owns the entire termination interest.

2. Where there is no widow or widower but there are surviving children, then the children own the entire termination interest.

3. Where both a widow or widower and a child or children survive, then the widow or widower own 50%, and the child or children own 50%. [Note: The rights of the author's children and grandchildren are, in all cases, divided among them and exercised on a *per stirpes* basis and the share of the children of a dead child, for example, can be only exercised by a majority of them. *Per stirpes*—when descendants take by representation of their parent—i.e., child or children take among them the share their parent would have taken, if living.]

An example is given on page 125 of the House Report. A deceased author leaves a widow, two living children, and three grandchildren by a third child who is dead.

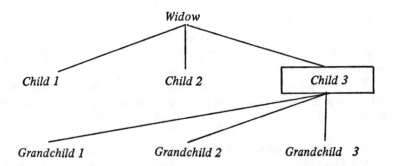

Widow gets 50% and the children of the author will divide 50%. Each of the three children would be entitled to 16 2/3% but Child 3 is dead. Per stirpes means that the three offspring of Child 3 will share Child 3's share. Thus, each of the three grandchildren get about 5 1/2%.

As the example points out, the widow is a necessary party in termination because she owns 50%. To get the majority she can be joined by either Child 1 or Child 2. But if neither join her she must get a majority of the grandchildren. Thus, even though the widow and one grandchild would own 55 1/2%, they would have to be joined by another child or grandchild to effect a termination or make a further transfer of reverted rights.

WHEN AND HOW TERMINATION IS EFFECTED (Section 203(3))

When may termination be effected?

Termination may be effected during the five years beginning at the end of 35 years from the date of the grant, or, if the grant covers the right of publication, 35 years from the date of publication or 40 years from the date of the grant, whichever is shorter.

How may termination be effected?

Termination may be effected by serving a written notice no less than two nor more than ten years before termination is to take effect. Notice must comply with Copyright Office regulations and a copy of the notice must be recorded in this Office before the effective date of the termination.

Two examples from the House Report are:

1. Contract for theatrical production signed on September 2, 1987. Termination of grant can be made to take effect between September 2, 2022 (35 years from execution) and September 1, 2027 (end of 5-year termination period). Assuming author decides to terminate on September 2, 2022 the advance notice must be filed between September 2, 2012 and September 2, 2020.

2. Contract for book publication executed on April 10, 1980; book finally published on August 23, 1987. Since contract covers the right of publication, the 5-year termination period would begin on April 10, 2020 (40 years from execution) rather than April 10, 2015 (35 years from execution) or August 23, 2022 (35 years from publication). Assuming that author decided to make the termination effective on January 1, 2024, the advance notice would have to be served between January 1, 2014 and January 1, 2022.

THE EFFECT OF TERMINATION

All rights revert to those with a right to terminate except that derivative works prepared before termination may continue to be utilized under the terms of the grant. Rights revert to everyone who owns termination interests on the date the notice was served, whether they joined in signing or not ·

Rights vest on the date that the notice is served. If beneficiary dies, his heirs would inherit his or her share.

In addition, the law provides that a further grant or agreement to make a further grant of any right covered by a terminated grant is valid only if it is signed by the same number and proportion of owners, in whom the right has vested . . . , as are required to terminate the grant. Section 203(b)(3).

Moreover, such further grant or agreement is valid only if made after the effective date of termination, except that a new transfer to the original grantee or his successor may be made after the notice of termination is served. Section 203(b)(4). In effect this gives the original grantee or his successor a right of first refusal and a preference over others since such grantee or successor may have a two to ten year lead time in dealing for the rights.

[NOTE: Section 203(a)(5) provides that "termination of the grant may be effected notwithstanding any agreement to the contrary, including an agreement to make a will or to make any future grant.]

TERMINATIONS OF TRANSFERS AND LICENSES COVERING THE EXTENDED RENEWAL TERM (Section 304(c))

What grants are covered?

Grants made by the author or grants executed by those beneficiaries of the author who could claim renewal under the present law may be terminated. Only grants covering the renewal copyright and only grants made prior to January 1, 1978 are covered. There are no termination rights in works made for hire.

Who may terminate?

The author, or if he or she is deceased, his family may terminate. The shares are the same as spelled out earlier under section 203.

When may termination be effected?

Termination may be effected during a five-year period which begins at the end of 56 years from the date copyright was originally secured, or on January 1, 1978, whichever is later.

How may termination be effected?

Termination may be effected by serving a written notice upon the grantee or the grantee's successor in title. Where grant is executed by a person or persons other than the author, all of those who executed the grant and survive, or their duly authorized agents, must sign the notice. Notice must comply with Copyright Office regulations. A copy of the notice must be recorded in the Copyright Office before the effective date of termination.

NOTE: Some works will not be subject to any termination rights. Section 304(c) applies only to grants made prior to January 1, 1978 and section 203 applies only to grants made on or after that date. Section 203 termination rights apply only to grants made by the author, and works made for hire are not subject to termination.

What is the effect of termination?

All rights revert to those with a right to terminate except that derivative works prepared before termination may continue to be utilized under the terms of the grant. No new derivative works may be prepared after the effective date of termination. Termination rights vest on the date the notice is served.

Examples:

1. A publishing company, on July 1, 1977, makes a contract with Norbert Novelist for a new book. The book is not written until July 20, 1979. The rights transferred in the July 1, 1977 contract would not be subject to termination. The grant was made before January 1, 1977 but not for a work in which copyright was subsisting on the effective date of the new law.

2. An author writes book in 1970; the work is never published and no rights in the work were assigned during the author's lifetime—author died in August of 1980. In june of 1981 the author's widow grants a publishing company certain rights. Those rights are not subject to termination. Only section 203 can apply and that section is limited to grants made by the author.

SCOPE OF THE EXCLUSIVE RIGHTS ACCORDED COPYRIGHT OWNERS

[Chapter I, Section 106]

The section setting forth the exclusive rights of the copyright owner is the heart of any copyright law. This section determines the limits of protection granted to authors and their successors in interest.

As the 1965 Supplementary Report of the Register states, "in a narrow view, all of the author's exclusive rights translate into money: whether he should be paid for a particular use or whether it should be free." This Report also notes that "[t]he basic legislative problem is to insure that the copyright law provides the necessary monetary incentive to write, produce, publish, and disseminate creative works, while at the same time guarding against the danger that these works will not be disseminated and used as fully as they should because of copyright restrictions."

The drafters of the new law took particular pains not to confine the scope of an author's rights on the basis of the present technology. Thus, the exclusive rights of an author are stated in broad terms.

Section 106 grants five basic and exclusive rights. The right to display a work publicly is specifically stated for the first time. Detailed limitations and exemptions follow in sections 107 through 118; these sections, therefore, must always be read in conjunction with section 106.

The House Report notes that the rights in section 106 are cumulative and to some extent overlap. For example, the preparation of a derivative work would usually also involve its reproduction.

The rights stated may be subdivided without limitation. Each subdivision of an exclusive right may be owned and enforced separately (section 201(d)(2)).

Reproduce the copyrighted work in copies or phonorecords

The right to reproduce the work is the most fundamental right granted by any copyright law. The terms "copies" and "phonorecords" include the first or original embodiment of the work (the prototype), as well as any other objects from which the work can be "perceived, reproduced, or otherwise communicated, either directly or with the aid of a machine or device."

Prepare derivative works

The right to prepare new versions of copyrighted works is a valuable one, and its existence permits the copyright owner to control uses of his work that might not otherwise be included in the reproduction. A derivative work is defined in section 101 as a work based upon one or more preexisting works such as a translation, musical arrangement, dramatization, fictionalization, motion picture version, sound recording, art reproduction, abridgment, condensation, or any other form in which a work may be recast, transformed, or adapted.

Public distribution

This right includes distribution by sale, gift, or other transfer of ownership of the material object embodying the work, or by rental, lease, or lending the material object. The exclusive right to sell a copyrighted work is terminated on the first authorized sale, and a copyright owner is not permitted to control future disposition of sold copies of the work. This is made clear by section 109 which draws a basic distinction between the rights of a copyright owner and the rights of someone who owns a physical object (a copy or phonorecord) that embodies a copyrighted work. Section 109 states that once a copy or phonorecord has been lawfully made, it can be disposed of by its owner without the copyright owner's permission.

Public performing right

For certain kinds of works, the right of public performance has become the most important. The right of public performance under 106(4) extends to "literary, musical, dramatic, and choreographic works, pantomimes, and motion pictures and other audiovisual works"; there is no such right for sound recordings.

140

Unlike the present law, this right is not limited by any "for profit" requirement. There are, however, a number of exemptions and limitations in sections 107 through 118.

The exclusive right of public performance has been expanded to include motion pictures and other audiovisual works. Performance of an audiovisual work means to show the images in any sequence and to make any sounds accompanying the work audible. The House and Senate Reports state that the showing of portions of motion pictures, filmstrips, or slide sets sequentially will constitute a "performance" rather than a "display."

Under the definition of "perform" in section 101 it is clear that the following would constitute a performance of a work: live renditions that are face to face, renditions from recordings, broadcasting, retransmission by loud-speakers, and transmission and retransmissions by cable, microwave, etc. To perform publicly is defined as performing at a place open to the public or at a place where a substantial number of persons outside of a normal circle of a family and its social acquaintances is gathered.

Right of public display

This is the only right granted under the new law whose existence is open to question under the old law.

By definition (section 101) to "display" a work means to show a copy of it, either directly or by means of a film, slide, television image, or any other device or process or, in the case of a motion picture or other audiovisual work, to show individual images nonsequentially. Thus, subject to the limitations imposed by section 109, the right of public display applies to any work embodied in manuscript or printed matter and in pictorial, graphic, and sculptural works, including "stills." Exhibition of a motion picture or other audiovisual work as a whole is a performance rather than a display.

Section 109(b) states that the owner of a lawfully-made copy can display it publicly to viewers present *at the same place as the copy.* Thus, the exclusive right of public display would not apply where the owner of a copy wishes to show it directly to the public, as in a gallery or display case, or indirectly through an opaque projector.

FAIR USE AND OTHER LIMITATIONS AND EXEMPTIONS ON EXCLUSIVE RIGHTS

[Sections 107, 108, 110, 112]

FAIR USE (Section 107)

Although fair use (a doctrine developed by the courts) was not included in any copyright statute prior to the 1976 Act, the concept is firmly established in everyday usage. The concept of "fair use" is not susceptible to exact definition. Generally speaking, however, it allows copying without permission from, or payment to, the copyright owner where the use is reasonable and not harmful to the rights of the copyright owner.

Section 107 is somewhat vague since it would be difficult to prescribe precise rules to cover all situations. It refers to "purposes such as criticism, comment, news reporting, teaching (including multiple copies for classroom use), scholarship, or research" and sets out four factors to be considered in determining whether ot not a particular use is fair. These are:

1. The purpose and character of the use, including whether such use is of a commercial nature or is for nonprofit educational purposes;

2. The amount and substantiality of the portion used in relation to the copyrighted work as a whole;

3. The nature of the copyrighted work; and

4. The effect of the use upon the potential market for or value of the copyrighted work.

These criteria are not necessarily the sole criteria that a court may consider. Section 107 makes it clear that the factors a court shall consider shall "include" these four; section 101, the definitional section of the new law, states that the terms "including" and "such as" are illustrative and not limitative.

The legislative reports state that section 107 as drafted is intended to restate the present judicial doctrine; it is not intended to change, narrow or enlarge it in any way.

One thing is clear—the language of section 107 does not provide specific tests by which one can determine with much certainty whether or not a particular use is fair. The difficulty of arriving at a clear-cut definition is inherent in the nature of the doctrine. The House and Senate Reports state:

> Although the courts have considered and ruled upon the doctrine of fair use over and over again, no real definition of this concept has ever emerged. Indeed, since the doctrine is an equitable rule of reason, no generally applicable definition is possible, and each case raising the question must be decided on its own facts.

Under these circumstances the various interest groups tried to work out some compromises. Three different educational groups, dealing respectively with copying for teacher and classroom use of print materials, photocopying of music, and audiovisual presentations met separately with authors' and publishers' organizations to work out guidelines. These efforts were successful in the music and print field. No agreement was reached on audiovisual works although attempts are still being made to resolve this issue.

The guidelines for books and periodicals appear in Appendix 3. They may be briefly summarized as covering: (1) single copies for teachers, (2) multiple classroom copies, and (3) prohibitions. Multiple classroom copying cannot exceed the number of pupils per class, must meet strict tests of

142

brevity, spontaneity and noncumulative effect, and must include a notice of copyright.

The prohibitions include:

1. the copies may not be used as a substitute for anthologies, compilations or collective works;

2. copies cannot be made of consumable material such as work books;

3. the copies cannot be a substitute for purchases, be "directed by higher authority" or be repeated by the same teacher from term to term; and

4. there can be no charge to the student beyond the actual copying cost.

The music guidelines follow much the same pattern. They allow emergency copying to replace previously purchased copies for use in an immediate performance. Copying of excerpts of no more than 10% of the whole work is allowed for academic purposes other than performance. The excerpts cannot constitute a performable unit such as a section, movement or aria. Editing and simplifying purchased works is allowed as is the production of single copies of certain sound recordings for certain educational purposes.

Both sets of guidelines state that they constitute the minimum and not the maximum standards of educational fair use under section 107. They also state:

> The parties agree that the conditions determining the extent of permissible copying for educational purposes may change in the future; that certain types of copying permitted under these guidelines may not be permissible in the future; and conversely that in the future other types of copying not permitted under these guidelines may be permissible under revised guidelines .... There may be instances in which copying which does not fall within the guidelines stated ... may nonetheless be permitted under the criteria of fair use.

The House Report states that the Judiciary Committee believes that the guidelines are a reasonable interpretation of the minimum standards of fair use. It notes that teachers will know that copying within the guidelines is fair use and that the guidelines, therefore, serve the purpose of fulfilling the need for greater certainty and protection for teachers. The House and Senate conferees accepted these guidelines as part of their understanding of fair use.

The problem of off-the-air taping for nonprofit use was left unresolved. The House Report states that the doctrine of fair use has some limited application in this area. The Senate Report, on the other hand, states that, "The committee does not intend to suggest however, that off-the-air taping for convenience would under any circumstances be considered 'fair use.'"

Certain non-educational materials receive attention in the legislative reports as well. In speaking of independent newsletters which are particularly vulnerable to mass photocopying practices, both the House and Senate Reports call for a narrower interpretation of fair use than might be applied to mass-circulation periodicals.

The legislative reports also state the belief that in the case of calligraphers, a single copy reproduction of an excerpt from a copyrighted work for a single client "does not represent an infringement of copyright."

REPRODUCTION BY LIBRARIES AND ARCHIVES
(Section 108)

Section 108 deals with a variety of situations involving photocopying and other forms of reproductions by libraries and archives. Subsection (a) provides that "... it is not an infringement of copyright for a library or archives, or any of its employees acting within the scope of their employment, to reproduce no more than one copy or phonorecord of a work, or to distribute such a copy or phonorecord, under the conditions specified by this section if–

1. the reproduction or distribution is made without any purpose of direct or indirect commercial advantage;

2. the collections of the library or archives are (i) open to the public, or (ii) available not only to researchers affiliated with the library or archives or with the institution of which it is a part, but also to other persons doing research in a specialized field; and

3. the reproduction or distribution of a work includes a notice of copyright."

Thus, (a) lays out the basic conditions under which a library or archives can claim an exemption. But this is only the beginning—for library activity to be exempt it must also qualify under one of the conditions laid out in subsection (b) through (f), must not run afoul of subsection (g), and must involve copying of a work that is not mentioned in subsection (h).

(b) *Archival preservation*—this exemption applies only to unpublished works in the current collection of a library or archives. It allows reproduction only in facsimile form, and only for "purposes of preservation or security or for deposit for research use in another library or archives."

(c) *Replacement*—libraries or archives are authorized to duplicate a published work in facsimile form solely for the purpose of replacement of a copy or phonorecord that is damaged, deteriorating, lost or stolen *but* only if it finds that an unused replacement copy cannot be obtained at a fair price. The legislative reports offer some guidance as to what is meant—they indicate that a reasonable investigation will always require recourse to commonly known trade sources in the United States, and in the normal situation also to the publisher or copyright owner or an authorized reproducing service.

(d) *Journal articles, small excerpts,* etc.—This subsection applies to "no more than one article or other contribution to a copyrighted collection or periodical issue, or to . . . a small part of any other copyrighted work." The only conditions for supplying a reproduction are that "the copy becomes the property of the user"; there is no reason to suppose that it "would be used for any purposes other than private study, scholarship, or research"; and the library or archives must display prominently, at the place where orders are accepted, a warning of copyright. The institution must also include a warning to be prescribed by a Copyright Office regulation on its order form.

(e) *Entire works or substantial parts*—With one addition, the conditions applicable under subsection (d) apply under subsection (e) to "the entire work," or "a substantial part of it." The added condition is that "the library or archives has first determined, on the basis of a reasonable investigation, that a copy or phonorecord of a copyrighted work cannot be obtained at a fair price."

(f) *General exemptions*—this subsection contains four clauses aimed at precluding certain interpretations of section 108.

  (1) The first clause makes clear that no liability attaches to a library or its staff for "unsupervised use of reproducing equipment located on its premises," as long as a copyright warning is posted on the machine.

  (2) Conversely, the second clause provides that the individual user of the reproducing equipment is not insulated from liability if the reproduction exceeds fair use, and the same is true if the library is asked to make the copy for the individual.

  (3) The third clause, which was added to the section during the floor debates in the Senate in September, 1974, reflects the controversy over the videotape archive of news programs at Vanderbilt University. It states that nothing in section 108 "shall be construed to limit the reproduction and distribution of a limited number of copies and excerpts by a library or archives of an audiovisual news program . . . ."

  The intent is to permit libraries and archives to make off-the-air videotape recordings of daily network newscasts for limited distribution to scholars and researchers. The House Report notes that it is an adjunct to the American Television and Radio Archive established in Section 113 of the Transitional and Supplementary Provisions.

  The House Report notes that this section does not apply to documentaries, magazine format or other public affairs broadcasts dealing with subjects of general interest to the viewing public. The report also states that this material is to be distributed only by lending. Performance, copying, or sale, whether or not for profit, by the recipient of a copy of a television broadcast taped off the air, is forbidden.

(4) The fourth clause is important. It declares that nothing in section 108 "in any way affects the right of fair use as provided by section 107." It also provides that the right of reproduction granted by section 108 does not override any contractual arrangements assumed by a library or archives when it obtained the work for its collections.

(g) *Multiple and systematic copying*—This subsection was one of the most controversial. It states that the rights of reproduction and distribution under section 108 extend to the "isolated and unrelated" reproduction or distribution of a single copy or phonorecord of the same material on separate occasions; they do not cover related or concerted multiple copying, even when done over a period of time for different users.

The exact language is: "that the rights under section 108 do not extend to cases where the library or archives, or its employees:

(1) is aware or has substantial reason to believe that it is engaging in the related or concerted reproduction or distribution of multiple copies or phonorecords of the same material, whether made on one occasion or over a period of time, and whether intended for aggregate use by one or more individuals or for separate use by the individual members of a group; or

(2) engages in the systematic reproduction or distribution of single or multiple copies or phonorecords of materials described in subsection (d) [an article or contribution to a periodical or copyrighted collection or a small part of any other copyrighted work]: PROVIDED, That nothing in this clause prevents a library or archives from participating in interlibrary arrangements that do not have, as their purpose or effect, that the library or archives receiving such copies or phonorecords for distribution does so in such aggregate quantities as to substitute for a subscription to or purchase of such work."

The National Commission on New Technological Uses of Copyrighted Works (CONTU) developed, with the assistance of representatives of library organizations and authors and publishers, a set of guidelines on interlibrary arrangements which were incorporated into the Conference Report. However, in the report the conferees stated:

". . . the guidelines are not intended as, and cannot be considered, explicit rules or directions governing any and all cases, now or in the future. It is recognized that their purpose is to provide guidance in the most commonly-encountered interlibrary photocopying situations, that they are not intended to be limiting or determinative in themselves or with respect to other situations, and that they deal with an evolving situation that will undoubtedly require their continuous reevaluation and adjustment."

Part of this reevaluation process will be the requirement in section 108(i) that the Register of Copyrights, five years after the effective date of the new Act, and at five-year intervals thereafter, issue reports on the extent to which section 108 has achieved the intended balancing of the rights of the creators and the needs of users. The guidelines themselves call for a five-year review also.

[NOTE: the CONTU guidelines are limited to one of the most frequent interlibrary loan practices—the making of copies of articles from periodicals whose issue dates are less than five years old. The question of guidelines or interpretations of making copies from articles more than five years old is left to future interpretation. Note, too, that the focus of the guidelines is on the requesting library rather than on the one which fills the orders.]

(h) *Material not covered*—This subsection narrows the scope of subsections (d) and (e) to exclude musical works, pictorial, graphic, and sculptural works, and audiovisual works (other than television news programs) from the reproduction privileges set out therein.

The exclusions under (h) do not apply to archival reproduction under (b); or to replacement of damaged or lost copies under (c); or to "pictorial or graphic works published as illustrations, diagrams, or similar adjuncts to works of which copies are reproduced or distributed in accordance with subsections (d) and (e)."

It is important to remember that the doctrine of fair use remains fully applicable under section 107 to musical works, pictorial, graphic and sculptural works and audiovisual works.

[NOTE: the Conference Report deals with the interpretation of "indirect commercial advantage" as used in section 108. With regard to libraries which are connected with industrial, profit-making, or proprietary institutions it says, "[a]s long as the library or archives meets the criteria in section 108(a) and the other requirements of the section, including the prohibitions against multiple and systematic copying in subsection (g), the conferees consider that isolated, spontaneous making of single photocopies by a library or archives in a for-profit organization without any commercial motivation, or participation by such a library in interlibrary arrangements, would come within the scope of section 108."]

EXEMPTIONS OF CERTAIN
PERFORMANCES AND DISPLAYS
(Section 110)

The general rights of public performance and display which are enunciated in clauses (4) and (5) of section 106 (see Chapter 7) are made subject to nine specific limitations in section 110. This section exempts the following types of public performances from copyright liability under specified conditions:

(1)   face-to-face teaching activities;

(2)   instructional broadcasting (broadcasts that are essentially an adjunct to actual classwork of educational institutions as opposed to public broadcasts which are of a cultural or educational nature and directed to the public at large);

(3)   religious services;

(4)   live performances without commercial advantage to anyone;

(5)   mere reception of broadcasts in a public place;

(6)   annual agricultural and horticultural fairs;

(7)   public performance in connection with sale of records or sheet music;

(8)   noncommercial broadcasts to the blind or deaf;

(9)   nonprofit performances of dramatic works transmitted to the blind by radio subcarrier.

As the legislative reports note, clauses (1) through (4) deal with performances and displays that were generally exempt under the "for profit" limitation or other provisions of the 1909 law.

(1)   *Face-to-face teaching activities*—This sets out the conditions under which performances or displays, in the course of instructional activities other than broadcasting, are to be exempt from copyright control. This clause covers all types of works.

To be exempt, the performance or display must be by a pupil or an instructor which would generally mean a teacher but it is intended to be broad enough to cover, for example, a guest lecturer. Performance by actors, singers or musicians brought in from outside would not be exempt.

"Face-to-face" was inserted to exclude broadcasting or other transmissions, whether radio or television, or open or closed circuit, from an outside location into a classroom. The exemption does, however, extend to the use of devices for amplifying or reproducing sound and for projecting visual images, as long as instructors and students are in the same building or general area.

"Teaching activities" is intended to mean systematic instruction; it would not include performances or displays that are given for the recreation or entertainment of any part of the audience. This is true even though the work performed or displayed has great cultural or intellectual appeal.

The phrase "classroom or similar place" limits the exemption to places devoted to instruction. The legislative reports indicate that such a place might be a studio, workshop, gymnasium, or library as long as it actually is used as a classroom for systematic instructional activities. Performances in an auditorium for a school assembly, a graduation exercise, etc. would be outside the scope of this exemption because the audience is not confined to members of a specific class, although they might be exempted under other provisions of section 110.

(2) *Instructional broadcasting*—This covers broadcasting which is an adjunct to the actual classwork of educational institutions; it exempts "the performance of a nondramatic literary or musical work or display of a work by or in the course of transmission" if three conditions are met. The first is that the performance or display must be a "regular part of the systematic instructional activities of a governmental body or a nonprofit educational institution." The second is that "the performance or display is directly related and of material assistance to the teaching content of the transmission." The third is that the transmission must be made "primarily" for: "(i) reception in classrooms or similar places normally devoted to instruction; or (ii) reception by persons to whom the transmission is directed because of their disabilities or other special circumstances prevent their attendance in classrooms or similar places normally devoted to instruction; or (iii) reception by officers or employees of governmental bodies as part of their official duties or employment."

Only performances of nondramatic literary or musical works would be exempt. The performance of a dramatico-musical work such as an opera or musical comedy, or a motion picture or other audiovisual work could occur lawfully only if the copyright owner's permission had been obtained.

With respect to exhibitions, the exemption would apply to any type of work which the right "to display . . . publicly" under section 106(5) applies (see Chapter 7).

The reports indicate that "systematic instructional activities" is intended as the general equivalent of "curriculums" but that it could be broader in certain cases.

The term "educational institution" was used because it is broad enough to cover a wide range of establishments engaged in teaching activities. It is not supposed to cover, however, "foundations," "associations," etc. who are not primarily and directly engaged in instruction.

110(2) ties in with section 112(b) (see below) which represents a response to instructional broadcasters' requests for special recording privileges. It permits a nonprofit organization that is entitled to transmit a performance or display of a work under section 110(2) to make not more than 30 copies or phonorecords and to use the "ephemeral recordings" for transmitting purposes for not more than seven years after the initial transmission. Thereafter, only one copy or phonorecord may be preserved exclusively for archival purposes.

(3) *Religious services*—This covers performances of a nondramatic literary or musical work and also performances of dramatico-musical works "of a religious nature" and displays of all kinds. This exemption only applies to performances and displays "in the course of services at a place of worship or other religious assembly." This clause does not cover the sequential showing of motion pictures and other audiovisual works.

The House Report indicates that oratorios, cantatas, and musical settings of the mass are covered by the exemption, but that secular operas, musical plays, motion pictures and the like, even if they have an underlying religious or philosophical theme and take place in the course of a religious service, are not.

This exemption would not extend to religious broadcasts or other transmissions to the public at large.

(4) *Certain other nonprofit performances*—This clause provides that the noncommercial performance of a nondramatic literary or musical work other than in an transmission to the public is generally exempt from copyright liability if no compensation is paid to its performers, promoters or organizers. If, however, proceeds are derived through a direct or indirect admission charge for exclusively educational, religious, or charitable purposes, then the copyright owner is given a chance to serve a notice of objection concerning the performance.

To prevent the performance, the notice must be in writing and be signed by the copyright owner or his duly authorized agent, must be served on the person responsible for the performance at least seven days prior to the performance, and must state the reasons for the objection. Also, the notice must comply in form, content and manner of service with regulations the Copyright Office is to promulgate.

(5) *Mere reception in public*—This clause applies to all types of works. Its basic purpose is to exempt from liability anyone who merely turns on, in a public place, an ordinary radio or television of a kind commonly sold to the public for private use. This clause is not supposed to have anything to do with cable systems; moreover, the exemption would be denied in any case where the audience is charged directly to see or hear the transmission.

[NOTE: with respect to *Twentieth Century Music Corp* v. *Aiken,* 422 U.S. 151 (1975), the House Report states that this fact situation represents the outer limit of the exemption and believes that the line should be drawn at this point. (Aiken had a small business and used a home receiver with four ordinary loudspeakers grouped within a relatively narrow circumference from the set.) A proprietor of a small commercial establishment who brings standard home equipment to the premises and plays it for the enjoyment of the customer would fall within the exemption. If the equipment were of a commercial nature, then liability would be imposed. In making this determination, the House Report indicates that factors to consider are the size, physical arrangement and noise level of the areas within the establishment where the transmissions are made audible or visible, and the extent to which the receiving apparatus is altered or augmented for the purpose of improving aural or visual quality of the performance for the public.

(6) *Agricultural Fairs*—This clause exempts "performance of a nondramatic musical work by a governmental body or a nonprofit agricultural or horticultural organization, in the course of an annual agricultural or horticultural fair or exhibition conducted by such body or organization."

This clause makes it clear that only the governmental body or nonprofit organization sponsoring the fair is covered. Concessionaires have no exemption under this clause.

(7) *Retail sale of phonorecords*—This provision allows the performance of a nondramatic musical work or of a sound recording by a vending establishment open to the public at large without any direct or indirect admission charge, where the sole purpose of the performance is to promote the retail sale of copies or phonorecords of the work.

(8) and (9) *Transmission for the blind and other handicapped persons*— Subsection (8) provides an exemption for the performance of a nondramatic literary work. To qualify, a broadcast must be specifically designed for, and directed to, blind or other sight or hearing impaired persons; must be made without any purpose of direct or indirect commercial advantage; and be broadcast through the facilities of either:

a)   a governmental body;

b)   a noncommercial educational broadcast station;

c)   a radio subcarrier authorization; or

d)   a cable system.

Clause (9) exempts nonprofit performances of dramatic works transmitted to audiences of the blind by radio subcarrier authorization, but only for a single performance of a dramatic work published at least ten years earlier.

EPHEMERAL RECORDINGS
(Section 112)

Ephemeral recordings are "copies or phonorecords of a work made for purposes of later transmission by a broadcasting organization legally entitled to transmit the work." Thus, an ephemeral recording is a tape or phonorecord of a work made by a broadcaster who either by license of the copyright owner or exemption in the statute has the right to perform a work, but not necessarily the right to make copies. Without an ephemeral recording right, the broadcaster who may have secured a license to perform a copyrighted work on radio or television would not be able to tape the performance of the work.

The new copyright law distinguishes between a broadcaster who acquires a license to transmit a work and an instructional broadcaster who is exempt under section 110(2).

Under 112(a) a licensed broadcaster is allowed to make one copy of a program provided that the copy is retained and used only by the transmitter who made it and used only within that transmitter's normal transmission area. Additionally, the broadcaster is required to either destroy the copy within six months or use it exclusively for archival purposes. Motion pictures and other audiovisual works are *not* included in this exemption.

112(b) covers recordings for instructional transmissions. It permits a nonprofit organization that is free to transmit a performance or display under 110(2) or 114(a) to make not more than 30 copies or phonorecords and to use the ephemeral recordings for transmitting purposes for not more than seven years after the initial transmission.

[NOTE: there is no reproduction privilege for motion pictures or other audiovisual works. 110(2) covers only nondramatic literary and musical works and displays of all types of works.]

It is important to realize that ephemeral recordings made by instructional broadcasters are in fact audiovisual works that often compete for the same market. As the reports indicate, it is unfair to allow instructional broadcasters to reproduce multiple copies of films and tapes, and to exchange them with other broadcasters without paying any copyright royalties; this was considered to injure the market of producers of audiovisual material who pay substantial fees to authors for the same uses. This was the main reason why limitations were placed on this exemption.

112(c) covers religious broadcasts. This clause states that "it is not an infringement for a government or nonprofit organization to make no more than one copy or phonorecord for each transmitting organization of a particular transmission program embodying a performance of a nondramatic musical work of a religious nature or a sound recording of such musical work" if: (a) there is no charge; (2) there is no use other than a single transmission by a transmitting organization entitled to transmit to the public under a license or (3) one copy only is kept for archival purposes. All other copies are to be destroyed within one year from the date the transmission was first transmitted to the public.

The case made by the religious program producers before Congress was that they are producing a nonprofit broadcast and are merely using the convenience of tape or disc rather than long lines because it is cheaper to do so in this manner.

112(d) grants an ephemeral recording right to transmissions to handicapped audiences. This subsection ties in with 110(8).

112(e) covers the copyright status of ephemeral recordings. It provides that ephemeral recordings are not to be copyrightable as derivative works except with the consent of the owners of the copyrighted material employed in them.

LIMITATIONS ON EXCLUSIVE RIGHTS IN SOUND RECORDINGS
(Section 114(b))

An exception to the exclusive rights in sound recordings granted in section 106 is that permission is not needed to use sound recordings in educational television and radio programs distributed or transmitted by or through public broadcasting entities as long as phonorecords of such programs are not commercially distributed by or through such entities to the public.

The rights in sound recordings are also limited by certain portions of sections 108 and 112 and of course by the doctrine of fair use, section 107.

THE COMPULSORY LICENSES AND THE COPYRIGHT ROYALTY TRIBUNAL

[Sections 111, 115, 116, 118 and Chapter 8]

SECONDARY TRANSMISSIONS (Section 111)

Section 111 covers the complex and economically important problem of "secondary transmissions." For the most part this section is directed at the operation of cable systems and the terms and conditions of their liability for the retransmissions of copyrighted works. It does, however, consider other forms of secondary transmission including apartment house and hotel systems, common carriers, and secondary transmissions of primary transmissions to controlled groups. Subsection (f) contains the definitions of the operative terms—e.g., "primary transmitter" and "secondary transmitter."

Cable television systems are commercial subscription services which pick up broadcasts of programs originated by others and retransmit them to paying subscribers. A typical system consists of three sections: the head end section, which is the point where the signal is introduced into the system; the trunk line section, which brings the signal from the head end to the local community; and the distribution system, which carries the signal from the trunk line to the various subscribers' homes. In an area where off-the-air reception is poor (e.g., where there is hilly terrain) the cable system may use microwave to bring TV signals to the head end. A growing number of cable systems also originate programs, such as movies and sports, and charge additional fees for this service (pay cable).

Subsection (c) establishes a compulsory license for cable systems. Generally it allows the retransmission of those over-the-air broadcast signals that a cable system is authorized to carry pursuant to the rules and regulations of the FCC. This license, however, is conditioned on compliance with the reporting and filing provisions of the law, payment of the royalties due, etc. The rationale for this provision is that Congress believed that cable systems are commercial enterprises whose basic retransmission operations are based on the carriage of copyrighted program material. Congress believed that royalties should be paid by cable operators to the creators of such programs; but Congress recognized that it would be too burdensome and impractical to require every cable system to negotiate with every copyright owner.

Basic Principles of the Compulsory License:

1. A cable system's retransmission is clearly a public "performance" of the copyrighted work.

2. As long as a cable operator is authorized by his FCC license to carry a particular signal, he is entitled to rely on the "compulsory license" with respect to the copyrighted material carried by the signal.

3. The new law makes distinctions between cable retransmission of local and distant signals and between cable carriage of network and non-network programming. Congress believed that the retransmission of local signals, essentially those already available over-the-air in the cable system's community, did not economically injure copyright owners since they were compensated for use of their programs in the local markets under their broadcast licenses. Congress also concluded that retransmission of network programming, whether local or distant, did not injure the copyright owner. The owner would be adequately compensated under its contract with the network. Payment in this situation is generally based on reaching all markets served by the network by any means. Congress did, however, find that the retransmission of *distant non-network* programming would damage the copyright owner. Where a cable system brings a distant, non-network signal into its community, the copyright owner's ability to subsequently license the use of its program in that community would be impaired. In effect, the copyright owner would find itself dealing in used goods. Thus, all signals are under the compulsory license but generally the statutory fee is based on the amount of carriage of distant, non-network programming.

4. Commercial substitution and program modification is prohibited. The law provides that if a cable system intentionally alters the content of the retransmitted program, or changes, deletes, or adds to commercial advertising or station announcements transmitted by the originating station, it loses the benefit of the compulsory license. The law permits suit to be brought by the originating broadcast station or any broadcast station within whose local service area the cable retransmission is made. In such a case the court may deprive the cable system of the compulsory license for a period of up to 30 days. The effect of this is to preclude a cable operator from deciding that the

154

economic benefits of commercial substitution or the like are significant enough to forego the compulsory license and negotiate directly with the copyright owner.

5. There are provisions governing the importation of foreign television signals. FCC rules permit certain border cable systems to retransmit certain Mexican and Canadian signals. The new law extends the compulsory license to the retransmission of Mexican and Canadian signals by cable systems located within limited zones in the U.S. In the case of Canadian signals the zone is defined geographically—it applies to areas located within 150 miles from the U.S.-Canadian border, or south from the border to the 42nd parallel of latitude, whichever distance is greater. Included within the compulsory license area: Detroit, Pittsburgh, Cleveland. Outside: New York, Philadelphia, Chicago and San Francisco.

The Mexican situation was harder to deal with because of the effect of the retransmission of Mexican signals on indigenous U.S. Spanish-language programming. With regard to Mexico, the zone is defined by technology. The compulsory license applies only in such areas where the signals may be received by a U.S. cable system by means of direct interception of a free space radio wave. Thus, the compulsory license is generally applicable only to systems which receive the program directly off-the-air and not to those systems which use microwave or other devices going beyond a mere receiving antenna.

Additionally, there is a grandfather clause. The new law permits cable systems authorized to carry Canadian or Mexican signals under FCC rules in effect on April 15, 1976 to continue to carry those signals under the compulsory license.

Cable systems operation outside the specified zones, and not grandfathered in, are not entitled to the compulsory license and must negotiate for the retransmission of the signals with the copyright owners.

6. Section 111 does not normally cover situations where someone tapes a program off-the-air and the program is later retransmitted from the tape. There is a complicated exception involving cable systems outside the continental United States, some of which are allowed to use tape because they cannot pick signals out of the air. See 111(e).

Exemptions

Subsection (a) contains four exemptions to the compulsory license. These are:

(1) Secondary transmissions consisting "entirely of the relaying, by the management of a hotel, apartment house, or similar establishment" of a transmission to the private rooms of guests or residents as long as no direct charges were made to see or hear it. Private rooms limit it to living quarters; it would not include dining rooms, meeting halls, theatres, ballrooms, or similar places that are outside of a normal circle of a family and its social acquaintances.

(2) Secondary transmissions of instructional broadcasts which are within the scope of section 110(2) [See Chapter Eight] .

(3) Secondary transmissions of a passive carrier—i.e., one which "has no direct or indirect control over the content or selection of the primary transmission or over the particular recipients of the secondary transmission."

(4) The operations of non-profit "translators" and "boosters" which do nothing more than amplify broadcast signals and retransmit them to everyone in an area for free reception if there is "no purpose of direct or indirect commercial advantage" and if there is no charge to the recipients "other than assessments necessary to defray the actual and reasonable costs" of maintenance and operation. This exemption does not apply to a cable television system.

Outside the scope of the compulsory license (must be licensed from the copyright owner(s) of the program(s)) — Secondary transmissions of primary transmission to a controlled group.

Subsection (b) makes it clear that the secondary transmission to the public of a primary transmission embodying a performance or display is actionable as an act of infringement if the primary transmission is not made for reception by the public at large but is controlled and limited to reception by particular members of the public. Examples include MUZAK, closed circuit broadcasts to theaters, subscription television, or pay cable.

Filing Requirements: Notices, Statements of Account and the Royalty Fees

111(d)(1) required all cable systems in operation on April 17, 1977, to file by April 18, 1977, an initial notice giving certain identifying information and listing all signals that it regularly carries. Cable systems that begin operations after April 18, 1977, must file such a notice 30 days prior to the commencement of operation. All cable systems are required to file supplemental notices within 30 days of any change in the information recorded.

The Copyright Office has adopted a regulation implementing this notification requirement [37 C.F.R. Section 201.11. Copies are available from the Copyright Office, request ML-142.]

This regulation requests that the notice be identified as such by prominently captioning the document as "An Initial Notice of Identity and Signal Carriage Complement." The notice should include: the identity and address of the person who, or entity which, owns or operates the system or has power to exercise primary control over it. The regulation suggests that the legal name be given with any fictitious or assumed name adopted for the purpose of conducting business. It also asks for the name and location of the primary transmitter or primary transmitters whose signals are regularly carried and suggests the station's call sign, accompanied by a brief statement of the type of signal carried (TV, "FM" etc.) be given. The location the Copyright Office would like is the name of the community to which the transmitter is licensed

156

by the FCC. The Office in its regulation suggests that the notices be dated and that they contain the individual signature of the person identified as the owner, etc. or his authorized agent.

The Initial Notices and Notices of Change will be placed in "the appropriate public files" of the Copyright Office. For a fee of $3 the Copyright Office will furnish a certified receipt.

Section 111(d)(2) requires all cable television to file semiannual statements of account. These statements must include a royalty fee for the six-month period covered; must list all signals carried during that period; and must provide information on the number of channels, the number of subscribers and gross receipts for basic service. Each statement must also be supplemented by a special statement of account covering distant non-network programming carried pursuant to FCC rules allowing for the addition or substitution of signals. Also, the Register is empowered to require, by regulation, the filing of "other data."

Section 111(d)(3) provides that the fees are to go to the Register, who, after deducting the reasonable costs incurred by the Office, shall deposit them in the Treasury. The Treasury is instructed to put the money into interest bearing U.S. securities.

Section 111(d)(4) lists the copyright owners entitled to royalty fees. They are: (1) copyright owners whose works were included ... by a cable system of a distant non-network television program; (2) any copyright owner whose work is included in a secondary transmission identified in a special statement of account; and (3) copyright owners whose works were included in distant non-network programming consisting exclusively of aural signals— i.e., radio.

No royalties may be claimed or distributed for "local" or "network" programs.

Every year during the month of July every person claiming to be entitled to royalties must file with the Copyright Royalty Tribunal (see below). After the first day of August of each year the Tribunal shall determine whether a controversy exists. If no controversy exists, the Tribunal, after deducting its reasonable administrative costs, shall distribute the fees to the owners or their agents. If a controversy exists, it must conduct a proceeding in accordance with chapter 8 of the 1976 Act.

Summary

In order to be covered by the compulsory license provided by Section 111, a cable system must:

- retransmit only those signals permitted under FCC rules
- comply with the filing and reporting requirements of the Copyright Office
- pay the royalties established by the formula in the law
- avoid program modification or commercial substitution

- restrict its retransmissions to programs that originate from FCC-licensed stations in the U.S.

- (in the case of a Canadian signal) be located in the appropriate zone; or

- (in the case of a Mexican signal) limit itself to the appropriate technology.

COMPULSORY LICENSE FOR MAKING AND DISTRIBUTING PHONO-RECORDS EMBODYING NONDRAMATIC MUSICAL COMPOSITIONS
(Section 115)

Sections 1(e) and 101(e) of the 1909 Act grant the copyright owner of a musical composition the exclusive right to make or license the first recording. After that anyone else may make a "similar use" of the work. The compulsory license provision of the old law required that the compulsory licensee notify the copyright owner of his intent, send a copy of the notice of intention to use to the Copyright Office for recordation, and pay the statutory royalties at the appropriate time.

A major issue in the revision effort was whether to retain this compulsory license. The Copyright Office originally suggested that the compulsory license provision be eliminated. This proposal was met with fierce opposition by record producers both small and large. Even copyright proprietors favored its retention in some form.

In 1967 the House Judiciary Committee noted in its report that it favored retention of the principle; it did, however, also state "that the present system is unfair and unnecessarily burdensome on copyright owners" and observed "that the present statutory rate is too low."

The compulsory license for making phonorecords of copyrighted nondramatic musical compositions is retained in section 115 of the new law; there are, however, substantial changes in the system.

Availability and Scope of the Compulsory License (Section 115(a))

This subsection makes the compulsory license available as soon as the copyright owner of the music distributes phonorecords to the public in the United States. The distribution must be authorized by the copyright owner of the music.

The compulsory license is available only if the purpose in making phonorecords is to distribute them to the public for private use. (Background music systems need the express consent of the copyright owner; they may not rely on this section.)

The compulsory license provided by section 115 is not available to an unauthorized duplicator. Moreover, the interpretation of *Duchess Music Corp.* v. *Stern,* 458 F.2d 1305 (9th Cir.), *cert. denied,* 409 U.S. 847 (1972) and its progeny—*Marks, Jondora* and *Fame*—is incorporated into the legislative reports. However, it is possible to duplicate the sounds fixed and owned by another as long as the owner of those sounds authorizes the duplication. If the owner of the sounds authorizes the use, section 115 is applicable.

Subsection (a) recognizes the practical need for a limited privilege to make new arrangements of the music being used under a compulsory license. It does not, however, allow the music to be "perverted, distorted, or travestied." [House Report 94-1476.] A new arrangement may be made as long as it doesn't change the basic melody or fundamental character of the work. There can be no copyright in the new arrangement unless the copyright owner of the music specifically authorizes the new arrangement.

Notice of Intention to Obtain a Compulsory License (Section 115(b))

The user must serve a notice of his or her intent on the copyright owner before or within 30 days after the phonorecords have been made; however, the notice must be served *before* any phonorecords are distributed. If the copyright owner is not identified in the registration or other records of the Copyright Office, the notice of intention should be filed with the Copyright Office.

The notice must comply with the form, content and manner of service required by the regulations of the Copyright Office.

Failure to file the required notice of intention rules out the compulsory license; in the absence of a negotiated license, the user is subject to the remedies applicable to other types of infringement.

Royalty Payable under the Compulsory License (Section 115(c))

A "notice of use," Form U, is not required under the new law. Instead, to receive royalties, the copyright owner must be "identified in the registration of other public records of the Copyright Office."

Proper identification is an important condition of recovery—the owner is entitled to royalties for phonorecords made and distributed after being so identified, but is not entitled to recover for any phonorecords previously made and distributed.

Royalty payments are to be made on or before the 20th day of each month. Each payment must be under oath and must comply with the requirements of the Copyright Office regulation on this subject.

The Register of Copyrights, by regulation, is to establish criteria for the detailed annual statements of account which must be certified by a Certified Public Accountant. A regulation will prescribe the form, content, manner of certification with respect to the number of records made, and the number of records distributed.

The royalty rate is 2 3/4 cents or 1/2 cent per minute or fraction of playing time, whichever is larger, for each work embodied in the phonorecord.

Under the old law, the royalty payment was for each phonorecord manufactured; under the new law, it's for each phonorecord "made and distributed." Congress believed it was unfair to require payment of license fees on records which merely go into inventory, which may later be destroyed and from which the record producer gains no economic benefit. A phonorecord is considered "distributed" if the compulsory licensee has voluntarily and permanently parted with possession.

The House Report notes that "made" is meant to be broader than "manufactured"; that it is meant to "include within its scope every possible manufacturing or other process capable of reproducing a sound recording in phonorecords."

The legislative reports make it clear that "even if a presser, manufacturer, or other maker had no role in the distribution process, that person would be jointly and severally liable where the provisions of section 115 were not complied with."

The Register of Copyrights is to issue a regulation prescribing a point in time when, for accounting purposes, under section 115, a phonorecord will be considered "permanently distributed," and situations in which a compulsory licensee is barred from maintaining reserves (e.g., situations in which the compulsory licensee has frequently failed to make payments in the past).

Subsection (4) allows the copyright owner to serve written notice on a defaulting licensee; the compulsory license is terminated if the default is not remedied in 30 days from the date of the notice. Termination makes the making or the distribution, or both, of all phonorecords for which the royalty has not been paid actionable as acts of infringement.

PUBLIC PERFORMANCE BY MEANS OF COIN-OPERATED PHONORECORD PLAYERS
(Section 116)

Section 1(e) of the 1909 law contains the "jukebox exemption." The position of the Copyright Office has been that this exemption is an historical anomaly. The 1961 Report of the Register notes that it was placed in the law in 1909 "at the last minute with virtually no discussion." The Report also observes that in 1909 coin-operated music machines were apparently a novelty of little economic consequence. The Copyright Office recommended that this exemption be repealed, or at least be replaced by a provision requiring jukebox operators to pay reasonable license fees for the public performance of music for profit.

Section 116(a)(2) provides that the operator of a coin-operated phonorecord player may obtain a compulsory license for the public performance of nondramatic musical works on that machine. A "coin-operated phonorecord player" is defined as one which is "activated by the insertion of coins, currency, tokens, or other monetary units or their equivalent." To come within the compulsory license provision the following must be present:

1. The establishment where the machine is located must make "no direct or indirect charge for admission";

2. The phonorecord player must be "accompanied by a list of titles of all musical works available for performance on it," and the list must be affixed to the machine itself or "posted in the establish-

ment in a prominent position where it can readily be examined by the public"; and

3. The machine must provide "a choice to be made by the patrons of the establishment in which it is located."

To obtain the compulsory license, the jukebox operator must file an application with the Copyright Office, send the royalty payment, and then affix the certificate to the jukebox in a way that it is readily visible to the public. The application must be filed within one month after the machine is placed in use and during the month of January in each succeeding year. The royalty payment for a full year is $8.00, or if filed for the first time after July 1 of any year the fee is $4.00.

Within twenty days after the Copyright Office receives an application and fee, the certificate must be issued. The certificate must be affixed to the machine on or before March 1 or within ten days after the date of issue.

Under 116(b)(2) the failure to file, affix the certificate or pay the royalty would make any public performance on that machine an infringement subject to all the remedies provided by Chapter Five of the law.

Section 116(c)(1) requires the Register, after deducting reasonable administrative costs, to deposit in the Treasury the fees collected. These fees are to be invested in interest-bearing securities for later distribution with interest by the Copyright Royalty Tribunal. The Register has to submit to the Tribunal an annual detailed statement accounting for all the fees received during the preceding year.

116(c)(2) provides that during each January every person claiming to be entitled to a portion of the fees collected under §116 shall file a claim with the Tribunal. The claim must include an agreement to accept the determination of the Tribunal as final in any controversy. Judicial review, however, is provided for in section 810.

After the first of October the Tribunal is to determine whether a controversy exists. If there is no controversy, it will distribute the fees after deducting "its reasonable administrative costs." If it decides that there is a controversy, it must conduct a hearing to determine the distribution of royalty fees.

116(4) directs the Tribunal to promulgate regulations whereby the persons who have reason to believe they will be entitled to file a claim for public performances of their works for a given year are permitted to have access to phonorecord players (jukebokes) to determine their share of the fees. A potential claimant could not harass an establishment proprietor, but if the claimant were denied access which is granted by this section, he or she may bring an action in the U.S. District Court for the District of Columbia for cancellation of the compulsory license of the jukebox to which he or she was denied access.

Under 116(d) certain actions which would fraudulently subvert the intent of this section would be subject to a criminal penalty. The falsification of material facts in the application, the alteration of the certificate, or knowingly affixing the certificate to a machine other than the one it covers, would subject the guilty party to a fine of up to $2,500.

[NOTE: it is the operator and not the proprietor of the establishment that section 116 is aimed at. The proprietor is exempt from liability unless he also is an operator of the machine or unless he fails or refuses to reveal the identity of the operator. (§116(a)(1))].

NONCOMMERCIAL, i.e., PUBLIC BROADCASTING
(Section 118)

Section 118 provides a compulsory license for public broadcasting for the use of published nondramatic musical works and published pictorial, sculptural and graphic works provided certain conditions are met.

Works Not Included

Materials which are excluded under this compulsory license are: nondramatic literary works, plays, operas, ballets, motion pictures and other audiovisual works including television programs.

Subsection (e), however, encourages the parties to conclude voluntary agreements for the use of nondramatic literary works, and the Register is to report to Congress on January 3, 1980 on the extent to which voluntary agreements have been reached. The report is also to include any problems that have arisen and to make appropriate legislative recommendations.

Subsection (f) clarifies that section 118 does not apply to unauthorized dramatizations of nondramatic musical works, to program productions based on published compilations of pictorial, graphic or sculptural works, or to the use of audiovisual works, except as such may be considered "fair uses" within the meaning of section 107.

Voluntary Negotiations

Although this section sets up a compulsory license, it strongly encourages voluntary agreements between public broadcasters and copyright owners. Voluntarily negotiated agreements shall prevail in every case provided they are filed in the Copyright Office within 30 days of execution in accordance with regulations prescribed by the Register of Copyrights. [37 C.F.R. Section 201.9; copies available from the Copyright Office request ML-146].

Voluntary agreements become effective upon their being filed in the Copyright Office. This applies not only to the categories of works included under the compulsory license, but also to nondramatic literary works which are not. The Regulation provides that the original instrument of agreement, or a legible photocopy or other full-size facsimile reproduction accompanied by a certification that the reproduction is a true copy be filed. All persons identified as parties in the document must sign it or have an authorized agent sign for them. The document must be complete on its face; it should be clearly identified as being submitted under section 118, and it must be accompanied by the appropriate fee. The date of recordation is the date on which all

162

elements have been received by the Copyright Office and after recordation, the document is returned to the sender with a certificate of record.

Components of Compulsory License

A compulsory license may be obtained for one or more of the following activities [subsection (d)]:

1. performances or displays of published music or graphics by a public broadcasting entity in the course of a noncommercial educational broadcast transmission;

2. production, reproduction and distribution of copies or phonorecords of such programs by a public broadcasting entity; and

3. simultaneous off-air videotaping and performance or display of such transmission by nonprofit institutions or governmental bodies for face-to-face teaching purposes within the condition of 110(1) for a period of seven days from the transmission.

There is a provision, however, that broadcasters are not liable for copies of programs they supplied which are not destroyed within this period if they inform the receiving institution of this destruction obligation.

The terms and rates of the compulsory license are to be established by the Copyright Royalty Tribunal between 120 days and six months after it publishes a notice of the initiation of proceedings. The notice is supposed to be published "not later than thirty days after the Copyright Royalty Tribunal has been constituted."

No initial rates have been established by the new law for public broadcasting licenses; nor does the Tribunal collect and distribute monies. Rather the Tribunal is to devise a schedule of rates and terms within 120 days or six months from the date of the publication of the initial notice. In addition, section 118 does not indicate when compulsory licensing rates must be paid.

A provision in subsection (b)(3) directs the Tribunal to establish requirements by which copyright owners may receive reasonable notice of the use of their works under section 118 — the records of such use are to be kept by public broadcasting entities.

Definitions

As used in section 118, "public broadcasting entity" means a noncommercial educational broadcast station as defined by the FCC. In addition, any "nonprofit institution or organization" is eligible if it is engaged in the activities described in section 118(d)(2).

COPYRIGHT ROYALTY TRIBUNAL
[Chapter 8 — Sections 801-810]

The Copyright Royalty Tribunal, an independent body in the legislative branch of the government, shall consist of five commissioners to be appointed by the President with the advise and consent of the Senate. The term of service is seven years; however, for start-up purposes three commissioners will have seven-year terms while the other two will be named to serve for five years.

The Copyright Royalty Tribunal was established for the purpose of distributing the royalties to those entitled to receive payment under sections 111 (secondary transmissions by cable systems) and 116 (performance by means of a jukebox). If disputes arise over the distribution of these royalties, the Tribunal is to resolve these disputes. In addition, the Royalty Tribunal is to make determinations as to reasonable terms and rates of royalty payments as provided in section 118 (public broadcasting), and to periodically review and adjust statutory royalty rates for the use of copyrighted materials pursuant to the four compulsory licenses.

Distribution of Royalties (Section 809)

The Tribunal is charged with distributing the royalties for cable and jukeboxes. If a controversy is determined to exist, the Tribunal must publish a notice of commencement of proceedings. The Tribunal is required to render a final decision in any such proceeding within one year from the date of publication of the notice.

The full scope of judicial review allowed by the Administrative Procedure Act is allowed. Section 810 specially provides that any final decision of the Tribunal under 801(b) is appealable to the U.S. Court of Appeals within 30 days after publication in the Federal Register.

Periodic Review (Section 804)

The new law provides for a periodic review of the established royalty rates as follows:

> Cable — section 111: 1980 and each subsequent fifth year.

> Mechanical license for music on phonorecords — section 115: 1980, 1987 and in each subsequent 10th year.

> Jukeboxes — section 116: 1980 and in each subsequent 10th year.

> Public broadcasting — section 118: rates established will be reviewed in 1982 and in each subsequent 5th year.

NOTICE OF COPYRIGHT

[Sections 401 – 406]

As the Supplementary Report of the Register points out, one of the principal criticisms of the 1909 Act concerns the provisions requiring a notice of copyright as a condition of protection. Unintentional omission of the notice and comparatively trivial errors in its form and position have caused forfeiture in a number of cases.

Both the 1961 *Report of the Register* and the 1965 *Supplementary Report* recommended, however, that the notice did serve several useful and definite purposes. They recognized four principal values of a copyright notice: (1) placing published material which no one is interested in protecting in the public domain; (2) showing whether a work is under copyright; (3) identifying the copyright owner; and (4) showing the year of publication. Therefore, these reports recommended that the new law continue to require a notice on published copies but suggested that there be provisions ameliorating the effect for inadvertent omissions and errors.

In general, sections 401 through 406 represent an effort to preserve the values of the notice by inducing its use while substantially ameliorating the effects of accidental or even deliberate errors or omissions. Subject to certain safeguards for innocent infringers, protection would not be lost by the complete omission of the notice from large numbers of copies or from a whole edition, if registration for the work is made before or within 5 years after publication. Error in the name or date in the notice would not be fatal and could be corrected.

Sections 401 and 402 set out the basic notice requirements—401 deals with "copies from which the work can be visually perceived," and 402 deals with "phonorecords" of sound recordings. As the legislative reports note, the notice requirements established by these parallel provisions apply only when copies or phonorecords of a work are "publicly distributed." They [the reports] state that no copyright notice would be required in connection with the public display of a copy by any means, including projectors, television or cathode ray tubes connected with information storage and retrieval systems, or in connection with the public performance of a work by means of copies or phonorecords, whether in the presence of an audience or through television, radio, computer transmission, or any other process.

Both sections 401 and 402 require that a notice be used whenever the work "is published in the United States or elsewhere by authority of the copyright owner." The phrase "or elsewhere," makes it clear that the notice requirements apply to copies or phonorecords distributed to the public anywhere in the world, regardless of where and when the work was first published.

NOTICE ON VISUALLY PERCEPTIBLE COPIES
(Section 401)

Subsections (b) and (c) set out the requirements concerning form and position.

Subsection (b) states the required elements. They are:

1. the symbol © (the letter C in a circle), or the word "Copyright,"
or the abbreviation "Copr."

2. the year of first publication fo the work

3. the name of the owner of copyright in the work, or an abbreviation by which the name can be recognized, or a generally known alternative designation of the owner.

There are two special provisions concerning compilations or derivative works and certain pictorial, graphic or sculptural works:

In *compilations* or *derivative works* incorporating previously published material the year of first publication of the compilation or derivative work is sufficient.

In *pictorial, graphic,* or *sculptural* works, with accompanying text matter, if any, the year date may be omitted where such a work is reproduced in or on greeting cards, postcards, stationery, jewelry, dolls, toys, or any useful articles.

Subsection (c) simply provides that the notice "shall be affixed to the copies in such manner and location as to give reasonable notice of the claim of copyright." This provision follows the flexible approach of the Universal Copyright Convention.

This subsection also provides that the Register of Copyrights is to set forth by regulation a list of examples of "specific methods of affixation and positions of the notice on various types of works that will satisfy this requirement." A notice placed or affixed in accordance with Copyright Office regulations would clearly meet the requirements but, since the Register's examples are not to be considered exhaustive, a notice placed or affixed in some other way might also comply with the law if it were found to give reasonable notice of the copyright claim.

NOTICE ON PHONORECORDS OF SOUND RECORDINGS
(Section 402)

Subsections (b) and (c) set out the requirements concerning form and position.

Subsection (b) requires three elements for the notice. They are:

1. the symbol ℗ (the letter P in a circle)

2. the year of first publication of the sound recording

3. the name of the owner of copyright in the sound recording, or an abbreviation by which the name can be recognized, or a generally known alternative designation of the owner.

With regard to the name requirement, the law also provides for a presumption in favor of the record producer. This subsection states "if the producer of the sound recording is named on the phonorecord labels or containers, and if no name appears in conjunction with the notice, the producer's name shall be considered a part of the notice.

Subsection (c) provides that "The notice shall be placed on the surface of the phonorecord, or on the phonorecord label or container, in such manner and location as to give reasonable notice of the claim of copyright."

The legislative reports note three of the reasons for prescribing use of the symbol "℗" rather than "©":

1. Need to avoid confusion between claims to copyright in the sound recording and in the musical or literary work embodied in it;

2. Need to distinguish between claims in the sound recording and in the printed text and art work appearing on the record label, album cover, liner notes, etc.

3. This symbol has been adopted as the international symbol for the protection of sound recordings by the "Phonograms Convention" (The Convention for the Protection of Producers of Phonograms Against Unauthorized Duplication of Their Phonograms, done at Geneva October 29, 1971) to which the U.S. is a party.

NOTICE FOR PUBLICATIONS INCORPORATING UNITED STATES GOVERNMENT WORKS
(Section 403)

This section requires a special notice for a publication that incorporates United States Government works. It provides that, when the copies or phonorecords consist "preponderantly of one or more works of the United States Government," the notice identify those parts of the work in which copyright is claimed—that is, the "new matter" added to the uncopyrightable United States Government work. A failure to meet this requirement would be treated as an omission of the notice subject to the provisions of section 405.

NOTICE FOR CONTRIBUTIONS TO COLLECTIVE WORKS
(Section 404)

In conjunction with section 201(c), section 404 deals with a serious problem under the 1909 law: the notice requirements applicable to contributions published in periodicals and other collective works. The basic approach of this section is to permit but not require a separate contribution to contain its own notice and to make a single notice, covering the collective work as a whole, sufficient to satisfy the notice requirement for the separate contributions it contains.

As the legislative reports indicate, the rights in an individual contribution to a collective work generally would not be affected by the lack of a separate notice as long as the collective work as a whole bears a notice. One exception is advertisements inserted on behalf of persons other than the owner of copyright in the collective work.

Subsection (b) provides that where a separate contribution does not bear its own notice and is published in a collective work with a general notice containing the name of someone other than the copyright owner of the contribution, it is treated as if it has been published with the wrong name in the notice. This means that this will be governed by section 406(a) and an innocent infringer who in good faith took a license from the person named in the general notice would be shielded from liability to some extent.

OMISSION OF COPYRIGHT NOTICE
(Section 405)

Subsection (a) makes it clear that the notice requirements of sections 401, 402 and 403 are not absolute and that, unlike the 1909 law, the outright omission of a copyright notice does not automatically forfeit protection and place the work into the public domain. Under this section a work published without a notice will still be eligible for statutory protection for at least five years, whether the omission was partial or total, unintentional or deliberate.

Subsection 405(a) provides that the omission of notice does not invalidate the copyright if either of two conditions is met:

(1) if "no more than a relatively small number" of copies or phonorecords have been publicly distributed without notice; or

(2) if registration for the work has previously been made, or is made within five years after publication without notice, and a reasonable effort is made to add notice to copies or phonorecords publicly distributed in the U.S. after the omission is discovered.

Thus, if the notice is omitted from more than a "relatively small number" of copies or phonorecords, copyright is not lost immediately, but the work will go into the public domain if no effort is made to correct the error and if the work is not registered within five years after copies or phonorecords were published without a notice.

Both the House and Senate Reports state that the phrase "relatively small number" is intended to be less restrictive than the phrase "a particular copy or copies" in section 21 of the old law.

[Note: the basic notice requirements are limited to cases where a work is published "by authority of the copyright owner" and 405(a), therefore, refers only to omission "from copies or phonorecords publicly distributed by authority of the copyright owner." Example: if the copyright owner authorized publication only on the express condition that all copies or phonorecords bear a prescribed notice, the notice provisions would not apply since the publication itself would not be authorized.]

Subsection (b) provides that an innocent infringer who acts "in reliance upon an authorized copy or phonorecord from which the copyright notice has been omitted" and who proves that he or she was misled by the omission is protected from liability for actual or statutory damages with respect to "any infringing acts committed before receiving actual notice" of registration. This is seen as a major inducement to use of the notice.

Subsection (c) deals with the removal, destruction or obliteration of the notice without the authorization of the copyright owner. It provides that this does not affect the copyright protection in the work.

ERROR WITH RESPECT TO NAME OR DATE IN NOTICE
(Section 406)

It was common under the 1909 law for a copyright notice to be fatally defective because the name or date had been omitted or wrongly stated. As the legislative reports indicate, this section is intended to avoid technical forfeitures in these cases, while at the same time inducing use of the correct name and date in protecting users who rely on erroneous information.

Wrong name: Under 406(a) the use of the wrong name in the notice would not affect the validity or ownership of the copyright. However, unless the error has been corrected in the records of the Copyright Office, an innocent infringer misled by the notice would have a complete defense if he infringed under the apparent authority of the person named in the notice.

Wrong date: 406(b)

a. *Antedated:* where the year is earlier than the year of first publication, any statutory term measured from the year of first publication will be computed from the year given in the notice. This is the established judicial principle which is codified in this subsection.

This would be applicable to anonymous works, pseudonymous works and works made for hire—see 302(c). The legislative reports indicate that this will also be applicable to the presumptive periods set forth in section 302(e).

b. *Postdated:* where the year in the notice is more than one year later than the year of first publication, the case is treated as if the notice had been omitted and is therefore governed by section 405.

The reports state that notices postdated by one year are quite common in works published near the end of the year, and it would be unnecessarily strict to equate cases of this sort with works published without a notice.

[Note: under the 1909 law claims are registered in cases where the year in the notice is postdated by one year. See 37 CFR 202.2. Where the year in the notice is postdated by more than one year the Copyright Office rejects the claim.]

Omission of name and date: Subsection (c) provides that, if copies or phonorecords "contain no name or no date that could reasonably be considered a part of the notice," the result is the same as though the notice had been omitted entirely and section 405 controls.

As the legislative reports point out, there is no requirement that the elements of the copyright notice "accompany" each other. The reports state that under this provision a name or date that could reasonably be read with the other elements may satisfy the notice requirements even if somewhat separated from them. "Direct contiguity or juxtaposition of the elements is no longer necessary; but if the elements are too widely separated for their relation to be apparent, or if uncertainty is created by the presence of other names or dates, the case would have to be treated as if the name or date, and hence the notice itself had been omitted altogether."

DEPOSIT AND REGISTRATION

[Sections 407–412]

Sections 407–412 mark another departure from the old law and bring the U.S. closer to international practice. Under the 1909 Act, deposit of copies for the collections of the Library and for purposes of copyright registration have been treated as the same thing. The new law's approach is to regard deposit and registration as separate though related requirements. Deposit of copies and phonorecords for the Library is generally required for material published in the United States. Copyright registration, as such, is not required but the new law has substantial inducements for registration. Deposit for the Library can be combined with registration.

DEPOSIT FOR THE LIBRARY OF CONTRESS
(Section 407)

The basic requirement of this provision is that within three months after a work has been published with notice in the United States, the owner of copyright must deposit two copies or phonorecords of the work in the Copyright Office. Exceptions to this requirement will be embodied in regulations promulgated by the Register which will be aimed at meeting the needs of the Library and adjusting the deposit obligations to meet special situations.

If the "owner of copyright or of the exclusive right of publication" does not deposit the copies or phonorecords and the work is not one of the categories that is exempted, the Register may demand deposit. Failure to comply would not invalidate the copyright; however, it would subject the owner to fines.

The legislative reports make it clear that section 407 applies to a foreign work as soon as such a work is first published in this country.

With respect to works, other than sound recordings, the basic obligation is to deposit "two complete copies of the best edition," as defined in section 101. Section 101 makes it clear that the Library is entitled to receive copies or phonorecords from the edition it believes best suits its needs regardless of quantity or quality of other U.S. editions that may also have been published before the time of deposit.

For sound recordings, two complete phonorecords of the best edition and any other visually perceptible material published with the phonorecords must be deposited. Thus, for example, text or pictorial matter appearing on record sleeves and album covers would have to be deposited too. As the legislative reports state, the required deposit in the case of a sound recording would extend to the "entire package" and not just to the disk, tape or other phonorecord.

407(c) is aimed at the special needs of artists whose works are published in expensive limited editions. Under the present law, optional deposit of photographs is permitted for various classes of works but not for fine prints. This subsection requires the Register to issue regulations under which such works would either be exempted entirely from mandatory deposit or would be subject to an appropriate alternative form of deposit.

Subsection (e) ties in with the American Television and Radio Archives after written demand has been made, the required copies (or copy) are not deposited within three months after the demand is received, the person or persons on whom the demand was made are liable:

1. to pay a fine of not more than $250 for each work; and

2. to pay to the Library's specially designated fund, the total retail price of the copies or phonorecords demanded, or, if no retail price has been fixed, the reasonable cost of the Library of Congress of acquiring them; and

3. if such person willfully or repeatedly refuses to comply with such a demand, to pay an additional fine of $2,500.

Subsection (3) ties in with the American Television and Radio Archives Act, 2 USC 170, which appears as section 113 of the Transitional and Supplementary Provisions. This subsection was added to provide a basis for the Librarian of Congress to acquire, as part of the copyright deposit system, copies or recordings of non-syndicated radio and television programs without imposing any hardships on broadcasters. Under this subsection the Library is authorized to tape programs off the air in all cases and may "demand" that the Library be supplied with a copy or phonorecord of a particular program. As the House Report notes, this "demand" authority is extremely limited for: 1. the broadcaster is not required to retain any recording of a program after it has been transmitted unless a demand has already been received. 2. the demand would cover only a particular program—"blanket" demands would not be permitted; 3. the broadcaster would have the option of supplying by gift, by loan for purposes of reproduction, or by sale at cost; and 4. the penalty for willful failure or refusal to comply is limited to the cost of reproducing and supplying the copy or phonorecord in question.

[*Note:* section 705 requires that records be kept of all deposits. For $2 the Office will provide a receipt of deposit—section 708(3).]

COPYRIGHT REGISTRATION IN GENERAL
(Section 408)

Permissive registration. Under 408(a) registration of a claim to copyright, whether published or unpublished, can be made voluntarily by "the owner of copyright or of any exclusive right in the work" at any time during the copyright term. The claim may be registered by depositing copies, phonorecords, or other materials specified by subsections (b) and (c), together with an application and fee.

Except where registration is made to preserve a copyright that would otherwise be invalidated because of omission of the notice, (section 405(a)), registration is not a condition of copyright protection.

Deposit for purpose of registration. In general, and subject to various exceptions, the material to be deposited should be one complete copy or phonorecord of an unpublished work, and two complete copies of the best edition in the case of a published work.

For works first published outside the United States, one complete copy or phonorecord "as so published" would be required.

[Note: the provision in the 1909 law, section 215, which allows waiver of the registration fee for foreign works if, within six months of first publication, two copies are deposited instead of the usual one, has been dropped. This provision was enacted in 1949 to meet the serious postwar problems of transferring funds from foreign countries to the United States. This waiver-of-fee option was found to be administratively burdensome and the 1965 Supplementary Report of the Register states that it "appears to have outlived its usefulness."]

For a contribution to a collective work, one complete copy or phonorecord of the best edition of the collective work will be required.

Subsection (b) also provides that copies or phonorecords deposited for the Library under 407 may be used to satisfy the deposit provisions of 408 "if they are accompanied by the prescribed application and fee, and by any additional identifying material that the Register may, by regulation, require."

Beginning on January 1, 1978, the effective date of the new law, . . .deposit copies or phonorecords must be accompanied by an application and fee if they are to be used for copyright registration. If copies or phonorecords are sent separately they will not be held to await connection with an application and fee. After this date, if copies or phonorecords are sent without simultaneously submitting an application and registration fee, the deposit will be used for the Library of Congress but not for registration.

The Register is authorized to issue regulations under which deposit of additional material, needed for identification of the work in which copyright is claimed, could be required in certain cases.

Classification and deposit regulations. Subsection (c) allows the Register, by regulation, to specify "the administrative classes into which works are to be placed for purposes of deposit and registration." The legislative reports state that it is important that the statutory provisions setting forth the subject matter of copyright be kept entirely separate from the administrative classification. Moreover, the law makes it clear that the administrative classification "has no significance with respect to the subject matter of copyright or the exclusive rights provided by this title."

The Register is also given latitude in adjusting the type of materials deposited to the needs of the registration system. The Register is authorized to issue regulations specifying "the nature of the copies or phonorecords to be deposited in the various classes" and for particular classes, to require or permit deposit of one copy or phonorecord rather than two.

The legislative reports note that under this provision the Register could, where appropriate, permit deposit of phonorecords rather than notated copies of musical compositions, allow or require deposit of print-outs of computer programs under certain circumstances, or permit deposit of one volume of an encyclopedia for purposes of registration of a single contribution.

The Register is also allowed to require or permit the substitute deposit of material that would better serve the purposes of identification where copies or phonorecords are bulky, unwieldy, easily broken, or otherwise impractical to file and retain as records identifying the work registered. Examples: billboard posters, toys and dolls, ceramics and glassware, costume jewelry and a wide range of three dimensional objects.

The Register's authority also extends to rare or extremely valuable copies which would be burdensome or impossible to deposit. The legislative reports note that deposit of one copy rather than two would probably be justifiable in the case of most motion pictures.

The Register also has the authority to allow a single registration for a "group of related works." The legislative reports include the following examples: the various editions or issues of a daily newspaper, a work published in serial installments, a group of related jewelry designs, a group of photographs by one photographer, a series of greeting cards related to each other in some way, or a group of poems by a single author.

Under 408(c)(2) the Register is directed to establish regulations permitting, under certain conditions, a single registration for a group of works by the same individual author, all first published as contributions to periodicals, including newspapers, within a 12 month period, on the basis of a single deposit, application and fee. Each of the works as first published must have contained a separate copyright notice, and the name of the owner must have been the same in each notice. Deposit of one copy of the entire issue of the periodical, or of the entire section in the case of a newspaper, in which each contribution is first published is required. The application must identify each work separately, including the periodical containing it and its date of first publication.

408(c)(3) provides, under certain conditions, an alternative to the separate renewal registrations under section 304(a). If the specified conditions are met, a single renewal registration may be made for a group of works by the same individual author, all first published as contributions to periodicals, including newspapers. The requirements are:

1. the renewal claimant or claimants and the basis for the claim or claims under 304(a) is the same for each of the works; and

2. the works were all copyrighted upon their first publication, either through separate copyright notice and registration or by virtue of a general notice in the periodical issue as a whole; and

3. the renewal application and fee are received not more than 28 or less than 27 years after the 31st day of December of the calendar year in which all of the works were first published; and

4. the renewal application identifies each work separately, including the periodical containing it and its date of first publication.

Corrections and amplifications: There is no provision in the present law for correcting or amplifying the information given in a completed registration. There is such a procedure provided by regulation—see 201.5 of the present Copyright Office Regulations.

Subsection (d) authorizes the Register to establish "formal procedures for filing of an application for supplementary registration," in order to correct an error or amplify the information in a copyright registration. The "error" to be corrected is an error made by the applicant that the Copyright Office could not have been expected to note during its examination.

A supplementary registration under subsection (d) is subject to payment of a separate fee and would be maintained as an independent record separate and apart from the record of the earlier registration. It would, however, be required to identify clearly "the registration to be corrected or amplified" so that the two registrations could be tied together by appropriate means in the Copyright Office records.

The original record would not be expunged or cancelled, rather it would be maintained to insure a complete public record.

APPLICATION FOR COPYRIGHT REGISTRATION
(Section 409)

This section provides that the form prescribed by the Register shall include:

(1) the name and address of the copyright claimant;

(2) in the case of a work other than an anonymous or pseudonymous work, the name and nationality or domicile of the author or authors, and, if one or more of the authors is dead, the dates of their deaths;

(3) if the work is anonymous or pseudonymous, the nationality or domicile of the author or authors;

(4) in the case of a work made for hire, a statement to this effect;

(5) if the copyright claimant is not the author, a brief statement of how the claimant obtained ownership of the copyright;

(6) the title of the work, together with any previous or alternative titles under which the work can be identified;

(7) the year in which creation of the work was completed;

(8) if the work has been published, the date and nation of its first publication;

(9) in the case of a compilation or derivative work, an identification of any preexisting work or works that it is based on or incorporates, and a brief, general statement of the additional material covered by the copyright claim being registered;

(10) in the case of a published work containing material of which copies are required by section 601 to be manufactured in the United States, the names of the persons or organizations who performed the processes specified by subsection (c) of section 601 with respect to that material, and the places where those processes were performed; and

(11) any other information regarded by the Register of Copyrights as bearing upon the preparation or identification of the work or the existence, ownership, or duration of the copyright.

The legislative reports indicate that the catchall phrase at the end of section 409 was included to enable the Register to obtain more specialized information, such as that bearing on whether the work contains material that is a "work of the United States Government." The reports also note that in the case of works subject to the manufacturing requirement, the application must also include information about the manufacture of copies.

REGISTRATION OF CLAIM AND ISSUANCE OF CERTIFICATE
(Section 410)

The Register is required to register the claim and issue a certificate if he or she determines that "the material deposited constitutes copyrightable subject matter and that the other legal and formal requirements ... have been met."

The Register is required to refuse registration and notify the applicant if he determines that "the material deposited for registration does not constitute copyrightable subject matter or that the claim is invalid for any other reason."

Subsection (c) deals with the probative effect of a certificate of registration. A certificate is required to be given prima facie weight in any judicial proceedings if the registration it covers was made "before or within five years after first publication of the work"; thereafter the court is given discretion to decide what evidentiary weight the certificate should be accorded.

The legislative reports note that the five-year period is based on a recognition that the longer the lapse of time between publication and registration the less likely the facts are to be reliable.

Under 410(c) a certificate is to "constitute prima facie evidence of the validity of the copyright and of the facts stated in the certificate." The principle that a certificate represents prima facie evidence of copyright validity has been established in a long line of court decisions. What this means is that the plaintiff should not ordinarily be forced in the first instance to provide all of the multitude of facts that underline the validity of copyright unless the defendant, by effectively challenging them, shifts the burden of proof to the plaintiff.

Section 401(d) makes the effective date of registration the day when the application, deposit, and fee ("which are later determined by the Register of Copyrights or by a court of competent jurisdiction to be acceptable for registration") have all been received. Where the three necessary items are received at different times, the date of receipt of the last of them is controlling regardless of when the Copyright Office acts on the claim.

REGISTRATION AS PREREQUISITE TO INFRINGEMENT SUIT
(Section 411)

This section restates the present statutory requirement that registration must be made before a suit for copyright infringement is instituted. A copyright owner who has not registered his claim can have a valid cause of action against someone who has infringed his copyright, but he cannot enforce his right in the courts until he has registered his claim.

The new law also provides that a rejected claimant who has properly applied for registration may bring an infringement suit if he serves notice on the Register, thus allowing the Register to intervene in on the issue of registrability. The Register has 60 days to enter. If the Register fails to join the action this will "not deprive the court of jurisdiction to determine that issue."

Subsection (b) is intended to deal with the special situation presented by works that are being transmitted "live" at the same time they are being fixed in tangible form for the first time. Under certain circumstances, where the would be infringer has been given advance notice that copyright is being claimed in the work, an injunction could be obtained to prevent the unauthorized use of the material included in the "live" transmission.

REGISTRATION AS PREREQUISITE TO CERTAIN REMEDIES
(Section 412)

This section offers an incentive to register; it allows the owner of a registered work a broader range of remedies. Remedies available are tied to the date of registration. If an infringement occurred before registration, the copyright owner would be entitled to the ordinary remedies of injunction and actual damages. If, however, infringement occurred after registration, the owner would be entitled to the extraordinary remedies of attorney's fees and statutory damages.

This provision, which would apply to both domestic and foreign works, is subject to a grace period. If the work is registered within three months of first publication, there is no loss of rights. Full remedies could be recovered for any infringement begun during the three months after publication if registration is made before that period has ended. The legislative reports indicate that this exception (the three-month grace period) was needed to take care of newsworthy or suddenly popular works which may be infringed almost as soon as they are published, before the owner has had a reasonable opportunity to register his claim.

MANUFACTURING REQUIREMENTS AND IMPORTATION OF COPIES OR PHONORECORDS

[Sections 601–603]

MANUFACTURING REQUIREMENTS
(Section 601)

Prior to the Copyright Act of 1891 no protection was afforded to foreign authors. Thus, the works of English authors were widely pirated in the United States. When a movement was started for protection for foreign authors one of the conditions mentioned was that their works must be printed in the United States to be protected here.

The Act of March 3, 1891 is commonly known as the "International Copyright Act." It contained a complicated compromise which the Second Supplementary Report of the Register characterizes as having "the effect of giving U.S. copyright protection to foreign authors with one hand and taking it away from many of them with the other." The Register was referring to the manufacturing clause, which was the price of support for the printers, book manufacturers and the labor unions in the printing trades.

The manufacturing clause in the 1909 law had its most direct impact upon English language books and periodicals by U.S. authors or by foreign authors who are not covered by the U.C.C.

Books and periodicals of "foreign origin" in a language other than English are exempted from the manufacturing requirements. The term "of foreign origin," is limited however, and if the first edition of a foreign language work is by a U.S. author and is printed abroad, it is denied U.S. copyright protection. Such a work cannot even be eligible for "ad interim copyright" – this is available only to a book or periodical in the English language.

The 1961 Report of the Register favored elimination of the manufacturing clause as a condition of copyright protection. However, as the 1965 Supplementary Report notes, the book manufacturing industry took a very strong position against complete elimination of the manufacturing requirements. The Supplementary Report notes that it was apparent for the sake of the revision program that a compromise on this issue would be necessary.

Under the new act, this section is scheduled to be phased out completely on July 1, 1982. Until that time, the manufacturing clause will continue, under a considerably limited scope. The Register is to report on the effect of this phase-out by July, 1981 so that Congress may reexamine the issue. It would apply only to "a work consisting preponderantly of nondramatic literary material that is in the English language and is protected under this title." It does not cover: (a) dramatic, musical, pictorial or graphic works; (b) foreign language, bilingual, or multilingual works; (c) material in the public domain; or (d) works consisting preponderantly of material that is not subject to the manufacturing requirement.

The legislative reports give the following examples:

1. Where the literary material in a work consists merely of a foreword or preface, and captions, headings, or brief descriptions or explanations of pictorial, graphic or other nonliterary material, the manufacturing requirement does not apply to the work in whole or in part. In such a case, the non-literary material clearly exceeds the literary material in importance, and the entire work is free of the manufacturing requirement.

2. Where a work contains pictorial, graphic or other nonliterary material which merely illustrates a textual narrative or exposition, the nondramatic literary material is subject to the manufacturing requirement regardless of the relative amount of space occupied by each kind of material. In such a case the narrative or exposition plainly exceeds in importance the nonliterary material. However, only the portions of the work consisting of copyrighted nondramatic literary material in English are required to be manufactured in the United States or Canada. The illustrations may be manufactured elsewhere without affecting their copyright status.

The manufacturing requirement does not apply where "the author of any substantial part" [of the work] is neither a citizen nor domiciliary of the United States. In other words, the manufacturing requirement would not apply to a work of which any substantial part was written by a foreign author. It would apply only to works of U.S. authors and only then when no co-author was foreign. Moreover, works by American nationals domiciled abroad for at least a year preceding the date when importation is sought would be exempted.

Works made for hire. Section 601(b)(1) makes it clear that the exemption does not apply unless a substantial part of the work was prepared for an employer or other person who is not a national or domiciliary of the United States, or a domestic corporation or enterprise. The reference to "a domestic corporation or enterprise," the reports say, is intended to include a subsidiary formed by the domestic corporation or enterprise primarily for the purpose of obtaining the exemption.

Section 601 adopts a proposal put forward by various segments of the U.S. and Canadian printing industries recommending an exemption for copies manufactured in Canada. The legislative reports note that the wage standards in Canada are substantially comparable to those in the U.S. and, therefore, equal treatment arguments were persuasive. Also persuasive, however, was the "Toronto Agreement." Indeed this is noted in the Conference Report.

> Canada is specifically exempted from the provisions of Section 601 . . . This exemption is included as a result of an agreement reached in Toronto in 1968 . . . Upon addition of the Canadian exemption in American legislation, that agreement contemplates Canadian adoption of the Florence Agreement and prompt joint action to remove high Canadian tariffs on printed matter and the removal of other Canadian restraints on printing and publishing trade between the two countries, as well as reciprocal prompt action by U.S. groups to remove any remaining U.S. barriers to Canadian printed matter. The Canadian exemption is included in Section 601 with the expectation that these changes will be made.

The Conference Report goes on to note that if for any reason Canadian trade groups and the Canadian Government do not move promptly in reciprocation with the U.S. trade groups and the U.S. government to remove such tariff and other trade barriers, Congress would be expected to remove the Canadian exemption.

Limitations on Importation and Distribution of Copies Manufactured Abroad (Subsection (b))

The basic objective of section 601 is to induce manufacture of an edition in the U.S. if more than 2,000 copies are to be imported or distributed in this country. Subsection (a) therefore provides in general that "the importation into or public distribution in the United States" of copies not complying with the manufacturing requirement is prohibited. Subsection (b) then sets out the exceptions and clause (2) fixes the limit of importation at 2,000 copies. The exemption is intended to allow an author or publisher to test the potential market for the work in America before an entire American edition is printed.

Additional exceptions to the copies affected by the manufacturing requirement are set out in clauses (3) through (7) of subsection (b). Clause (3) permits importation of copies for governmental use, other than in schools, by the U.S. or by any state or political subdivision of a state. Clause (4) allows importation for personal use of "no more than one copy of any work at any one time." It also exempts copies in the baggage of persons arriving from abroad and copies intended for the library collection of nonprofit scholarly, educational, or religious organizations. Braille copies are exempted under clause (5), and clause (6) permits the public distribution in the U.S. of copies allowed entry by the other clauses of that subsection. Clause (7) covers cases in which an individual American author has, through choice or necessity arranged for publication of his work by a foreign rather than a domestic publisher.

Defining the Manufacturing Requirement (Subsection (c))

As the legislative reports note, restrictions to be imposed on foreign typesetting or composition posed a difficult problem. A number of publishers, under what they regard as a loophole in the present law, have been having their manuscripts typeset abroad, importing "reproduction proofs," then printing their books from offset plates "by lithographic process . . . wholly performed in the U.S." The language in the 1909 law is ambiguous; the practice had been considered to have support from the Copyright Office since it registered such claims under its rule of doubt.

The book publishers strenuously opposed any definition that would have closed this so-called loophole or would interfere with their use of new techniques, including use of imported computer tapes for composition here. Subsection (c) is a compromise between the book publishers and authors and the typographical firms and printing trade unions.

Under subsection (c) the manufacturing requirement is confined to the following processes;

1. Typesetting and platemaking "where the copies are printed directly from type that has been set, or directly from plates made from such type."

2. The making of plates "where the making of plates by a lithographic or photoengraving process is a final or intermediate step preceding the printing of copies."

3. In all other cases, the "printing or other final process of producing multiple copies and any binding of the copies."

Thus, there is nothing to prevent the importation of reproduction proofs, however prepared, as long as the plates from which the copies are printed are made in the U.S. and are not themselves imported. Also, computer tapes from which plates can be prepared here could be imported. However, regardless of the process involved, the actual duplication of multiple copies, together with any binding, are required to be done in the United States or Canada.

Effect of Noncompliance (Subsection (d))

Subsection (d) makes it clear that compliance with the manufacturing requirement no longer constitutes a condition of copyright protection; moreover, the consequences of noncompliance would affect only reproduction and distribution rights. The present "*ad interim*" copyright limitations and registration requirements are eliminated.

If copies are imported or distributed in violation of section 601, the copyright owner is not precluded from making and distributing phonorecords of the work, or from making derivative works (including dramatizations and motion pictures), or from performing or displaying the work publicly. Even the rights to reproduce copies are not lost in cases of violation, although their enforcement is limited against certain infringers.

An infringer of the exclusive rights of making and distributing copies would be given a complete defense if: (1) the copyright owner authorized or acquiesced in an importation or public distribution of copies in violation of the manufacturing requirement, and (2) the infringing copies were manufactured in the United States. The burden of proof is on the infringer.

Subsection (d) also provides, in effect, that a copyright owner can reclaim his full exclusive rights by manufacturing an edition in the U.S. and registering his claim in the Copyright Office.

INFRINGING INFORMATION
(Section 602)

This section has nothing to do with the manufacturing requirement in section 601, rather it deals with two situations—importation of "piratical" articles (copies or phonorecords made without any authorization of the copyright owner), and unauthorized importation of copies or phonorecords that were lawfully made. The general approach of this section is to make unauthorized importation an act of infringement in both cases, but to permit the Customs Service to prohibit importation of only "piratical" articles.

Subsection (a) states that unauthorized importation is an infringement but then spells out three exceptions: 1. importation under the authority or for the use of the U.S. government or of any State or political subdivision of a State, but not including copies or phonorecords for use in schools or copies of any audiovisual work imported for purposes other than archival use; 2. importation, for the private use of the importer and not for distribution, by any person with respect to no more than one copy or phonorecord of any one work at any one time, or by any person arriving from outside the U.S. with respect to copies or phonorecords forming part of such person's personal baggage; or 3. importation by or for an organization operated for scholarly, educational, or religious purposes and not for private gain, with respect to no more than one copy of an audiovisual work solely for its archival purposes, and no more than five copies or phonorecords of any other work for its library lending or archival purposes, unless the importation of such copies or phonorecords is part of an activity consisting of systematic reproduction or distribution, engaged in by such organization in violation of the provisions of section 108(g)(2).

ENFORCEMENT OF IMPORTATION PROHIBITIONS
(Section 603)

The importation prohibitions of both sections 601 and 602 would be enforced under section 603. Subsection (a) authorizes the Secretary of the Treasury and the U.S. Postal Service to make regulations for this purpose, and subsection (c) provides for the disposition of excluded articles.

Subsection (b) deals only with the prohibition against importation of "piratical" copies or phonorecords, and is aim· 1 at solving problems that have arisen under the 1909 statute. Since the Customs Service is usually not in a position to make determinations as to whether particular articles are "piratical," this subsection allows the Customs regulations to require the person seeking exclusion either to obtain a court order enjoining importation, or to furnish proof of his claim and to post bond.

COPYRIGHT INFRINGEMENT AND REMEDIES

[Sections 501-510]

INFRINGEMENT OF COPYRIGHT
(Section 501)

This section contains a statement of what constitutes an infringement. Subsection (a) identifies an infringer as someone who "violates any of the exclusive rights of the copyright owner as provided by sections 106 through 118" or "who imports copies or phonorecords in violation of section 602."

Because section 201(d) establishes the principle of divisibility of copyrights, there was a need to provide protection for the rights of all copyright owners and to avoid a multiplicity of suits. Subsection (b), the reports note, enables the owner of a particular right to bring an infringement action in that owner's name alone, while at the same time insuring (to the extent possible) that the other owners whose rights may be affected are notified and given a chance to join the action.

501(b) empowers the "legal or beneficial owner" of an exclusive right to institute a suit for "any infringement of that particular right committed while he is the owner of it." A "beneficial owner" is defined in the legislative reports as one who has parted with his legal title in exchange for percentage royalties based on sales or license fees.

INJUNCTIONS
(Section 502)

Courts are given discretionary power to grant injunctions and restraining orders, whether "preliminary," "temporary," etc. to prevent or stop infringements.

IMPOUNDING AND DISPOSITION OF INFRINGING ARTICLES
(Section 503)

Courts are given the power to impound allegedly infringing articles during the time the action is pending. The court is also empowered to order the destruction or other disposition of articles found to be infringing.

In both cases the articles affected include "all copies or phonorecords" and also "all plates, molds, matrices, masters, tapes, film negatives, or other articles by means of which such copies or phonorecords may be reproduced."

DAMAGES AND PROFITS
(Section 504)

The legislalative reports state that this is the cornerstone of the remedies sections and of the new law as a whole. Two basic aims of the section are: (1) to give the courts specific unambiguous directions concerning monetary awards, and at the same time, (2) to provide the courts with reasonable latitude to adjust recovery to the circumstances of the case.

Subsection (a) establishes the liability of the infringer for either "the copyright owner's actual damages and any additional profits of the infringer," or statutory damages. Recovery of actual damages and profits, under subsection (b), or of statutory damages, under subsection (c), is alternative and for the copyright owner to elect.

This section recognizes that an award of damages serves a different purpose from an award of profits—it provides: "The copyright owner is entitled to recover the actual damages suffered by him or her as a result of the infringement, and any profits of the infringer that are attributable to the infringement and are not taken into account in computing the actual damages." Damages would be paid to compensate the copyright owner for his losses caused by the infringement, while an award of profits is intended to prevent the infringer from unjustly benefiting from his wrongful act. If profits alone are used as a measure of the plaintiff's damages, however, only one or the other could be awarded. Where the copyright owner has suffered damages not reflected in the infringer's profits, or where there have been profits attributable to the copyrighted work but not used as a measure of damages, both may be awarded.

Subsection (c) covers *statutory* damages. It provides that the plaintiff's election to recover statutory damages may take place at any time during the trial before the court has rendered its final judgment.

Basic provisions:

1. Generally, where the plaintiff elects to recover statutory damages, the court is obliged to award between $250 and $10,000. The court may exercise its discretion within that range, but unless one of the exceptions in clause (2) is applicable, it cannot make an award of less than $250 or more than $10,000.

2. An award of minimum statutory damages may be multiplied if separate works and separately liable infringers are involved in the suit; however, a single award in the $250-$10,000 range is to be made "for all infringements involved in the action."

A single infringer of a single work is liable for a single amount no matter how many acts of infringement are involved and regardless of whether the acts were separate, isolated, or occurred in a related series.

3. Where the suit involves infringement of more than one separate and independent work, minimum statutory damages must be awarded for each work. An example is given in the legislative reports—if one defendant has infringed three copyrighted works, the copyright owner is entitled to statutory damages of at least $750 and may be awarded up to $30,000. Subsection (c)(1) makes it clear that "all parts of a compilation or derivative work constitute one work" for the purpose of assessing damages. Moreover, although minimum and maximum amounts are to be multiplied where multiple "works" are involved, the same is not true with respect to multiple copyrights, multiple owners, multiple registrations, or multiple exclusive rights. This is important since under a scheme of divisible copyright, it is possible to have the rights of a number of owners of separate "copyrights" in a single "work" infringed by one act of a defendant.

Clause (2) provides for exceptional cases in which the maximum award could be raised to $50,000 and the minimum could be reduced to $100. Courts are given discretion to increase statutory damages in cases of willful infringement and to lower the minimum where the infringer is innocent. The burden of proof in each instance is on the infringer.

The innocent infringer provision is where the infringer "was not aware and had no reason to believe that his or her acts constituted an infringement of copyright." It was felt that this provision offered adequate insulation to broadcasters and newspaper publishers who are particularly vulnerable to this type of infringement suit.

Also, there is a special clause dealing with the special situation of teachers, librarians, archivists and public broadcasters, and the nonprofit institutions of which they are a part. Where such person or instituion infringes copyrighted material in the honest belief that what they were doing constituted fair use, the court is precluded from awarding any statutory damages. In these cases, the burden of proof with respect to the defendant's good faith is said to rest on the plaintiff.

COSTS AND ATTORNEY'S FEES
(Section 505)

This section leaves the award of costs and attorney's fees (as part of the costs) entirely in the court's discretion. Attorney's fees may be awarded to the prevailing party. An exception to this section is where "the United States or an officer thereof" is a party.

CRIMINAL OFFENSES
(Section 506)

Four specific types of activities constitute a criminal offense:

1. *Criminal infringement*—infringement of "a copyright willfully and for purposes of commercial advantage or private financial gain";

2. *Fraudulent use of copyright notice*—with fraudulent intent, to place on an article a notice that the defendant "knows to be false" or to publicly distribute or import any article bearing such a notice;

3. *Fraudulent removal of copyright notice*—also requires fraudulent intent in removing or altering a notice;

4. *False representation*—knowingly making a false representation in connection with an application for copyright registration.

This section provides for a fine, imprisonment or both.

There is a special provision applying to any person who infringes willfully and for purposes of commercial advantage the copyright in a sound recording or a motion picture. First offense: fine of not more than $25,000 or imprisonment for not more than one year, or both. For each subsequent offense, fine of not more than $50,000 or imprisonment for not more than 2 years, or both.

STATUTE OF LIMITATIONS
(Section 507)

This section, which deals with both criminal proceedings and civil actions, is substantially identical with section 115 of the 1909 law. It establishes a three-year statute of limitations.

NOTIFICATION OF FILING AND DETERMINATION OF ACTIONS
(Section 508)

This section is intended to establish a method for notifying the Copyright Office and the public of the filing and disposition of copyright cases. The clerks of the federal courts are to notify the Copyright Office of the filing of any copyright actions and of their final disposition. Courts are also to send a copy of the written opinion if there is one. The Copyright Office is to make these notifications a part of its public records.

SEIZURE AND FORFEITURE
(Section 509)

This provision allows for the seizure and forfeiture to the United States of all copies or phonorecords and all the implements of reproduction, manufacture, or assemblage, used, or intended for use or possessed with the intent to use in violation of section 506(a) (criminal infringement).

Subsection (b) states that the applicable procedures for seizures and forfeitures under Title 19 (customs) shall apply to forfeitures and seizures under this section insofar as appropriate and consistent with the terms of this section. For the items described in subsection (a), however, the actions necessary are to be performed by such officers, agents or other persons authorized by the Attorney General rather than employees or officers of the Treasury Department.

REMEDIES FOR ALTERATION OF PROGRAMMING
BY CABLE SYSTEMS
(Section 510)

This section allows a remedy for the alteration of or substitution of programming by cable systems in violation of section 111(c)(3). The court may deprive the system of the compulsory license for one or more of its distant signals for a period not exceeding 30 days.

ADMINISTRATIVE PROVISIONS

[Chapter 7, Sections 701-710]

Chapter 7, entitled "Copyright Office," contains the administrative or "housekeeping" provisions of the new law.

ADMINISTRATIVE PROCEDURE ACT
(Section 701)

Section 701(d) makes the Copyright Office fully subject to the Administrative Procedure Act (with one exception: under 706(b), reproduction and distribution of deposit copies would be made under the Freedom of Information Act only to the extent permitted by the Copyright Office regulations.

REGULATIONS
(Section 702)

Section 702 states that the Register of Copyrights is authorized to establish regulations "not inconsistent with law." All regulations are subject to the approval of the Librarian of Congress.

EFFECTIVE DATE OF ACTIONS IN THE COPYRIGHT OFFICE
(Section 703)

This section provides that where an action is to be performed on a specified date and that date falls on a Saturday, Sunday, holiday, or other nonbusiness day within the District of Columbia, the action may be taken on the next succeeding business day. It also provides that the action is effective as of the date when the period expired.

RETENTION AND DISPOSITION OF ARTICLES DEPOSITED IN THE COPYRIGHT OFFICE
(Section 704)

As the Reports of the Register indicate, a practical problem of concern to both the Office and the copyright bar concerns the storage limitations of the Copyright Office. Also mentioned was the need to retain copies and phonorecords for the identification of works in which a claim to copyright has been registered. The legislative reports note that aside from its indisputable utility to future historians and scholars, a substantially complete collection of both published and unpublished deposits (other than those selected by the Library) would avoid the many difficulties encountered when copies needed for identification in connection with litigation or other purposes have been destroyed.

The basic policy behind section 704 is copyright deposits that should be retained as long as possible. The Register and the Librarian of Congress, however, are empowered to dispose of deposits under appropriate safeguards when they jointly decide that it has become necessary to do so.

Section 704(a) makes it clear that any copy or phonorecord, or identifying material deposited for registration, whether registered or not, becomes "the property of the United States Government." The legislative reports state that this means that the copyright owner or person who made the deposit cannot demand its return as a matter of right, even in rejection cases.

Section 704(b) deals in the first instance with published works. It makes all deposits available to the Library of Congress "for its collections, or for exchanges or transfer to any other library."

With respect to unpublished works, the Library is authorized to select any deposit for its own collections or for transfer to the National Archives or to a federal records center.

704(c) authorizes the Register to make "facsimile" copies of all or any part of the material deposited under section 408 and to make such reproductions part of the Copyright Office records of the registration. This is to be done before transferring or otherwise disposing of the copies or phonorecords.

Subsection (d) deals with deposits not selected by the Library. It provides that they are to be retained under the control of the Copyright Office "for the longest period considered practicable and desirable" by the Register and the Librarian. The aim is to preserve copyright deposits of all classes of material for as long a period as is reasonably possible by any practical means of storage. The 1965 Supplementary Report of the Register states the reference to "government storage facilities" contemplates that "dead storage" available in or out of Washington would be considered preferable to outright destruction.

Because of their unique value and irreplaceable nature, intentional destruction of unpublished works is prohibited during their copyright term unless a facsimile reproduction has been made.

Subsection (e) establishes a new procedure whereby a copyright owner can request retention of deposited material for the full term of copyright. The Register is authorized to issue regulations prescribing the fees for this service and the "conditions under which such requests are to be made and granted."

COPYRIGHT OFFICE RECORDS
(Section 705)

Subsection (a) requires the Register to keep records of all deposits, registrations, recordations, and "other actions taken under this title." The Register must also prepare indexes of all such records.

Subsection (b) provides that these records and indexes, as well as the deposits within the control of the Copyright Office, be open to public inspection.

Subsection (c) provides that upon request and payment of the prescribed fee, the office shall search its public records, indexes, and deposits, and furnish a report of the information they disclose.

COPIES OF COPYRIGHT OFFICE RECORDS
(Section 706)

Subsection (a) provides that copies may be made of any public records or indexes. It also provides for additional certificates.

Subsection (b) provides that copies or reproductions of deposited articles which are under the Copyright Office's control shall be furnished only under conditions specified in its regulations.

COPYRIGHT OFFICE FORMS AND PUBLICATIONS
(Section 707)

(a) *Catalog of Copyright Entries.* Sections 210 and 211 of the 1909 law require that an indexed catalog of all copyright registrations be printed at periodic intervals, and that it be distributed to customs and postal officials and offered for sale to the public.

The Reports of the Register noted that this catalog is extremely expensive to prepare and that some parts of it are used much less than others. The 1961 Report suggested that the purposes of the catalog might be served better and at less cost if the Register were given discretion to decide when and in what form the various parts should be issued.

Thus, the new law retains the 1909 law's basic requirement that the Register compile and publish catalogs of all copyright registrations at periodic intervals, but provides for "discretion to determine on the basis of practicability and usefulness the form and frequency of publication of each particular part."

As the legislative reports note, this will in no way diminish the utility or value of the present catalogs, and the flexibility allowed, coupled with the use of new mechanical and electronic devices now becoming available, will avoid waste.

(b) *Other publications.* Register is to furnish application forms and general informational material. The Register is also authorized to publish other material that may be of value to the public.

COPYRIGHT OFFICE FEES
(Section 708)

(1) for the registration of a copyright claim or a supplementary registration under section 408, including the issuance of a certificate of registration, $10;

(2) for the registration of a claim to renewal of a subsisting copyright in its first term under section 304(a), including the issuance of a certificate of registration, $6;

(3) for the issuance of a receipt for a deposit under section 407, $2;

(4) for the recordation, as provided by section 205, of a transfer of copyright ownership or other document of six pages or less, covering no more than one title, $10; for each page over six and each title over one, 50 cents additional;

(5) for the filing, under section 115(b), of a notice of intention to make phonorecords, $6;

(6) for the recordation, under section 302(c), of a statement revealing the identity of an author of an anonymous or pseudonymous work, or for the recordation, under section 3u2(d), of a statement relating to the death of an author, $10 for a document of six pages or less, covering no more than one title; for each page over six and for each title over one, $1 additional;

(7) for the issuance, under section 601, of an import statement, $3;

(8) for the issuance, under section 706, of an additional certificate of registration, $4;

(9) for the issuance of any other certification, $4; the Register of Copyrights has discretion, on the basis of their cost, to fix the fees for preparing copies of Copyright Office records, whether they are to be certified or not;

(10) for the making and reporting of a search as provided by section 705, and for any related services, $10 for each hour or fraction of an hour consumed;

(11) for any other special services requiring a substantial amount of time or expense, such fees as the Register of Copyrights may fix on the basis of the cost of providing the service.

Subsection (b) states that except for the possibility of waivers in "occasional or isolated cases involving relative small amounts," the Register is to charge fees for services rendered to other government agencies.

Subsection (c) provides that the Register may, in accordance with regulation, refund any sum paid by mistake or in excess of the required fee. However, before refunding in a rejection case, the Register "may deduct all or any part of the prescribed registration fee to cover the reasonable administrative costs of processing the claim."

DELAY IN DELIVERY CAUSED BY DISRUPTION OF
POSTAL OR OTHER SERVICES
(Section 709)

This section authorizes the Register to issue regulations to permit the acceptance of material which is delivered after the close of the prescribed period if the delay was caused by a general disruption or suspension of postal or other transportation or communications services.

VOLUNTARY LICENSING FOR REPRODUCTIONS FOR THE USE OF
THE BLIND AND PHYSICALLY HANDICAPPED
(Section 710)

Section 710 directs the Register, after consulting with the Chief of the Division for the Blind and Physically Handicapped and other appropriate officials of the Library of Congress, to establish, by regulation, forms and procedures by which copyright owners of certain specified categories of nondramatic literary works may voluntarily grant to the Library a license to reproduce and distribute copies or phonorecords of the work solely for the use of the blind and physically handicapped.

APPENDIX

Full Text of the
New Copyright Law

Public Law 94–553
94th Congress

An Act

For the general revision of the Copyright Law, title 17 of the United States Code, and for other purposes.

Oct. 19, 1976
[S. 22]

Be it enacted by the Senate and House of Representatives of the United States of America in Congress assembled,

Title 17, USC, Copyrights.

TITLE I—GENERAL REVISION OF COPYRIGHT LAW

SEC. 101. Title 17 of the United States Code, entitled "Copyrights", is hereby amended in its entirety to read as follows:

TITLE 17—COPYRIGHTS

Chapter 1.—SUBJECT MATTER AND SCOPE OF COPYRIGHT

§ 101. Definitions

17 USC 101.

As used in this title, the following terms and their variant forms mean the following:

An "anonymous work" is a work on the copies or phonorecords of which no natural person is identified as author.

"Audiovisual works" are works that consist of a series of related images which are intrinsically intended to be shown by the use of machines or devices such as projectors, viewers, or electronic equipment, together with accompanying sounds, if any, regardless of the nature of the material objects, such as films or tapes, in which the works are embodied.

The "best edition" of a work is the edition, published in the United States at any time before the date of deposit, that the Library of Congress determines to be most suitable for its purposes.

A person's "children" are that person's immediate offspring, whether legitimate or not, and any children legally adopted by that person.

A "collective work" is a work, such as a periodical issue, anthology, or encyclopedia, in which a number of contributions, constituting separate and independent works in themselves, are assembled into a collective whole.

A "compilation" is a work formed by the collection and assembling of preexisting materials or of data that are selected, coordinated, or arranged in such a way that the resulting work as a whole constitutes an original work of authorship. The term "compilation" includes collective works.

"Copies" are material objects, other than phonorecords, in which a work is fixed by any method now known or later developed, and from which the work can be perceived, reproduced, or otherwise communicated, either directly or with the aid of a machine or device. The term "copies" includes the material object, other than a phonorecord, in which the work is first fixed.

"Copyright owner", with respect to any one of the exclusive rights comprised in a copyright, refers to the owner of that particular right.

A work is "created" when it is fixed in a copy or phonorecord for the first time; where a work is prepared over a period of time, the portion of it that has been fixed at any particular time constitutes the work as of that time, and where the work has been prepared in different versions, each version constitutes a separate work.

A "derivative work" is a work based upon one or more preexisting works, such as a translation, musical arrangement, dramatization, fictionalization, motion picture version, sound recording, art reproduction, abridgment, condensation, or any other form in which a work may be recast, transformed, or adapted. A work consisting of editorial revisions, annotations, elaborations, or other modifications which, as a whole, represent an original work of authorship, is a "derivative work".

A "device", "machine", or "process" is one now known or later developed.

To "display" a work means to show a copy of it, either directly or by means of a film, slide, television image, or any other device or process or, in the case of a motion picture or other audiovisual work, to show individual images nonsequentially.

A work is "fixed" in a tangible medium of expression when its embodiment in a copy or phonorecord, by or under the authority of the author, is sufficiently permanent or stable to permit it to be perceived, reproduced, or otherwise communicated for a period of more than transitory duration. A work consisting of sounds, images, or both, that are being transmitted, is "fixed" for purposes of this title if a fixation of the work is being made simultaneously with its transmission.

The terms "including" and "such as" are illustrative and not limitative.

194

A "joint work" is a work prepared by two or more authors with the intention that their contributions be merged into inseparable or interdependent parts of a unitary whole.

"Literary works" are works, other than audiovisual works, expressed in words, numbers, or other verbal or numerical symbols or indicia, regardless of the nature of the material objects, such as books, periodicals, manuscripts, phonorecords, film, tapes, disks, or cards, in which they are embodied.

"Motion pictures" are audiovisual works consisting of a series of related images which, when shown in succession, impart an impression of motion, together with accompanying sounds, if any.

To "perform" a work means to recite, render, play, dance, or act it, either directly or by means of any device or process or, in the case of a motion picture or other audiovisual work, to show its images in any sequence or to make the sounds accompanying it audible.

"Phonorecords" are material objects in which sounds, other than those accompanying a motion picture or other audiovisual work, are fixed by any method now known or later developed, and from which the sounds can be perceived, reproduced, or otherwise communicated, either directly or with the aid of a machine or device. The term "phonorecords" includes the material object in which the sounds are first fixed.

"Pictorial, graphic, and sculptural works" include two-dimensional and three-dimensional works of fine, graphic, and applied art, photographs, prints and art reproductions, maps, globes, charts, technical drawings, diagrams, and models. Such works shall include works of artistic craftsmanship insofar as their form but not their mechanical or utilitarian aspects are concerned; the design of a useful article, as defined in this section, shall be considered a pictorial, graphic, or sculptural work only if, and only to the extent that, such design incorporates pictorial, graphic, or sculptural features that can be identified separately from, and are capable of existing independently of, the utilitarian aspects of the article.

A "pseudonymous work" is a work on the copies or phonorecords of which the author is identified under a fictitious name.

"Publication" is the distribution of copies or phonorecords of a work to the public by sale or other transfer of ownership, or by rental, lease, or lending. The offering to distribute copies or phonorecords to a group of persons for purposes of further distribution, public performance, or public display, constitutes publication. A public performance or display of a work does not of itself constitute publication.

To perform or display a work "publicly" means—

(1) to perform or display it at a place open to the public or at any place where a substantial number of persons outside of a normal circle of a family and its social acquaintances is gathered; or

(2) to transmit or otherwise communicate a performance or display of the work to a place specified by clause (1) or to the public, by means of any device or processs, whether the members of the public capable of receiving the performance or display receive it in the same place or in separate places and at the same time or at different times.

"Sound recordings" are works that result from the fixation
of a series of musical, spoken, or other sounds, but not including
the sounds accompanying a motion picture or other audiovisual
work, regardless of the nature of the material objects, such as
disks, tapes, or other phonorecords, in which they are embodied.

"State" includes the District of Columbia and the Common
wealth of Puerto Rico, and any territories to which this title
is made applicable by an Act of Congress.

A "transfer of copyright ownership" is an assignment, mort
gage, exclusive license, or any other conveyance, alienation, or
hypothecation of a copyright or of any of the exclusive rights
comprised in a copyright, whether or not it is limited in time or
place of effect, but not including a nonexclusive license.

A "transmission program" is a body of material that, as an
aggregate, has been produced for the sole purpose of transmis
sion to the public in sequence and as a unit.

To "transmit" a performance or display is to communicate it
by any device or process whereby images or sounds are received
beyond the place from which they are sent.

The "United States", when used in a geographical sense, com
prises the several States, the District of Columbia and the Com
monwealth of Puerto Rico, and the organized territories unde
the jurisdiction of the United States Government.

A "useful article" is an article having an intrinsic utilitaria
function that is not merely to portray the appearance of the
article or to convey information. An article that is normally
part of a useful article is considered a "useful article".

The author's "widow" or "widower" is the author's surviving
spouse under the law of the author's domicile at the time of his
or her death, whether or not the spouse has later remarried.

A "work of the United States Government" is a work prepare
by an officer or employee of the United States Government as
part of that person's official duties.

A "work made for hire" is—

(1) a work prepared by an employee within the scope of
his or her employment; or

(2) a work specially ordered or commissioned for use as
a contribution to a collective work, as a part of a motion
picture or other audiovisual work, as a translation, as a sup
plementary work, as a compilation, as an instructional text,
as a test, as answer material for a test, or as an atlas, if the
parties expressly agree in a written instrument signed by
them that the work shall be considered a work made for hire.
For the purpose of the foregoing sentence, a "supplementary
work" is a work prepared for publication as a secondary
adjunct to a work by another author for the purpose of
introducing, concluding, illustrating, explaining, revising,
commenting upon, or assisting in the use of the other work,
such as forewords, afterwords, pictorial illustrations, maps,
charts, tables, editorial notes, musical arrangements, answer
material for tests, bibliographies, appendixes, and indexes,
and an "instructional text" is a literary, pictorial, or graphic
work prepared for publication and with the purpose of use
in systematic instructional activities.

17 USC 102.

§ 102. Subject matter of copyright: In general

(a) Copyright protection subsists, in accordance with this title,
original works of authorship fixed in any tangible medium of expr

sion, now known or later developed, from which they can be perceived, reproduced, or otherwise communicated, either directly or with the aid of a machine or device. Works of authorship include the following categories:

Works of authorship.

(1) literary works;
(2) musical works, including any accompanying words;
(3) dramatic works, including any accompanying music;
(4) pantomimes and choreographic works;
(5) pictorial, graphic, and sculptural works;
(6) motion pictures and other audiovisual works; and
(7) sound recordings.

(b) In no case does copyright protection for an original work of authorship extend to any idea, procedure, process, system, method of operation, concept, principle, or discovery, regardless of the form in which it is described, explained, illustrated, or embodied in such work.

§ 103. Subject matter of copyright: Compilations and derivative works

17 USC 103.

(a) The subject matter of copyright as specified by section 102 includes compilations and derivative works, but protection for a work employing preexisting material in which copyright subsists does not extend to any part of the work in which such material has been used unlawfully.

(b) The copyright in a compilation or derivative work extends only to the material contributed by the author of such work, as distinguished from the preexisting material employed in the work, and does not imply any exclusive right in the preexisting material. The copyright in such work is independent of, and does not affect or enlarge the scope, duration, ownership, or subsistence of, any copyright protection in the preexisting material.

§ 104. Subject matter of copyright: National origin

17 USC 104.

(a) UNPUBLISHED WORKS.—The works specified by sections 102 and 103, while unpublished, are subject to protection under this title without regard to the nationality or domicile of the author.

(b) PUBLISHED WORKS.—The works specified by sections 102 and 103, when published, are subject to protection under this title if—

(1) on the date of first publication, one or more of the authors is a national or domiciliary of the United States, or is a national, domiciliary, or sovereign authority of a foreign nation that is a party to a copyright treaty to which the United States is also a party, or is a stateless person, wherever that person may be domiciled; or

(2) the work is first published in the United States or in a foreign nation that, on the date of first publication, is a party to the Universal Copyright Convention; or

(3) the work is first published by the United Nations or any of its specialized agencies, or by the Organization of American States; or

(4) the work comes within the scope of a Presidential proclamation. Whenever the President finds that a particular foreign nation extends, to works by authors who are nationals or domiciliaries of the United States or to works that are first published in the United States, copyright protection on substantially the same basis as that on which the foreign nation extends protection to works of its own nationals and domiciliaries and works first published in that nation, the President may by proclamation extend protection under this title to works of which one or more

of the authors is, on the date of first publication, a national, domiciliary, or sovereign authority of that nation, or which was first published in that nation. The President may revise, suspend, or revoke any such proclamation or impose any conditions or limitations on protection under a proclamation.

17 USC 105.

§ 105. Subject matter of copyright: United States Government works

Copyright protection under this title is not available for any work of the United States Government, but the United States Government is not precluded from receiving and holding copyrights transferred to it by assignment, bequest, or otherwise.

17 USC 106.

§ 106. Exclusive rights in copyrighted works

Subject to sections 107 through 118, the owner of copyright under this title has the exclusive rights to do and to authorize any of the following:

(1) to reproduce the copyrighted work in copies or phonorecords;

(2) to prepare derivative works based upon the copyrighted work;

(3) to distribute copies or phonorecords of the copyrighted work to the public by sale or other transfer of ownership, or by rental, lease, or lending;

(4) in the case of literary, musical, dramatic, and choreographic works, pantomimes, and motion pictures and other audiovisual works, to perform the copyrighted work publicly; and

(5) in the case of literary, musical, dramatic, and choreographic works, pantomimes, and pictorial, graphic, or sculptural works, including the individual images of a motion picture or other audiovisual work, to display the copyrighted work publicly.

17 USC 107.

§ 107. Limitations on exclusive rights: Fair use

Notwithstanding the provisions of section 106, the fair use of a copyrighted work, including such use by reproduction in copies or phonorecords or by any other means specified by that section, for purposes such as criticism, comment, news reporting, teaching (including multiple copies for classroom use), scholarship, or research, is not an infringement of copyright. In determining whether the use made of a work in any particular case is a fair use the factors to be considered shall include—

(1) the purpose and character of the use, including whether such use is of a commercial nature or is for nonprofit educational purposes;

(2) the nature of the copyrighted work;

(3) the amount and substantiality of the portion used in relation to the copyrighted work as a whole; and

(4) the effect of the use upon the potential market for or value of the copyrighted work.

17 USC 108.

§ 108. Limitations on exclusive rights: Reproduction by libraries and archives

(a) Notwithstanding the provisions of section 106, it is not an infringement of copyright for a library or archives, or any of its employees acting within the scope of their employment, to reproduce no more than one copy or phonorecord of a work, or to distribute such copy or phonorecord, under the conditions specified by this section if—

(1) the reproduction or distribution is made without any purpose of direct or indirect commercial advantage;

(2) the collections of the library or archives are (i) open to the public, or (ii) available not only to researchers affiliated with the library or archives or with the institution of which it is a part, but also to other persons doing research in a specialized field; and

(3) the reproduction or distribution of the work includes a notice of copyright.

(b) The rights of reproduction and distribution under this section apply to a copy or phonorecord of an unpublished work duplicated in facsimile form solely for purposes of preservation and security or for deposit for research use in another library or archives of the type described by clause (2) of subsection (a), if the copy or phonorecord reproduced is currently in the collections of the library or archives.

(c) The right of reproduction under this section applies to a copy or phonorecord of a published work duplicated in facsimile form solely for the purpose of replacement of a copy or phonorecord that is damaged, deteriorating, lost, or stolen, if the library or archives has, after a reasonable effort, determined that an unused replacement cannot be obtained at a fair price.

(d) The rights of reproduction and distribution under this section apply to a copy, made from the collection of a library or archives where the user makes his or her request or from that of another library or archives, of no more than one article or other contribution to a copyrighted collection or periodical issue, or to a copy or phonorecord of a small part of any other copyrighted work, if—

(1) the copy or phonorecord becomes the property of the user, and the library or archives has had no notice that the copy or phonorecord would be used for any purpose other than private study, scholarship, or research; and

(2) the library or archives displays prominently, at the place where orders are accepted, and includes on its order form, a warning of copyright in accordance with requirements that the Register of Copyrights shall prescribe by regulation.

(e) The rights of reproduction and distribution under this section apply to the entire work, or to a substantial part of it, made from the collection of a library or archives where the user makes his or her request or from that of another library or archives, if the library or archives has first determined, on the basis of a reasonable investigation, that a copy or phonorecord of the copyrighted work cannot be obtained at a pair price, if—

(1) the copy or phonorecord becomes the property of the user, and the library or archives has had no notice that the copy or phonorecord would be used for any purpose other than private study, scholarship, or research; and

(2) the library or archives displays prominently, at the place where orders are accepted, and includes on its order form, a warning of copyright in accordance with requirements that the Register of Copyrights shall prescribe by regulation.

(f) Nothing in this section—

(1) shall be construed to impose liability for copyright infringement upon a library or archives or its employees for the unsupervised use of reproducing equipment located on its premises: *Provided,* That such equipment displays a notice that the making of a copy may be subject to the copyright law;

(2) excuses a person who uses such reproducing equipment or who requests a copy or phonorecord under subsection (d) from liability for copyright infringement for any such act, or for any later use of such copy or phonorecord, if it exceeds fair use as provided by section 107;

(3) shall be construed to limit the reproduction and distribution by lending of a limited number of copies and excerpts by a library or archives of an audiovisual news program, subject to clauses (1), (2), and (3) of subsection (a) ; or

(4) in any way affects the right of fair use as provided by section 107, or any contractual obligations assumed at any time by the library or archives when it obtained a copy or phonorecord of a work in its collections.

(g) The rights of reproduction and distribution under this section extend to the isolated and unrelated reproduction or distribution of a single copy or phonorecord of the same material on separate occasions, but do not extend to cases where the library or archives, or its employee—

(1) is aware or has substantial reason to believe that it is engaging in the related or concerted reproduction or distribution of multiple copies or phonorecords of the same material, whether made on one occasion or over a period of time, and whether intended for aggregate use by one or more individuals or for separate use by the individual members of a group; or

(2) engages in the systematic reproduction or distribution of single or multiple copies or phonorecords of material described in subsection (d) : *Provided*, That nothing in this clause prevents a library or archives from participating in interlibrary arrangements that do not have, as their purpose or effect, that the library or archives receiving such copies or phonorecords for distribution does so in such aggregate quantities as to substitute for a subscription to or purchase of such work.

(h) The rights of reproduction and distribution under this section do not apply to a musical work, a pictorial, graphic or sculptural work, or a motion picture or other audiovisual work other than an audiovisual work dealing with news, except that no such limitation shall apply with respect to rights granted by subsections (b) and (c), or with respect to pictorial or graphic works published as illustrations, diagrams, or similar adjuncts to works of which copies are reproduced or distributed in accordance with subsections (d) and (e).

Report to Congress.

(i) Five years from the effective date of this Act, and at five-year intervals thereafter, the Register of Copyrights, after consulting with representatives of authors, book and periodical publishers, and other owners of copyrighted materials, and with representatives of library users and librarians, shall submit to the Congress a report setting forth the extent to which this section has achieved the intended statutory balancing of the rights of creators, and the needs of users. The report should also describe any problems that may have arisen, and present legislative or other recommendations, if warranted.

17 USC 109.

§ 109. Limitations on exclusive rights: Effect of transfer of particular copy or phonorecord

Disposal.

(a) Notwithstanding the provisions of section 106(3), the owner of a particular copy or phonorecord lawfully made under this title, or any person authorized by such owner, is entitled, without the authority of the copyright owner, to sell or otherwise dispose of the possession of that copy or phonorecord.

Public display.

(b) Notwithstanding the provisions of section 106(5), the owner of a particular copy lawfully made under this title, or any person authorized by such owner, is entitled, without the authority of the copyright owner, to display that copy publicly, either directly or by the projection of no more than one image at a time, to viewers present at the place where the copy is located.

(c) The privileges prescribed by subsections (a) and (b) do not, unless authorized by the coyright owner, extend to any person who has acquired possession of the copy or phonorecord from the copyright owner, by rental, lease, loan, or otherwise, without acquiring ownership of it.

§ 110. Limitations on exclusive rights: Exemption of certain performances and displays   17 USC 110.

Notwithstanding the provisions of section 106, the following are not infringements of copyright:

(1) performance or display of a work by instructors or pupils in the course of face-to-face teaching activities of a nonprofit educational institution, in a classroom or similar place devoted to instruction, unless, in the case of a motion picture or other audiovisual work, the performance, or the display of individual images, is given by means of a copy that was not lawfully made under this title, and that the person responsible for the performance knew or had reason to believe was not lawfully made;

(2) performance of a nondramatic literary or musical work or display of a work, by or in the course of a transmission, if—

(A) the performance or display is a regular part of the systematic instructional activities of a governmental body or a nonprofit educational institution; and

(B) the performance or display is directly related and of material assistance to the teaching content of the transmission; and

(C) the transmission is made primarily for—

(i) reception in classrooms or similar places normally devoted to instruction, or

(ii) reception by persons to whom the transmission is directed because their disabilities or other special circumstances prevent their attendance in classrooms or similar places normally devoted to instruction, or

(iii) reception by officers or employees of governmental bodies as a part of their official duties or employment;

(3) performance of a nondramatic literary or musical work or of a dramatico-musical work of a religious nature, or display of a work, in the course of services at a place of worship or other religious assembly;

(4) performance of a nondramatic literary or musical work otherwise than in a transmission to the public, without any purpose of direct or indirect commercial advantage and without payment of any fee or other compensation for the performance to any of its performers, promoters, or organizers, if—

(A) there is no direct or indirect admission charge; or

(B) the proceeds, after deducting the reasonable costs of producing the performance, are used exclusively for educational, religious, or charitable purposes and not for private financial gain, except where the copyright owner has served notice of objection to the performance under the following conditions;   Notice of objection to performance.

(i) the notice shall be in writing and signed by the copyright owner or such owner's duly authorized agent; and

(ii) the notice shall be served on the person responsible for the performance at least seven days before the date of the performance, and shall state the reasons for the objection; and

Regulation.

      (iii) the notice shall comply, in form, content, and manner of service, with requirements that the Register of Copyrights shall prescribe by regulation;

(5) communication of a transmission embodying a performance or display of a work by the public reception of the transmission on a single receiving apparatus of a kind commonly used in private homes, unless—

      (A) a direct charge is made to see or hear the transmission; or

      (B) the transmission thus received is further transmitted to the public;

(6) performance of a nondramatic musical work by a governmental body or a nonprofit agricultural or horticultural organization, in the course of an annual agricultural or horticultural fair or exhibition conducted by such body or organization; the exemption provided by this clause shall extend to any liability for copyright infringement that would otherwise be imposed on such body or organization, under doctrines of vicarious liability or related infringement, for a performance by a concessionnaire, business establishment, or other person at such fair or exhibition, but shall not excuse any such person from liability for the performance;

(7) performance of a nondramatic musical work by a vending establishment open to the public at large without any direct or indirect admission charge, where the sole purpose of the performance is to promote the retail sale of copies or phonorecords of the work, and the performance is not transmitted beyond the place where the establishment is located and is within the immediate area where the sale is occurring;

(8) performance of a nondramatic literary work, by or in the course of a transmission specifically designed for and primarily directed to blind or other handicapped persons who are unable to read normal printed material as a result of their handicap, or deaf or other handicapped persons who are unable to hear the aural signals accompanying a transmission of visual signals, if the performance is made without any purpose of direct or indirect commercial advantage and its transmission is made through the facilities of: (i) a governmental body; or (ii) a noncommercial educational broadcast station (as defined in section 397 of title 47); or (iii) a radio subcarrier authorization (as defined in 47 CFR 73.293–73.295 and 73.593–73.595); or (iv) a cable system (as defined in section 111(f)).

(9) performance on a single occasion of a dramatic literary work published at least ten years before the date of the performance, by or in the course of a transmission specifically designed for and primarily directed to blind or other handicapped persons who are unable to read normal printed material as a result of their handicap, if the performance is made without any purpose of direct or indirect commercial advantage and its transmission is made through the facilities of a radio subcarrier authorization referred to in clause (8)(iii), *Provided*, That the provisions of this clause shall not be applicable to more than one performance of the same work by the same performers or under the auspices of the same organization.

§ 111. Limitations on exclusive rights: Secondary transmissions

(a) CERTAIN SECONDARY TRANSMISSIONS EXEMPTED.—The secondary transmission of a primary transmission embodying a performance or display of a work is not an infringement of copyright if—

(1) the secondary transmission is not made by a cable system, and consists entirely of the relaying, by the management of a hotel, apartment house, or similar establishment, of signals transmitted by a broadcast station licensed by the Federal Communications Commission, within the local service area of such station, to the private lodgings of guests or residents of such establishment, and no direct charge is made to see or hear the secondary transmission; or

(2) the secondary transmission is made solely for the purpose and under the conditions specified by clause (2) of section 110; or

(3) the secondary transmission is made by any carrier who has no direct or indirect control over the content or selection of the primary transmission or over the particular recipients of the secondary transmission, and whose activities with respect to the secondary transmission consist solely of providing wires, cables, or other communications channels for the use of others: *Provided*, That the provisions of this clause extend only to the activities of said carrier with respect to secondary transmissions and do not exempt from liability the activities of others with respect to their own primary or secondary transmissions; or

(4) the secondary transmission is not made by a cable system but is made by a governmental body, or other nonprofit organization, without any purpose of direct or indirect commercial advantage, and without charge to the recipients of the secondary transmission other than assessments necessary to defray the actual and reasonable costs of maintaining and operating the secondary transmission service.

(b) SECONDARY TRANSMISSION OF PRIMARY TRANSMISSION TO CONTROLLED GROUP.—Notwithstanding the provisions of subsections (a) and (c), the secondary transmission to the public of a primary transmission embodying a performance or display of a work is actionable as an act of infringement under section 501, and is fully subject to the remedies provided by sections 502 through 506 and 509, if the primary transmission is not made for reception by the public at large but is controlled and limited to reception by particular members of the public: *Provided*, however, That such secondary transmission is not actionable as an act of infringement if—

(1) the primary transmission is made by a broadcast station licensed by the Federal Communications Commission; and

(2) the carriage of the signals comprising the secondary transmission is required under the rules, regulations, or authorizations of the Federal Communications Commission; and

(3) the signal of the primary transmitter is not altered or changed in any way by the secondary transmitter.

(c) SECONDARY TRANSMISSIONS BY CABLE SYSTEMS.—

(1) Subject to the provisions of clauses (2), (3), and (4) of this subsection, secondary transmissions to the public by a cable system of a primary transmission made by a broadcast station licensed by the Federal Communications Commission or by an appropriate governmental authority of Canada or Mexico and embodying a performance or display of a work shall be subject to compulsory licensing upon compliance with the requirements of subsection (d) where the carriage of the signals comprising the secondary transmission is permissible under the rules, regulations, or authorizations of the Federal Communications Commission.

(2) Notwithstanding the provisions of clause (1) of this subsection, the willful or repeated secondary transmission to the public by a cable system of a primary transmission made by a

broadcast station licensed by the Federal Communications Commission or by an appropriate governmental authority of Canada or Mexico and embodying a performance or display of a work is actionable as an act of infringement under section 501, and is fully subject to the remedies provided by sections 502 through 506 and 509, in the following cases:

(A) where the carriage of the signals comprising the secondary transmission is not permissible under the rules, regulations, or authorizations of the Federal Communications Commission; or

(B) where the cable system has not recorded the notice specified by subsection (d) and deposited the statement of account and royalty fee required by subsection (d).

Alteration, deletion, or substitution.

(3) Notwithstanding the provisions of clause (1) of this subsection and subject to the provisions of subsection (e) of this section, the secondary transmission to the public by a cable system of a primary transmission made by a broadcast station licensed by the Federal Communications Commission or by an appropriate governmental authority of Canada or Mexico and embodying a performance or display of a work is actionable as an act of infringement under section 501, and is fully subject to the remedies provided by sections 502 through 506 and sections 509 and 510, if the content of the particular program in which the performance or display is embodied, or any commercial advertising or station announcements transmitted by the primary transmitter during, or immediately before or after, the transmission of such program, is in any way willfully altered by the cable system through changes, deletions, or additions, except for the alteration, deletion, or substitution of commercial advertisements performed by those engaged in television commercial advertising market research: *Provided,* That the research company has obtained the prior consent of the advertiser who has purchased the original commercial advertisement, the television station broadcasting that commercial advertisement, and the cable system performing the secondary transmission: *And provided further,* That such commercial alteration, deletion, or substitution is not performed for the purpose of deriving income from the sale of that commercial time.

Prior consent of advertiser.

(4) Notwithstanding the provisions of clause (1) of this subsection, the secondary transmission to the public by a cable system of a primary transmission made by a broadcast station licensed by an appropriate governmental authority of Canada or Mexico and embodying a performance or display of a work is actionable as an act of infringement under section 501, and is fully subject to the remedies provided by sections 502 through 506 and section 509, if (A) with respect to Canadian signals, the community of the cable system is located more than 150 miles from the United States-Canadian border and is also located south of the forty-second parallel of latitude, or (B) with respect to Mexican signals, the secondary transmission is made by a cable system which received the primary transmission by means other than direct interception of a free space radio wave emitted by such broadcast television station, unless prior to April 15, 1976, such cable system was actually carrying, or was specifically authorized to carry, the signal of such foreign station on the system pursuant to the rules, regulations, or authorizations of the Federal Communications Commission.

(d) COMPULSORY LICENSE FOR SECONDARY TRANSMISSIONS BY CABLE SYSTEMS.—

(1) For any secondary transmission to be subject to compulsory licensing under subsection (c), the cable system shall, at least one month before the date of the commencement of operations of the cable system or within one hundred and eighty days after the enactment of this Act, whichever is later, and thereafter within thirty days after each occasion on which the ownership or control or the signal carriage complement of the cable system changes, record in the Copyright Office a notice including a statement of the identity and address of the person who owns or operates the secondary transmission service or has power to exercise primary control over it, together with the name and location of the primary transmitter or primary transmitters whose signals are regularly carried by the cable system, and thereafter, from time to time, such further information as the Register of Copyrights, after consultation with the Copyright Royalty Tribunal (if and when the Tribunal has been constituted), shall prescribe by regulation to carry out the purpose of this clause.

Notice.

(2) A cable system whose secondary transmissions have been subject to compulsory licensing under subsection (c) shall, on a semiannual basis, deposit with the Register of Copyrights, in accordance with requirements that the Register shall, after consultation with the Copyright Royalty Tribunal (if and when the Tribunal has been constituted), prescribe by regulation—

(A) a statement of account, covering the six months next preceding, specifying the number of channels on which the cable system made secondary transmissions to its subscribers, the names and locations of all primary transmitters whose transmissions were further transmitted by the cable system, the total number of subscribers, the gross amounts paid to the cable system for the basic service of providing secondary transmissions of primary broadcast transmitters, and such other data as the Register of Copyrights may, after consultation with the Copyright Royalty Tribunal (if and when the Tribunal has been constituted), from time to time prescribe by regulation. Such statement shall also include a special statement of account covering any nonnetwork television programming that was carried by the cable system in whole or in part beyond the local service area of the primary transmitter, under rules, regulations, or authorizations of the Federal Communications Commission permitting the substitution or addition of signals under certain circumstances, together with logs showing the times, dates, stations, and programs involved in such substituted or added carriage; and

Statement of account.

Nonnetwork television programming.

(B) except in the case of a cable system whose royalty is specified in subclause (C) or (D), a total royalty fee for the period covered by the statement, computed on the basis of specified percentages of the gross receipts from subscribers to the cable service during said period for the basic service of providing secondary transmissions of primary broadcast transmitters, as follows:

Total royalty fee.

(i) 0.675 of 1 per centum of such gross receipts for the privilege of further transmitting any nonnetwork programing of a primary transmitter in whole or in part beyond the local service area of such primary transmitter, such amount to be applied against the fee, if any, payable pursuant to paragraphs (ii) through (iv);

205

(ii) 0.675 of 1 per centum of such gross receipts for the first distant signal equivalent;

(iii) 0.425 of 1 per centum of such gross receipts for each of the second, third, and fourth distant signal equivalents;

(iv) 0.2 of 1 per centum of such gross receipts for the fifth distant signal equivalent and each additional distant signal equivalent thereafter; and

in computing the amounts payable under paragraph (ii) through (iv), above, any fraction of a distant signal equivalent shall be computed at its fractional value and, in the case of any cable system located partly within and partly without the local service area of a primary transmitter, gross receipts shall be limited to those gross receipts derived from subscribers located without the local service area of such primary transmitter; and

(C) if the actual gross receipts paid by subscribers to a cable system for the period covered by the statement for the basic service of providing secondary transmissions of primary broadcast transmitters total $80,000 or less, gross receipts of the cable system for the purpose of this subclause shall be computed by subtracting from such actual gross receipts the amount by which $80,000 exceeds such actual gross receipts, except that in no case shall a cable system's gross receipts be reduced to less than $3,000. The royalty fee payable under this subclause shall be 0.5 of 1 per centum, regardless of the number of distant signal equivalents, if any; and

(D) if the actual gross receipts paid by subscribers to a cable system for the period covered by the statement, for the basic service of providing secondary transmissions of primary broadcast transmitters, are more than $80,000 but less than $160,000, the royalty fee payable under this subclause shall be (i) 0.5 of 1 per centum of any gross receipts up to $80,000; and (ii) 1 per centum of any gross receipts in excess of $80,000 but less than $160,000, regardless of the number of distant signal equivalents, if any.

(3) The Register of Copyrights shall receive all fees deposited under this section and, after deducting the reasonable costs incurred by the Copyright Office under this section, shall deposit the balance in the Treasury of the United States, in such manner as the Secretary of the Treasury directs. All funds held by the Secretary of the Treasury shall be invested in interest-bearing United States securities for later distribution with interest by the Copyright Royalty Tribunal as provided by this title. The Register shall submit to the Copyright Royalty Tribunal, on a semiannual basis, a compilation of all statements of account covering the relevant six-month period provided by clause (2) of this subsection.

Statements of account, submittal to Copyright Royalty Tribunal.

Royalty fees, distribution.

(4) The royalty fees thus deposited shall, in accordance with the procedures provided by clause (5), be distributed to those among the following copyright owners who claim that their works were the subject of secondary transmissions by cable systems during the relevant semiannual period:

(A) any such owner whose work was included in a secondary transmission made by a cable system of a nonnetwork television program in whole or in part beyond the local service area of the primary transmitter; and

(B) any such owner whose work was included in a secondary transmission identified in a special statement of account deposited under clause (2)(A); and

(C) any such owner whose work was included in nonnetwork programing consisting exclusively of aural signals carried by a cable system in whole or in part beyond the local service area of the primary transmitter of such programs.

(5) The royalty fees thus deposited shall be distributed in accordance with the following procedures:

Distribution procedures.

(A) During the month of July in each year, every person claiming to be entitled to compulsory license fees for secondary transmissions shall file a claim with the Copyright Royalty Tribunal, in accordance with requirements that the Tribunal shall prescribe by regulation. Notwithstanding any provisions of the antitrust laws, for purposes of this clause any claimants may agree among themselves as to the proportionate division of compulsory licensing fees among them, may lump their claims together and file them jointly or as a single claim, or may designate a common agent to receive payment on their behalf.

(B) After the first day of August of each year, the Copyright Royalty Tribunal shall determine whether there exists a controversy concerning the distribution of royalty fees. If the Tribunal determines that no such controversy exists, it shall, after deducting its reasonable administrative costs under this section, distribute such fees to the copyright owners entitled, or to their designated agents. If the Tribunal finds the existence of a controversy, it shall, pursuant to chapter 8 of this title, conduct a proceeding to determine the distribution of royalty fees.

(C) During the pendency of any proceeding under this subsection, the Copyright Royalty Tribunal shall withhold from distribution an amount sufficient to satisfy all claims with respect to which a controversy exists, but shall have discretion to proceed to distribute any amounts that are not in controversy.

(e) NONSIMULTANEOUS SECONDARY TRANSMISSIONS BY CABLE SYSTEMS.—

(1) Notwithstanding those provisions of the second paragraph of subsection (f) relating to nonsimultaneous secondary transmissions by a cable system, any such transmissions are actionable as an act of infringement under section 501, and are fully subject to the remedies provided by sections 502 through 506 and sections 509 and 510, unless—

(A) the program on the videotape is transmitted no more than one time to the cable system's subscribers; and

(B) the copyrighted program, episode, or motion picture videotape, including the commercials contained within such program, episode, or picture, is transmitted without deletion or editing; and

(C) an owner or officer of the cable system (i) prevents the duplication of the videotape while in the possession of the system, (ii) prevents unauthorized duplication while in the possession of the facility making the videotape for the system if the system owns or controls the facility, or takes reasonable precautions to prevent such duplication if it does not own or control the facility, (iii) takes adequate precautions to prevent duplication while the tape is being transported, and (iv) subject to clause (2), erases or destroys, or causes the erasure or destruction of, the videotape; and

(D) within forty-five days after the end of each calendar quarter, an owner or officer of the cable system executes an affidavit attesting (i) to the steps and precautions taken to prevent duplication of the videotape, and (ii) subject to clause (2), to the erasure or destruction of all videotapes made or used during such quarter; and

(E) such owner or officer places or causes each such affidavit, and affidavits received pursuant to clause (2)(C), to be placed in a file, open to public inspection, at such system's main office in the community where the transmission is made or in the nearest community where such system maintains an office; and

(F) the nonsimultaneous transmission is one that the cable system would be authorized to transmit under the rules, regulations, and authorizations of the Federal Communications Commission in effect at the time of the nonsimultaneous transmission if the transmission had been made simultaneously, except that this subclause shall not apply to inadvertent or accidental transmissions.

(2) If a cable system transfers to any person a videotape of a program nonsimultaneously transmitted by it, such transfer is actionable as an act of infringement under section 501, and is fully subject to the remedies provided by sections 502 through 506 and 509, except that, pursuant to a written, nonprofit contract providing for the equitable sharing of the costs of such videotape and its transfer, a videotape nonsimultaneously transmitted by it, in accordance with clause (1), may be transferred by one cable system in Alaska to another system in Alaska, by one cable system in Hawaii permitted to make such nonsimultaneous transmissions to another such cable system in Hawaii, or by one cable system in Guam, the Northern Mariana Islands, or the Trust Territory of the Pacific Islands, to another cable system in any of those three territories, if—

(A) each such contract is available for public inspection in the offices of the cable systems involved, and a copy of such contract is filed, within thirty days after such contract is entered into, with the Copyright Office (which Office shall make each such contract available for public inspection); and

(B) the cable system to which the videotape is transferred complies with clause (1)(A), (B), (C)(i), (iii), and (iv), and (D) through (F); and

(C) such system provides a copy of the affidavit required to be made in accordance with clause (1)(D) to each cable system making a previous nonsimultaneous transmission of the same videotape.

(3) This subsection shall not be construed to supersede the exclusivity protection provisions of any existing agreement, or any such agreement hereafter entered into, between a cable system and a television broadcast station in the area in which the cable system is located, or a network with which such station is affiliated.

"Videotape."

(4) As used in this subsection, the term "videotape", and each of its variant forms, means the reproduction of the images and

208

sounds of a program or programs broadcast by a television broadcast station licensed by the Federal Communications Commission, regardless of the nature of the material objects, such as tapes or films, in which the reproduction is embodied.

(f) DEFINITIONS.—As used in this section, the following terms and their variant forms mean the following:

A "primary transmission" is a transmission made to the public by the transmitting facility whose signals are being received and further transmitted by the secondary transmission service, regardless of where or when the performance or display was first transmitted.

A "secondary transmission" is the further transmitting of a primary transmission simultaneously with the primary transmission, or nonsimultaneously with the primary transmission if by a "cable system" not located in whole or in part within the boundary of the forty-eight contiguous States, Hawaii, or Puerto Rico: *Provided, however*, That a nonsimultaneous further transmission by a cable system located in Hawaii of a primary transmission shall be deemed to be a secondary transmission if the carriage of the television broadcast signal comprising such further transmission is permissible under the rules, regulations, or authorizations of the Federal Communications Commission.

A "cable system" is a facility, located in any State, Territory, Trust Territory, or Possession, that in whole or in part receives signals transmitted or programs broadcast by one or more television broadcast stations licensed by the Federal Communications Commission, and makes secondary transmissions of such signals or programs by wires, cables, or other communications channels to subscribing members of the public who pay for such service. For purposes of determining the royalty fee under subsection (d)(2), two or more cable systems in contiguous communities under common ownership or control or operating from one headend shall be considered as one system.

The "local service area of a primary transmitter", in the case of a television broadcast station, comprises the area in which such station is entitled to insist upon its signal being retransmitted by a cable system pursuant to the rules, regulations, and authorizations of the Federal Communications Commission in effect on April 15, 1976, or in the case of a television broadcast station licensed by an appropriate governmental authority of Canada or Mexico, the area in which it would be entitled to insist upon its signal being retransmitted if it were a television broadcast station subject to such rules, regulations, and authorizations. The "local service area of a primary transmitter", in the case of a radio broadcast station, comprises the primary service area of such station, pursuant to the rules and regulations of the Federal Communications Commission.

A "distant signal equivalent" is the value assigned to the secondary transmission of any nonnetwork television programing carried by a cable system in whole or in part beyond the local service area of the primary transmitter of such programing. It is computed by assigning a value of one to each independent station and a value of one-quarter to each network station and noncommercial educational station for the nonnetwork programing so carried pursuant to the rules, regulations, and authorizations of the Federal Communications Commission. The foregoing values for independent, network, and noncommercial

educational stations are subject, however, to the following exceptions and limitations. Where the rules and regulations of the
Federal Communications Commission require a cable system to
omit the further transmission of a particular program and such
rules and regulations also permit the substitution of another program embodying a performance or display of a work in place of
the omitted transmission, or where such rules and regulations in
effect on the date of enactment of this Act permit a cable system,
at its election, to effect such deletion and substitution of a nonlive
program or to carry additional programs not transmitted by
primary transmitters within whose local service area the cable
system is located, no value shall be assigned for the substituted or
additional program; where the rules, regulations, or authorizations of the Federal Communications Commission in effect on the
date of enactment of this Act permit a cable system, at its election,
to omit the further transmission of a particular program and such
rules, regulations, or authorizations also permit the substitution
of another program embodying a performance or display of a
work in place of the omitted transmission, the value assigned for
the substituted or additional program shall be, in the case of a live
program, the value of one full distant signal equivalent multiplied by a fraction that has as its numerator the number of days
in the year in which such substitution occurs and as its denomi-
nator the number of days in the year. In the case of a station
carried pursuant to the late-night or specialty programing rules
of the Federal Communications Commission, or a station carried
on a part-time basis where full-time carriage is not possible
because the cable system lacks the activated channel capacity to
retransmit on a full-time basis all signals which it is authorized
to carry, the values for independent, network, and noncommercial
educational stations set forth above, as the case may be, shall be
multiplied by a fraction which is equal to the ratio of the broadcast hours of such station carried by the cable system to the total
broadcast hours of the station.

A "network station" is a television broadcast station that is
owned or operated by, or affiliated with, one or more of the television networks in the United States providing nationwide trans-
missons, and that transmits a substantial part of the programing
supplied by such networks for a substantial part of that station's
typical broadcast day.

An "independent station" is a commercial television broadcast
station other than a network station.

A "noncommercial educational station" is a television station
that is a noncommercial educational broadcast station as defined
in section 397 of title 47.

47 USC 397.

17 USC 112.

§ 112. Limitations on exclusive rights: Ephemeral recordings

(a) Notwithstanding the provisions of section 106, and except in
the case of a motion picture or other audiovisual work, it is not an
infringement of copyright for a transmitting organization entitled to
transmit to the public a performance or display of a work, under a
license or transfer of the copyright or under the limitations on exclusive rights in sound recordings specified by section 114(a), to make no
more than one copy or phonorecord of a particular transmission program embodying the performance or display, if—

(1) the copy or phonorecord is retained and used solely by the
transmitting organization that made it, and no further copies or
phonorecords are reproduced from it; and

(2) the copy or phonorecord is used solely for the transmitting organization's own transmissions within its local service area, or for purposes of archival preservation or security; and

(3) unless preserved exclusively for archival purposes, the copy or phonorecord is destroyed within six months from the date the transmission program was first transmitted to the public.

(b) Notwithstanding the provisions of section 106, it is not an infringement of copyright for a governmental body or other nonprofit organization entitled to transmit a performance or display of a work, under section 110(2) or under the limitations on exclusive rights in sound recordings specified by section 114(a), to make no more than thirty copies or phonorecords of a particular transmission program embodying the performance or display, if—

(1) no further copies or phonorecords are reproduced from the copies or phonorecords made under this clause; and

(2) except for one copy or phonorecord that may be preserved exclusively for archival purposes, the copies or phonorecords are destroyed within seven years from the date the transmission program was first transmitted to the public.

(c) Notwithstanding the provisions of section 106, it is not an infringment of copyright for a governmental body or other nonprofit organization to make for distribution no more than one copy or phonorecord, for each transmitting organization specified in clause (2) of this subsection, of a particular transmission program embodying a performance of a nondramatic musical work of a religious nature, or of a sound recording of such a musical work, if—

(1) there is no direct or indirect charge for making or distributing any such copies or phonorecords; and

(2) none of such copies or phonorecords is used for any performance other than a single transmission to the public by a transmitting organization entitled to transmit to the public a performance of the work under a license or transfer of the copyright; and

(3) except for one copy or phonorecord that may be preserved exclusively for archival purposes, the copies or phonorecords are all destroyed within one year from the date the transmission program was first transmitted to the public.

(d) Notwithstanding the provisions of section 106, it is not an infringement of copyright for a governmental body or other nonprofit organization entitled to transmit a performance of a work under section 110(8) to make no more than ten copies or phonorecords embodying the performance, or to permit the use of any such copy or phonorecord by any governmental body or nonprofit organization entitled to transmit a performance of a work under section 110(8), if—

(1) any such copy or phonorecord is retained and used solely by the organization that made it, or by a governmental body or nonprofit organization entitled to transmit a performance of a work under section 110(8), and no further copies or phonorecords are reproduced from it; and

(2) any such copy or phonorecord is used solely for transmissions authorized under section 110(8), or for purposes of archival preservation or security; and

(3) the governmental body or nonprofit organization permitting any use of any such copy or phonorecord by any governmental body or nonprofit organization under this subsection does not make any charge for such use.

(e) The transmission program embodied in a copy or phonorecord made under this section is not subject to protection as a derivative

211

work under this title except with the express consent of the owners of copyright in the preexisting works employed in the program.

17 USC 113.

§ 113. Scope of exclusive rights in pictorial, graphic, and sculptural works

(a) Subject to the provisions of subsections (b) and (c) of this section, the exclusive right to reproduce a copyrighted pictorial, graphic, or sculptural work in copies under section 106 includes the right to reproduce the work in or on any kind of article, whether useful or otherwise.

(b) This title does not afford, to the owner of copyright in a work that portrays a useful article as such, any greater or lesser rights with respect to the making, distribution, or display of the useful article so portrayed than those afforded to such works under the law, whether

17 USC 1 et seq.

title 17 or the common law or statutes of a State, in effect on December 31, 1977, as held applicable and construed by a court in an action brought under this title.

(c) In the case of a work lawfully reproduced in useful articles that have been offered for sale or other distribution to the public, copyright does not include any right to prevent the making, distribution, or display of pictures or photographs of such articles in connection with advertisements or commentaries related to the distribution or display of such articles, or in connection with news reports.

17 USC 114.

§ 114. Scope of exclusive rights in sound recordings

(a) The exclusive rights of the owner of copyright in a sound recording are limited to the rights specified by clauses (1), (2), and (3) of section 106, and do not include any right of performance under section 106(4).

(b) The exclusive right of the owner of copyright in a sound recording under clause (1) of section 106 is limited to the right to duplicate the sound recording in the form of phonorecords, or of copies of motion pictures and other audiovisual works, that directly or indirectly recapture the actual sounds fixed in the recording. The exclusive right of the owner of copyright in a sound recording under clause (2) of section 106 is limited to the right to prepare a derivative work in which the actual sounds fixed in the sound recording are rearranged, remixed, or otherwise altered in sequence or quality. The exclusive rights of the owner of copyright in a sound recording under clauses (1) and (2) of section 106 do not extend to the making or duplication of another sound recording that consists entirely of an independent fixation of other sounds, even though such sounds imitate or simulate those in the copyrighted sound recording. The exclusive rights of the owner of copyright in a sound recording under clauses (1), (2), and (3) of section 106 do not apply to sound recordings included in educational

47 USC 397.

television and radio programs (as defined in section 397 of title 47) distributed or transmitted by or through public broadcasting entities (as defined by section 118(g)) : *Provided*, That copies or phonorecords of said programs are not commercially distributed by or through public broadcasting entities to the general public.

(c) This section does not limit or impair the exclusive right to perform publicly, by means of a phonorecord, any of the works specified by section 106(4).

Report to Congress.

(d) On January 3, 1978, the Register of Copyrights, after consulting with representatives of owners of copyrighted materials, representatives of the broadcasting, recording, motion picture, entertainment industries, and arts organizations, representatives of organized labor and performers of copyrighted materials, shall submit to the Congress a report setting forth recommendations as to whether this section should be amended to provide for performers and copyright owners of copyrighted material any performance rights in such material. The report should describe the status of such rights in foreign countries, the views of major interested parties, and specific legislative or other recommendations, if any.

§ 115. Scope of exclusive rights in nondramatic musical works: Compulsory license for making and distributing phonorecords

17 USC 115.

In the case of nondramatic musical works, the exclusive rights provided by clauses (1) and (3) of section 106, to make and to distribute phonorecords of such works, are subject to compulsory licensing under the conditions specified by this section.

(a) AVAILABILITY AND SCOPE OF COMPULSORY LICENSE.—

(1) When phonorecords of a nondramatic musical work have been distributed to the public in the United States under the authority of the copyright owner, any other person may, by complying with the provisions of this section, obtain a compulsory license to make and distribute phonorecords of the work. A person may obtain a compulsory license only if his or her primary purpose in making phonorecords is to distribute them to the public for private use. A person may not obtain a compulsory license for use of the work in the making of phonorecords duplicating a sound recording fixed by another, unless: (i) such sound recording was fixed lawfully; and (ii) the making of the phonorecords was authorized by the owner of copyright in the sound recording or, if the sound recording was fixed before February 15, 1972, by any person who fixed the sound recording pursuant to an express license from the owner of the copyright in the musical work or pursuant to a valid compulsory license for use of such work in a sound recording.

(2) A compulsory license includes the privilege of making a musical arrangement of the work to the extent necessary to conform it to the style or manner of interpretation of the performance involved, but the arrangement shall not change the basic melody or fundamental character of the work, and shall not be subject to protection as a derivative work under this title, except with the express consent of the copyright owner.

(b) NOTICE OF INTENTION TO OBTAIN COMPULSORY LICENSE.—

(1) Any person who wishes to obtain a compulsory license under this section shall, before or within thirty days after making, and before distributing any phonorecords of the work, serve notice of intention to do so on the copyright owner. If the registration or other public records of the Copyright Office do not identify the copyright owner and include an address at which notice can be served, it shall be sufficient to file the notice of intention in the Copyright Office. The notice shall comply, in form, content, and manner of service, with requirements that the Register of Copyrights shall prescribe by regulation.

(2) Failure to serve or file the notice required by clause (1) forecloses the possibility of a compulsory license and, in the absence of a negotiated license, renders the making and distribution of phonorecords actionable as acts of infringement under section 501 and fully subject to the remedies provided by sections 502 through 506 and 509.

Failure to serve or file notice, penalty.

(c) ROYALTY PAYABLE UNDER COMPULSORY LICENSE.—

(1) To be entitled to receive royalties under a compulsory license, the copyright owner must be identified in the registration or other public records of the Copyright Office. The owner is entitled to royalties for phonorecords made and distributed after

213

being so identified, but is not entitled to recover for any phono-records previously made and distributed.

(2) Except as provided by clause (1), the royalty under a compulsory license shall be payable for every phonorecord made and distributed in accordance with the license. For this purpose, a phonorecord is considered "distributed" if the person exercising the compulsory license has voluntarily and permanently parted with its possession. With respect to each work embodied in the phonorecord, the royalty shall be either two and three-fourths cents, or one-half of one cent per minute of playing time or fraction thereof, whichever amount is larger.

Royalty
payments.
Regulations.

(3) Royalty payments shall be made on or before the twentieth day of each month and shall include all royalties for the month next preceding. Each monthly payment shall be made under oath and shall comply with requirements that the Register of Copyrights shall prescribe by regulation. The Register shall also prescribe regulations under which detailed cumulative annual statements of account, certified by a certified public accountant, shall be filed for every compulsory license under this section. The regulations covering both the monthly and the annual statements of account shall prescribe the form, content, and manner of certification with respect to the number of records made and the number of records distributed.

(4) If the copyright owner does not receive the monthly payment and the monthly and annual statements of account when due, the owner may give written notice to the licensee that, unless the default is remedied within thirty days from the date of the notice, the compulsory license will be automatically terminated. Such termination renders either the making or the distribution, or both, of all phonorecords for which the royalty has not been paid, actionable as acts of infringement under section 501 and fully subject to the remedies provided by sections 502 through 506 and 509.

17 USC 116.

§ 116. Scope of exclusive rights in nondramatic musical works: Public performances by means of coin-operated phono-record players

(a) LIMITATION ON EXCLUSIVE RIGHT.—In the case of a nondramatic musical work embodied in a phonorecord, the exclusive right under clause (4) of section 106 to perform the work publicly by means of a coin-operated phonorecord player is limited as follows:

(1) The proprietor of the establishment in which the public performance takes place is not liable for infringement with respect to such public performance unless—

(A) such proprietor is the operator of the phonorecord player; or

(B) such proprietor refuses or fails, within one month after receipt by registered or certified mail of a request, at a time during which the certificate required by clause (1)(C) of subsection (b) is not affixed to the phonorecord player, by the copyright owner, to make full disclosure, by registered or certified mail, of the identity of the operator of the phonorecord player.

(2) The operator of the coin-operated phonorecord player may obtain a compulsory license to perform the work publicly on that phonorecord player by filing the application, affixing the certificate, and paying the royalties provided by subsection (b).

(b) RECORDATION OF COIN-OPERATED PHONORECORD PLAYER, AFFIXATION OF CERTIFICATE, AND ROYALTY PAYABLE UNDER COMPULSORY LICENSE.—

214

(1) Any operator who wishes to obtain a compulsory license for the public performance of works on a coin-operated phonorecord player shall fulfill the following requirements:

(A) Before or within one month after such performances are made available on a particular phonorecord player, and during the month of January in each succeeding year that such performances are made available on that particular phonorecord player, the operator shall file in the Copyright Office, in accordance with requirements that the Register of Copyrights, after consultation with the Copyright Royalty Tribunal (if and when the Tribunal has been constituted), shall prescribe by regulation, an application containing the name and address of the operator of the phonorecord player and the manufacturer and serial number or other explicit identification of the phonorecord player, and deposit with the Register of Copyrights a royalty fee for the current calendar year of $8 for that particular phonorecord player. If such performances are made available on a particular phonorecord player for the first time after July 1 of any year, the royalty fee to be deposited for the remainder of that year shall be $4.

(B) Within twenty days of receipt of an application and a royalty fee pursuant to subclause (A), the Register of Copyrights shall issue to the applicant a certificate for the phonorecord player.

(C) On or before March 1 of the year in which the certificate prescribed by subclause (B) of this clause is issued, or within ten days after the date of issue of the certificate, the operator shall affix to the particular phonorecord player, in a position where it can be readily examined by the public, the certificate, issued by the Register of Copyrights under subclause (B), of the latest application made by such operator under subclause (A) of this clause with respect to that phonorecord player.

(2) Failure to file the application, to affix the certificate, or to pay the royalty required by clause (1) of this subsection renders the public performance actionable as an act of infringement under section 501 and fully subject to the remedies provided by sections 502 through 506 and 509.

(c) DISTRIBUTION OF ROYALTIES.—

(1) The Register of Copyrights shall receive all fees deposited under this section and, after deducting the reasonable costs incurred by the Copyright Office under this section, shall deposit the balance in the Treasury of the United States, in such manner as the Secretary of the Treasury directs. All funds held by the Secretary of the Treasury shall be invested in interest-bearing United States securities for later distribution with interest by the Copyright Royalty Tribunal as provided by this title. The Register shall submit to the Copyright Royalty Tribunal, on an annual basis, a detailed statement of account covering all fees received for the relevant period provided by subsection (b).

Statements of account, submittal to Copyright Royalty Tribunal. Claims.

(2) During the month of January in each year, every person claiming to be entitled to compulsory license fees under this section for performances during the preceding twelve-month period shall file a claim with the Copyright Royalty Tribunal, in accordance with requirements that the Tribunal shall prescribe by regulation. Such claim shall include an agreement to accept as final,

except as provided in section 810 of this title, the determination of the Copyright Royalty Tribunal in any controversy concerning the distribution of royalty fees deposited under subclause (A) of subsection (b)(1) of this section to which the claimant is a party. Notwithstanding any provisions of the antitrust laws, for purposes of this subsection any claimants may agree among themselves as to the proportionate division of compulsory licensing fees among them, may lump their claims together and file them jointly or as a single claim, or may designate a common agent to receive payment on their behalf.

(3) After the first day of October of each year, the Copyright Royalty Tribunal shall determine whether there exists a controversy concerning the distribution of royalty fees deposited under subclause (A) of subsection (b)(1). If the Tribunal determines that no such controversy exists, it shall, after deducting its reasonable administrative costs under this section, distribute such fees to the copyright owners entitled, or to their designated agents. If it finds that such a controversy exists, it shall, pursuant to chapter 8 of this title, conduct a proceeding to determine the distribution of royalty fees.

Distribution procedures.

(4) The fees to be distributed shall be divided as follows:

(A) to every copyright owner not affiliated with a performing rights society, the pro rata share of the fees to be distributed to which such copyright owner proves entitlement.

(B) to the performing rights societies, the remainder of the fees to be distributed in such pro rata shares as they shall by agreement stipulate among themselves, or, if they fail to agree, the pro rata share to which such performing rights societies prove entitlement.

(C) during the pendency of any proceeding under this section, the Copyright Royalty Tribunal shall withhold from distribution an amount sufficient to satisfy all claims with respect to which a controversy exists, but shall have discretion to proceed to distribute any amounts that are not in controversy.

Regulations.

(5) The Copyright Royalty Tribunal shall promulgate regulations under which persons who can reasonably be expected to have claims may, during the year in which performances take place, without expense to or harassment of operators or proprietors of establishments in which phonorecord players are located, have such access to such establishments and to the phonorecord players located therein and such opportunity to obtain information with respect thereto as may be reasonably necessary to determine, by sampling procedures or otherwise, the proportion of contribution of the musical works of each such person to the earnings of the phonorecord players for which fees shall have been deposited.

Civil action.

Any person who alleges that he or she has been denied the access permitted under the regulations prescribed by the Copyright Royalty Tribunal may bring an action in the United States District Court for the District of Columbia for the cancellation of the compulsory license of the phonorecord player to which such access has been denied, and the court shall have the power to declare the compulsory license thereof invalid from the date of issue thereof.

(d) CRIMINAL PENALTIES.—Any person who knowingly makes a false representation of a material fact in an application filed under clause (1)(A) of subsection (b), or who knowingly alters a certificate issued under clause (1)(B) of subsection (b) or knowingly affixes such a certificate to a phonorecord player other than the one it covers, shall be fined not more than $2,500.

(e) DEFINITIONS.—As used in this section, the following terms and their variant forms mean the following:

(1) A "coin-operated phonorecord player" is a machine or device that—

(A) is employed solely for the performance of nondramatic musical works by means of phonorecords upon being activated by insertion of coins, currency, tokens, or other monetary units or their equivalent;

(B) is located in an establishment making no direct or indirect charge for admission;

(C) is accompanied by a list of the titles of all the musical works available for performance on it, which list is affixed to the phonorecord player or posted in the establishment in a prominent position where it can be readily examined by the public; and

(D) affords a choice of works available for performance and permits the choice to be made by the patrons of the establishment in which it is located.

(2) An "operator" is any person who, alone or jointly with others:

(A) owns a coin-operated phonorecord player; or

(B) has the power to make a coin-operated phonorecord player available for placement in an establishment for purposes of public performance; or

(C) has the power to exercise primary control over the selection of the musical works made available for public performance on a coin-operated phonorecord player.

(3) A "performing rights society" is an association or corporation that licenses the public performance of nondramatic musical works on behalf of the copyright owners, such as the American Society of Composers, Authors and Publishers, Broadcast Music, Inc., and SESAC, Inc.

§ 117. Scope of exclusive rights: Use in conjunction with computers and similar information systems

17 USC 117.

Notwithstanding the provisions of sections 106 through 116 and 118, this title does not afford to the owner of copyright in a work any greater or lesser rights with respect to the use of the work in conjunction with automatic systems capable of storing, processing, retrieving, or transferring information, or in conjunction with any similar device, machine, or process, than those afforded to works under the law, whether title 17 or the common law or statutes of a State, in effect on December 31, 1977, as held applicable and construed by a court in an action brought under this title.

§ 118. Scope of exclusive rights: Use of certain works in connection with noncommercial broadcasting

17 USC 118.

(a) The exclusive rights provided by section 106 shall, with respect to the works specified by subsection (b) and the activities specified by subsection (d), be subject to the conditions and limitations prescribed by this section.

(b) Not later than thirty days after the Copyright Royalty Tribunal has been constituted in accordance with section 802, the Chairman of the Tribunal shall cause notice to be published in the Federal Register of the initiation of proceedings for the purpose of determining reasonable terms and rates of royalty payments for the activities specified by subsection (d) with respect to published nondramatic

Notice, publication in Federal Register.

217

musical works and published pictorial, graphic, and sculptural works during a period beginning as provided in clause (3) of this subsection and ending on December 31, 1982. Copyright owners and public broadcasting entities shall negotiate in good faith and cooperate fully with the Tribunal in an effort to reach reasonable and expeditious results. Notwithstanding any provision of the antitrust laws, any owners of copyright in works specified by this subsection and any public broadcasting entities, respectively, may negotiate and agree upon the terms and rates of royalty payments and the proportionate division of fees paid among various copyright owners, and may designate common agents to negotiate, agree to, pay, or receive payments.

(1) Any owner of copyright in a work specified in this subsection or any public broadcasting entity may, within one hundred and twenty days after publication of the notice specified in this subsection, submit to the Copyright Royalty Tribunal proposed licenses covering such activities with respect to such works. The Copyright Royalty Tribunal shall proceed on the basis of the proposals submitted to it as well as any other relevant information. The Copyright Royalty Tribunal shall permit any interested party to submit information relevant to such proceedings.

(2) License agreements voluntarily negotiated at any time between one or more copyright owners and one or more public broadcasting entities shall be given effect in lieu of any determination by the Tribunal: *Provided*, That copies of such agreements are filed in the Copyright Office within thirty days of execution in accordance with regulations that the Register of Copyrights shall prescribe.

Rates and terms, publication in Federal Register.

(3) Within six months, but not earlier than one hundred and twenty days, from the date of publication of the notice specified in this subsection the Copyright Royalty Tribunal shall make a determination and publish in the Federal Register a schedule of rates and terms which, subject to clause (2) of this subsection, shall be binding on all owners of copyright in works specified by this subsection and public broadcasting entities, regardless of whether or not such copyright owners and public broadcasting entities have submitted proposals to the Tribunal. In establishing such rates and terms the Copyright Royalty Tribunal may consider the rates for comparable circumstances under voluntary license agreements negotiated as provided in clause (2) of this subsection. The Copyright Royalty Tribunal shall also establish requirements by which copyright owners may receive reasonable notice of the use of their works under this section, and under which records of such use shall be kept by public broadcasting entities.

(4) With respect to the period beginning on the effective date of this title and ending on the date of publication of such rates and terms, this title shall not afford to owners of copyright or public broadcasting entities any greater or lesser rights with respect to the activities specified in subsection (d) as applied to works specified in this subsection than those afforded under the law in effect on December 31, 1977, as held applicable and construed by a court in an action brought under this title.

(c) The initial procedure specified in subsection (b) shall be repeated and concluded between June 30 and December 31, 1982, and at five-year intervals thereafter, in accordance with regulations that the Copyright Royalty Tribunal shall prescribe.

(d) Subject to the transitional provisions of subsection (b) (4), and to the terms of any voluntary license agreements that have been negotiated as provided by subsection (b) (2), a public broadcasting entity may, upon compliance with the provisions of this section, including the rates and terms established by the Copyright Royalty Tribunal under subsection (b) (3), engage in the following activities with respect to published nondramatic musical works and published pictorial, graphic, and sculptural works:

(1) performance or display of a work by or in the course of a transmission made by a noncommercial educational broadcast station referred to in subsection (g) ; and

(2) production of a transmission program, reproduction of copies or phonorecords of such a transmission program, and distribution of such copies or phonorecords, where such production, reproduction, or distribution is made by a nonprofit institution or organization solely for the purpose of transmissions specified in clause (1) ; and

(3) the making of reproductions by a governmental body or a nonprofit institution of a transmission program simultaneously with its transmission as specified in clause (1), and the performance or display of the contents of such program under the conditions specified by clause (1) of section 110, but only if the reproductions are used for performances or displays for a period of no more than seven days from the date of the transmission specified in clause (1), and are destroyed before or at the end of such period. No person supplying, in accordance with clause (2), a reproduction of a transmission program to governmental bodies or nonprofit institutions under this clause shall have any liability as a result of failure of such body or institution to destroy such reproduction: *Provided,* That it shall have notified such body or institution of the requirement for such destruction pursuant to this clause: *And provided further,* That if such body or institution itself fails to destroy such reproduction it shall be deemed to have infringed.

(e) Except as expressly provided in this subsection, this section shall have no applicability to works other than those specified in subsection (b).

(1) Owners of copyright in nondramatic literary works and public broadcasting entities may, during the course of voluntary negotiations, agree among themselves, respectively, as to the terms and rates of royalty payments without liability under the antitrust laws. Any such terms and rates of royalty payments shall be effective upon filing in the Copyright Office, in accordance with regulations that the Register of Copyrights shall prescribe.

(2) On January 3, 1980, the Register of Copyrights, after consulting with authors and other owners of copyright in nondramatic literary works and their representatives, and with public broadcasting entities and their representatives, shall submit to the Congress a report setting forth the extent to which voluntary licensing arrangements have been reached with respect to the use of nondramatic literary works by such broadcast stations. The report should also describe any problems that may have arisen, and present legislative or other recommendations, if warranted. **Report to Congress.**

(f) Nothing in this section shall be construed to permit, beyond the limits of fair use as provided by section 107, the unauthorized dramatization of a nondramatic musical work, the production of a transmission program drawn to any substantial extent from a published compilation of pictorial, graphic, or sculptural works, or the unauthorized use of any portion of an audiovisual work.

"Public broadcasting entity."

47 USC 397.

(g) As used in this section, the term "public broadcasting entity" means a noncommercial educational broadcast station as defined in section 397 of title 47 and any nonprofit institution or organization engaged in the activities described in clause (2) of subsection (d).

Chapter 2.—COPYRIGHT OWNERSHIP AND TRANSFER

17 USC 201.

§ 201. Ownership of copyright

(a) INITIAL OWNERSHIP.—Copyright in a work protected under this title vests initially in the author or authors of the work. The authors of a joint work are coowners of copyright in the work.

(b) WORKS MADE FOR HIRE.—In the case of a work made for hire, the employer or other person for whom the work was prepared is considered the author for purposes of this title, and, unless the parties have expressly agreed otherwise in a written instrument signed by them, owns all of the rights comprised in the copyright.

(c) CONTRIBUTIONS TO COLLECTIVE WORKS.—Copyright in each separate contribution to a collective work is distinct from copyright in the collective work as a whole, and vests initially in the author of the contribution. In the absence of an express transfer of the copyright or of any rights under it, the owner of copyright in the collective work is presumed to have acquired only the privilege of reproducing and distributing the contribution as part of that particular collective work, any revision of that collective work, and any later collective work in the same series.

(d) TRANSFER OF OWNERSHIP.—

(1) The ownership of a copyright may be transferred in whole or in part by any means of conveyance or by operation of law, and may be bequeathed by will or pass as personal property by the applicable laws of intestate succession.

(2) Any of the exclusive rights comprised in a copyright, including any subdivision of any of the rights specified by section 106, may be transferred as provided by clause (1) and owned separately. The owner of any particular exclusive right is entitled, to the extent of that right, to all of the protection and remedies accorded to the copyright owner by this title.

(e) INVOLUNTARY TRANSFER.—When an individual author's ownership of a copyright, or of any of the exclusive rights under a copyright, has not previously been transferred voluntarily by that individual author, no action by any governmental body or other official or organization purporting to seize, expropriate, transfer, or exercise rights of ownership with respect to the copyright, or any of the exclusive rights under a copyright, shall be given effect under this title.

17 USC 202.

§ 202. Ownership of copyright as distinct from ownership of material object

Ownership of a copyright, or of any of the exclusive rights under a copyright, is distinct from ownership of any material object in which the work is embodied. Transfer of ownership of any material object, including the copy or phonorecord in which the work is first fixed, does not of itself convey any rights in the copyrighted work embodied in the object; nor, in the absence of an agreement, does transfer of ownership of a copyright or of any exclusive rights under a copyright convey property rights in any material object.

§ 203. Termination of transfers and licenses granted by the author

17 USC 203.

(a) CONDITIONS FOR TERMINATION.—In the case of any work other than a work made for hire, the exclusive or nonexclusive grant of a transfer or license of copyright or of any right under a copyright, executed by the author on or after January 1, 1978, otherwise than by will, is subject to termination under the following conditions:

(1) In the case of a grant executed by one author, termination of the grant may be effected by that author or, if the author is dead, by the person or persons who, under clause (2) of this subsection, own and are entitled to exercise a total of more than one-half of that author's termination interest. In the case of a grant executed by two or more authors of a joint work, termination of the grant may be effected by a majority of the authors who executed it; if any of such authors is dead, the termination interest of any such author may be exercised as a unit by the person or persons who, under clause (2) of this subsection, own and are entitled to exercise a total of more than one-half of that author's interest.

(2) Where an author is dead, his or her termination interest is owned, and may be exercised, by his widow or her widower and his or her children or grandchildren as follows:

(A) the widow or widower owns the author's entire termination interest unless there are any surviving children or grandchildren of the author, in which case the widow or widower owns one-half of the author's interest;

(B) the author's surviving children, and the surviving children of any dead child of the author, own the author's entire termination interest unless there is a widow or widower, in which case the ownership of one-half of the author's interest is divided among them;

(C) the rights of the author's children and grandchildren are in all cases divided among them and exercised on a per stirpes basis according to the number of such author's children represented; the share of the children of a dead child in a termination interest can be exercised only by the action of a majority of them.

(3) Termination of the grant may be effected at any time during a period of five years beginning at the end of thirty-five years from the date of execution of the grant; or, if the grant covers the right of publication of the work, the period begins at the end of thirty-five years from the date of publication of the work under the grant or at the end of forty years from the date of execution of the grant, whichever term ends earlier.

(4) The termination shall be effected by serving an advance notice in writing, signed by the number and proportion of owners of termination interests required under clauses (1) and (2) of this subsection, or by their duly authorized agents, upon the grantee or the grantee's successor in title.

Notice.

(A) The notice shall state the effective date of the termination, which shall fall within the five-year period specified by clause (3) of this subsection, and the notice shall be served not less than two or more than ten years before that date. A copy of the notice shall be recorded in the Copyright Office before the effective date of termination, as a condition to its taking effect.

(B) The notice shall comply, in form, content, and manner of service, with requirements that the Register of Copyrights shall prescribe by regulation.

(5) Termination of the grant may be effected notwithstanding any agreement to the contrary, including an agreement to make a will or to make any future grant.

(b) EFFECT OF TERMINATION.—Upon the effective date of termination, all rights under this title that were covered by the terminated grants revert to the author, authors, and other persons owning termination interests under clauses (1) and (2) of subsection (a), including those owners who did not join in signing the notice of termination under clause (4) of subsection (a), but with the following limitations:

Limitations.

(1) A derivative work prepared under authority of the grant before its termination may continue to be utilized under the terms of the grant after its termination, but this privilege does not extend to the preparation after the termination of other derivative works based upon the copyrighted work covered by the terminated grant.

(2) The future rights that will revert upon termination of the grant become vested on the date the notice of termination has been served as provided by clause (4) of subsection (a). The rights vest in the author, authors, and other persons named in, and in the proportionate shares provided by, clauses (1) and (2) of subsection (a).

(3) Subject to the provisions of clause (4) of this subsection, a further grant, or agreement to make a further grant, of any right covered by a terminated grant is valid only if it is signed by the same number and proportion of the owners, in whom the right has vested under clause (2) of this subsection, as are required to terminate the grant under clauses (1) and (2) of subsection (a). Such further grant or agreement is effective with respect to all of the persons in whom the right it covers has vested under clause (2) of this subsection, including those who did not join in signing it. If any person dies after rights under a terminated grant have vested in him or her, that person's legal representatives, legatees, or heirs at law represent him or her for purposes of this clause.

(4) A further grant, or agreement to make a further grant, of any right covered by a terminated grant is valid only if it is made after the effective date of the termination. As an exception, however, an agreement for such a further grant may be made between the persons provided by clause (3) of this subsection and the original grantee or such grantee's successor in title, after the notice of termination has been served as provided by clause (4) of subsection (a).

(5) Termination of a grant under this section affects only those rights covered by the grants that arise under this title, and in no way affects rights arising under any other Federal, State, or foreign laws.

(6) Unless and until termination is effected under this section, the grant, if it does not provide otherwise, continues in effect for the term of copyright provided by this title.

17 USC 204.

§ 204. Execution of transfers of copyright ownership

(a) A transfer of copyright ownership, other than by operation of law, is not valid unless an instrument of conveyance, or a note or memorandum of the transfer, is in writing and signed by the owner of the rights conveyed or such owner's duly authorized agent.

(b) A certificate of acknowledgement is not required for the validity of a transfer, but is prima facie evidence of the execution of the transfer if—

(1) in the case of a transfer executed in the United States, the certificate is issued by a person authorized to administer oaths within the United States; or

(2) in the case of a transfer executed in a foreign country, the certificate is issued by a diplomatic or consular officer of the United States, or by a person authorized to administer oaths whose authority is proved by a certificate of such an officer.

§ 205. Recordation of transfers and other documents

17 USC 205.

(a) CONDITIONS FOR RECORDATION.—Any transfer of copyright ownership or other document pertaining to a copyright may be recorded in the Copyright Office if the document filed for recordation bears the actual signature of the person who executed it, or if it is accompanied by a sworn or official certification that it is a true copy of the original, signed document.

(b) CERTIFICATE OF RECORDATION.—The Register of Copyrights shall, upon receipt of a document as provided by subsection (a) and of the fee provided by section 708, record the document and return it with a certificate of recordation.

(c) RECORDATION AS CONSTRUCTIVE NOTICE.—Recordation of a document in the Copyright Office gives all persons constructive notice of the facts stated in the recorded document, but only if—

(1) the document, or material attached to it, specifically identifies the work to which it pertains so that, after the document is indexed by the Register of Copyrights, it would be revealed by a reasonable search under the title or registration number of the work; and

(2) registration has been made for the work.

(d) RECORDATION AS PREREQUISITE TO INFRINGEMENT SUIT.—No person claiming by virtue of a transfer to be the owner of copyright or of any exclusive right under a copyright is entitled to institute an infringement action under this title until the instrument of transfer under which such person claims has been recorded in the Copyright Office, but suit may be instituted after such recordation on a cause of action that arose before recordation.

(e) PRIORITY BETWEEN CONFLICTING TRANSFERS.—As between two conflicting transfers, the one executed first prevails if it is recorded, in the manner required to give constructive notice under subsection (c), within one month after its execution in the United States or within two months after its execution outside the United States, or at any time before recordation in such manner of the later transfer. Otherwise the later transfer prevails if recorded first in such manner, and if taken in good faith, for valuable consideration or on the basis of a binding promise to pay royalties, and without notice of the earlier transfer.

(f) PRIORITY BETWEEN CONFLICTING TRANSFER OF OWNERSHIP AND NONEXCLUSIVE LICENSE.—A nonexclusive license, whether recorded or not, prevails over a conflicting transfer of copyright ownership if the license is evidenced by a written instrument signed by the owner of the rights licensed or such owner's duly authorized agent, and if—

(1) the license was taken before execution of the transfer; or

(2) the license was taken in good faith before recordation of the transfer and without notice of it.

Chapter 3.—DURATION OF COPYRIGHT

17 USC 301.

§ 301. Preemption with respect to other laws

(a) On and after January 1, 1978, all legal or equitable rights that are equivalent to any of the exclusive rights within the general scope of copyright as specified by section 106 in works of authorship that are fixed in a tangible medium of expression and come within the subject matter of copyright as specified by sections 102 and 103, whether created before or after that date and whether published or unpublished, are governed exclusively by this title. Thereafter, no person is entitled to any such right or equivalent right in any such work under the common law or statutes of any State.

(b) Nothing in this title annuls or limits any rights or remedies under the common law or statutes of any State with respect to—

(1) subject matter that does not come within the subject matter of copyright as specified by sections 102 and 103, including works of authorship not fixed in any tangible medium of expression; or

(2) any cause of action arising from undertakings commenced before January 1, 1978; or

(3) activities violating legal or equitable rights that are not equivalent to any of the exclusive rights within the general scope of copyright as specified by section 106.

(c) With respect to sound recordings fixed before February 15, 1972, any rights or remedies under the common law or statutes of any State shall not be annulled or limited by this title until February 15, 2047. The preemptive provisions of subsection (a) shall apply to any such rights and remedies pertaining to any cause of action arising from undertakings commenced on and after February 15, 2047. Notwithstanding the provisions of section 303, no sound recording fixed before February 15, 1972, shall be subject to copyright under this title before, on, or after February 15, 2047.

(d) Nothing in this title annuls or limits any rights or remedies under any other Federal statute.

17 USC 302.

§ 302. Duration of copyright: Works created on or after January 1, 1978

(a) IN GENERAL.—Copyright in a work created on or after January 1, 1978, subsists from its creation and, except as provided by the following subsections, endures for a term consisting of the life of the author and fifty years after the author's death.

(b) JOINT WORKS.—In the case of a joint work prepared by two or more authors who did not work for hire, the copyright endures for a term consisting of the life of the last surviving author and fifty years after such last surviving author's death.

(c) ANONYMOUS WORKS, PSEUDONYMOUS WORKS, AND WORKS MADE FOR HIRE.—In the case of an anonymous work, a pseudonymous work, or a work made for hire, the copyright endures for a term of seventy-five years from the year of its first publication, or a term of one hundred years from the year of its creation, whichever expires first. If, before the end of such term, the identity of one or more of the authors of an anonymous or pseudonymous work is revealed in the records of a registration made for that work under subsections (a) or (d) of section 408, or in the records provided by this subsection, the copyright in the work endures for the term specified by subsection (a) or (b), based on the life of the author or authors whose identity has been revealed. Any person having an interest in the copyright in an anonymous or pseudonymous work may at any time record, in records to be maintained by the Copyright Office for that purpose, a statement identifying one or more authors of the work; the statement shall also identify the person filing it, the nature of that person's interest, the source of the information recorded, and the particular work affected, and shall comply in form and content with requirements that the Register of Copyrights shall prescribe by regulation.

(d) RECORDS RELATING TO DEATH OF AUTHORS.—Any person having an interest in a copyright may at any time record in the Copyright Office a statement of the date of death of the author of the copyrighted work, or a statement that the author is still living on a particular date. The statement shall identify the person filing it, the nature of that person's interest, and the source of the information recorded, and shall comply in form and content with requirements that the Register of Copyrights shall prescribe by regulation. The Register shall maintain current records of information relating to the death of authors of copyrighted works, based on such recorded statements and, to the extent the Register considers practicable, on data contained in any of the records of the Copyright Office or in other reference sources. Recordkeeping.

(e) PRESUMPTION AS TO AUTHOR'S DEATH.—After a period of seventy-five years from the year of first publication of a work, or a period of one hundred years from the year of its creation, whichever expires first, any person who obtains from the Copyright Office a certified report that the records provided by subsection (d) disclose nothing to indicate that the author of the work is living, or died less than fifty years before, is entitled to the benefit of a presumption that the author has been dead for at least fifty years. Reliance in good faith upon this presumption shall be a complete defense to any action for infringement under this title.

§ 303. Duration of copyright: Works created but not published or copyrighted before January 1, 1978
17 USC 303.

Copyright in a work created before January 1, 1978, but not theretofore in the public domain or copyrighted, subsists from January 1, 1978, and endures for the term provided by section 302. In no case, however, shall the term of copyright in such a work expire before December 31, 2002; and, if the work is published on or before December 31, 2002, the term of copyright shall not expire before December 31, 2027.

§ 304. Duration of copyright: Subsisting copyrights
17 USC 304.

(a) COPYRIGHTS IN THEIR FIRST TERM ON JANUARY 1, 1978.—Any copyright, the first term of which is subsisting on January 1, 1978, shall endure for twenty-eight years from the date it was originally secured: *Provided,* That in the case of any posthumous work or of any periodical, cyclopedic, or other composite work upon which the copyright was originally secured by the proprietor thereof, or of any work copyrighted by a corporate body (otherwise than as assignee or licensee of the individual author) or by an employer for whom such work is made for hire, the proprietor of such copyright shall be entitled to a renewal and extension of the copyright in such work for the further term of forty-seven years when application for such renewal and extension shall have been made to the Copyright Office and duly registered therein within one year prior to the expiration of the original term of copyright: *And provided further,* That in the case of any other copyrighted work, including a contribution by an individual author to a periodical or to a cyclopedic or other composite work, the author of such work, if still living, or the widow, widower, or children of the author, if the author be not living, or if such author, widow, widower, or children be not living, then the author's executors, or in the absence of a will, his or her next of kin shall be entitled to a renewal and extension of the copyright in such work for a further term of forty-seven years when application for such renewal and extension shall have been made to the Copyright Office and duly registered therein within one year prior to the expiration of the original term of copyright: *And provided further*, That in default of the registration of such application for renewal and extension, the copyright in any work shall terminate at the expiration of twenty-eight years from the date copyright was originally secured.

(b) COPYRIGHTS IN THEIR RENEWAL TERM OR REGISTERED FOR RENEWAL BEFORE JANUARY 1, 1978.—The duration of any copyright, the renewal term of which is subsisting at any time between December 31, 1976, and December 31, 1977, inclusive, or for which renewal registration is made between December 31, 1976, and December 31, 1977, inclusive, is extended to endure for a term of seventy-five years from the date copyright was originally secured.

(c) TERMINATION OF TRANSFERS AND LICENSES COVERING EXTENDED RENEWAL TERM.—In the case of any copyright subsisting in either its first or renewal term on January 1, 1978, other than a copyright in a work made for hire, the exclusive or nonexclusive grant of a transfer or license of the renewal copyright or any right under it, executed before January 1, 1978, by any of the persons designated by the second proviso of subsection (a) of this section, otherwise than by will, is subject to termination under the following conditions:

(1) In the case of a grant executed by a person or persons other than the author, termination of the grant may be effected by the surviving person or persons who executed it. In the case of a grant executed by one or more of the authors of the work, termination of the grant may be effected, to the extent of a particular author's share in the ownership of the renewal copyright, by the author who executed it or, if such author is dead, by the person or persons who, under clause (2) of this subsection, own and are entitled to exercise a total of more than one-half of that author's termination interest.

(2) Where an author is dead, his or her termination interest is owned, and may be exercised, by his widow or her widower and his or her children or grandchildren as follows:

(A) the widow or widower owns the author's entire termination interest unless there are any surviving children or grandchildren of the author, in which case the widow or widower owns one-half of the author's interest;

(B) the author's surviving children, and the surviving children of any dead child of the author, own the author's entire termination interest unless there is a widow or widower, in which case the ownership of one-half of the author's interest is divided among them;

(C) the rights of the author's children and grandchildren are in all cases divided among them and exercised on a per stirpes basis according to the number of such author's children represented; the share of the children of a dead child in a termination interest can be exercised only by the action of a majority of them.

(3) Termination of the grant may be effected at any time during a period of five years beginning at the end of fifty-six years from the date copyright was originally secured, or beginning on January 1, 1978, whichever is later.

(4) The termination shall be effected by serving an advance notice in writing upon the grantee or the grantee's successor in title. In the case of a grant executed by a person or persons other than the author, the notice shall be signed by all of those entitled to terminate the grant under clause (1) of this subsection, or by their duly authorized agents. In the case of a grant executed by one or more of the authors of the work, the notice as to any one author's share shall be signed by that author or his or her duly authorized agent or, if that author is dead, by the number and proportion of the owners of his or her termination interest required under clauses (1) and (2) of this subsection, or by their duly authorized agents.

Advance notice.

(A) The notice shall state the effective date of the termination, which shall fall within the five-year period specified by clause (3) of this subsection, and the notice shall be served not less than two or more than ten years before that date. A copy of the notice shall be recorded in the Copyright Office before the effective date of termination, as a condition to its taking effect.

(B) The notice shall comply, in form, content, and manner of service, with requirements that the Register of Copyrights shall prescribe by regulation.

(5) Termination of the grant may be effected notwithstanding any agreement to the contrary, including an agreement to make a will or to make any future grant.

(6) In the case of a grant executed by a person or persons other than the author, all rights under this title that were covered by the terminated grant revert, upon the effective date of termination, to all of those entitled to terminate the grant under clause (1) of this subsection. In the case of a grant executed by one or more of the authors of the work, all of a particular author's rights under this title that were covered by the terminated grant revert, upon the effective date of termination, to that author or, if that author is dead, to the persons owning his or her termination interest under clause (2) of this subsection, including those owners who did not join in signing the notice of termination under clause (4) of this subsection. In all cases the reversion of rights is subject to the following limitations:

Reversion.

Limitations.

(A) A derivative work prepared under authority of the grant before its termination may continue to be utilized under the terms of the grant after its termination, but this privilege does not extend to the preparation after the termination of other derivative works based upon the copyrighted work covered by the terminated grant.

(B) The future rights that will revert upon termination of the grant become vested on the date the notice of termination has been served as provided by clause (4) of this subsection.

(C) Where the author's rights revert to two or more persons under clause (2) of this subsection, they shall vest in those persons in the proportionate shares provided by that clause. In such a case, and subject to the provisions of subclause (D) of this clause, a further grant, or agreement to make a further grant, of a particular author's share with

227

respect to any right covered by a terminated grant is valid only if it is signed by the same number and proportion of the owners, in whom the right has vested under this clause, as are required to terminate the grant under clause (2) of this subsection. Such further grant or agreement is effective with respect to all of the persons in whom the right it covers has vested under this subclause, including those who did not join in signing it. If any person dies after rights under a terminated grant have vested in him or her, that person's legal representatives, legatees, or heirs at law represent him or her for purposes of this subclause.

(D) A further grant, or agreement to make a further grant, of any right covered by a terminated grant is valid only if it is made after the effective date of the termination. As an exception, however, an agreement for such a further grant may be made between the author or any of the persons provided by the first sentence of clause (6) of this subsection, or between the persons provided by subclause (C) of this clause, and the original grantee or such grantee's successor in title, after the notice of termination has been served as provided by clause (4) of this subsection.

(E) Termination of a grant under this subsection affects only those rights covered by the grant that arise under this title, and in no way affects rights arising under any other Federal, State, or foreign laws.

(F) Unless and until termination is effected under this subsection, the grant, if it does not provide otherwise, continues in effect for the remainder of the extended renewal term.

17 USC 305.

§ 305. Duration of copyright: Terminal date

All terms of copyright provided by sections 302 through 304 run to the end of the calendar year in which they would otherwise expire.

Chapter 4.—COPYRIGHT NOTICE, DEPOSIT, AND REGISTRATION

Sec.
401. Notice of copyright: Visually perceptible copies.
402. Notice of copyright: Phonorecords of sound recordings.
403. Notice of copyright: Publications incorporating United States Government works.
404. Notice of copyright: Contributions to collective works.
405. Notice of copyright: Omission of notice.
406. Notice of copyright: Error in name or date.
407. Deposit of copies or phonorecords for Library of Congress.
408. Copyright registration in general.
409. Application for copyright registration.
410. Registration of claim and issuance of certificate.
411. Registration as prerequisite to infringement suit.
412. Registration as prerequisite to certain remedies for infringement.

17 USC 401.

§ 401. Notice of copyright: Visually perceptible copies

(a) GENERAL REQUIREMENT.—Whenever a work protected under this title is published in the United States or elsewhere by authority of the copyright owner, a notice of copyright as provided by this section shall be placed on all publicly distributed copies from which the work can be visually perceived, either directly or with the aid of a machine or device.

(b) FORM OF NOTICE.—The notice appearing on the copies shall consist of the following three elements:

(1) the symbol © (the letter C in a circle), or the word "Copyright", or the abbreviation "Copr."; and

(2) the year of first publication of the work; in the case of compilations or derivative works incorporating previously published material, the year date of first publication of the compilation or derivative work is sufficient. The year date may be omitted where a pictorial, graphic, or sculptural work, with accompanying text matter, if any, is reproduced in or on greeting cards, postcards, stationery, jewelry, dolls, toys, or any useful articles; and

(3) the name of the owner of copyright in the work, or an abbreviation by which the name can be recognized, or a generally known alternative designation of the owner.

(c) POSITION OF NOTICE.—The notice shall be affixed to the copies in such manner and location as to give reasonable notice of the claim of copyright. The Register of Copyrights shall prescribe by regulation, as examples, specific methods of affixation and positions of the notice on various types of works that will satisfy this requirement, but these specifications shall not be considered exhaustive.

§ 402. Notice of copyright: Phonorecords of sound recordings   17 USC 402.

(a) GENERAL REQUIREMENT.—Whenever a sound recording protected under this title is published in the United States or elsewhere by authority of the copyright owner, a notice of copyright as provided by this section shall be placed on all publicly distributed phonorecords of the sound recording.

(b) FORM OF NOTICE.—The notice appearing on the phonorecords shall consist of the following three elements:

(1) the symbol ℗ (the letter P in a circle); and

(2) the year of first publication of the sound recording; and

(3) the name of the owner of copyright in the sound recording, or an abbreviation by which the name can be recognized, or a generally known alternative designation of the owner; if the producer of the sound recording is named on the phonorecord labels or containers, and if no other name appears in conjunction with the notice, the producer's name shall be considered a part of the notice.

(c) POSITION OF NOTICE.—The notice shall be placed on the surface of the phonorecord, or on the phonorecord label or container, in such manner and location as to give reasonable notice of the claim of copyright.

§ 403. Notice of copyright: Publications incorporating United   17 USC 403.
States Government works

Whenever a work is published in copies or phonorecords consisting preponderantly of one or more works of the United States Government, the notice of copyright provided by sections 401 or 402 shall also include a statement identifying, either affirmatively or negatively, those portions of the copies or phonorecords embodying any work or works protected under this title.

§ 404. Notice of copyright: Contributions to collective works   17 USC 404.

(a) A separate contribution to a collective work may bear its own notice of copyright, as provided by sections 401 through 403. However, a single notice applicable to the collective work as a whole is sufficient to satisfy the requirements of sections 401 through 403 with respect to the separate contributions it contains (not including advertisements inserted on behalf of persons other than the owner of copyright in the collective work), regardless of the ownership of copyright in the contributions and whether or not they have been previously published.

(b) Where the person named in a single notice applicable to a collective work as a whole is not the owner of copyright in a separate contribution that does not bear its own notice, the case is governed by the provisions of section 406(a).

17 USC 405.

§ 405. Notice of copyright: Omission of notice

(a) EFFECT OF OMISSION ON COPYRIGHT.—The omission of the copyright notice prescribed by sections 401 through 403 from copies or phonorecords publicly distributed by authority of the copyright owner does not invalidate the copyright in a work if—

(1) the notice has been omitted from no more than a relatively small number of copies or phonorecords distributed to the public; or

(2) registration for the work has been made before or is made within five years after the publication without notice, and a reasonable effort is made to add notice to all copies or phonorecords that are distributed to the public in the United States after the omission has been discovered; or

(3) the notice has been omitted in violation of an express requirement in writing that, as a condition of the copyright owner's authorization of the public distribution of copies or phonorecords, they bear the prescribed notice.

(b) EFFECT OF OMISSION ON INNOCENT INFRINGERS.—Any person who innocently infringes a copyright, in reliance upon an authorized copy or phonorecord from which the copyright notice has been omitted, incurs no liability for actual or statutory damages under section 504 for any infringing acts committed before receiving actual notice that registration for the work has been made under section 408, if such person proves that he or she was misled by the omission of notice. In a suit for infringement in such a case the court may allow or disallow recovery of any of the infringer's profits attributable to the infringement, and may enjoin the continuation of the infringing undertaking or may require, as a condition or permitting the continuation of the infringing undertaking, that the infringer pay the copyright owner a reasonable license fee in an amount and on terms fixed by the court.

(c) REMOVAL OF NOTICE.—Protection under this title is not affected by the removal, destruction, or obliteration of the notice, without the authorization of the copyright owner, from any publicly distributed copies or phonorecords.

17 USC 406.

§ 406. Notice of copyright: Error in name or date

(a) ERROR IN NAME.—Where the person named in the copyright notice on copies or phonorecords publicly distributed by authority of the copyright owner is not the owner of copyright, the validity and ownership of the copyright are not affected. In such a case, however, any person who innocently begins an undertaking that infringes the copyright has a complete defense to any action for such infringement if such person proves that he or she was misled by the notice and began the undertaking in good faith under a purported transfer or license from the person named therein, unless before the undertaking was begun—

(1) registration for the work had been made in the name of the owner of copyright; or

(2) a document executed by the person named in the notice and showing the ownership of the copyright had been recorded.

The person named in the notice is liable to account to the copyright owner for all receipts from transfers or licenses purportedly made under the copyright by the person named in the notice.

(b) ERROR IN DATE.—When the year date in the notice on copies or phonorecords distributed by authority of the copyright owner is earlier than the year in which publication first occurred, any period

230

computed from the year of first publication under section 302 is to be computed from the year in the notice. Where the year date is more than one year later than the year in which publication first occurred, the work is considered to have been published without any notice and is governed by the provisions of section 405.

(c) OMISSION OF NAME OR DATE.—Where copies or phonorecords publicly distributed by authority of the copyright owner contain no name or no date that could reasonably be considered a part of the notice, the work is considered to have been published without any notice and is governed by the provisions of section 405.

§ 407. Deposit of copies or phonorecords for Library of Congress
17 USC 407.

(a) Except as provided by subsection (c), and subject to the provisions of subsection (e), the owner of copyright or of the exclusive right of publication in a work published with notice of copyright in the United States shall deposit, within three months after the date of such publication—

(1) two complete copies of the best edition; or

(2) if the work is a sound recording, two complete phonorecords of the best edition, together with any printed or other visually perceptible material published with such phonorecords.

Neither the deposit requirements of this subsection nor the acquisition provisions of subsection (e) are conditions of copyright protection.

(b) The required copies or phonorecords shall be deposited in the Copyright Office for the use or disposition of the Library of Congress. The Register of Copyrights shall, when requested by the depositor and upon payment of the fee prescribed by section 708, issue a receipt for the deposit.

(c) The Register of Copyrights may by regulation exempt any categories of material from the deposit requirements of this section, or require deposit of only one copy or phonorecord with respect to any categories. Such regulations shall provide either for complete exemption from the deposit requirements of this section, or for alternative forms of deposit aimed at providing a satisfactory archival record of a work without imposing practical or financial hardships on the depositor, where the individual author is the owner of copyright in a pictorial, graphic, or sculptural work and (i) less than five copies of the work have been published, or (ii) the work has been published in a limited edition consisting of numbered copies, the monetary value of which would make the mandatory deposit of two copies of the best edition of the work burdensome, unfair, or unreasonable.

Exemption.

(d) At any time after publication of a work as provided by subsection (a), the Register of Copyrights may make written demand for the required deposit on any of the persons obligated to make the deposit under subsection (a). Unless deposit is made within three months after the demand is received, the person or persons on whom the demand was made are liable—

Penalties.

(1) to a fine of not more than $250 for each work; and

(2) to pay into a specially designated fund in the Library of Congress the total retail price of the copies or phonorecords demanded, or, if no retail price has been fixed, the reasonable cost of the Library of Congress of acquiring them; and

(3) to pay a fine of $2,500, in addition to any fine or liability imposed under clauses (1) and (2), if such person willfully or repeatedly fails or refuses to comply with such a demand.

(e) With respect to transmission programs that have been fixed and transmitted to the public in the United States but have not been published, the Register of Copyrights shall, after consulting with the Librarian of Congress and other interested organizations and officials,

Regulations.

establish regulations governing the acquisition, through deposit or otherwise, of copies or phonorecords of such programs for the collections of the Library of Congress.

(1) The Librarian of Congress shall be permitted, under the standards and conditions set forth in such regulations, to make a fixation of a transmission program directly from a transmission to the public, and to reproduce one copy or phonorecord from such fixation for archival purposes.

(2) Such regulations shall also provide standards and procedures by which the Register of Copyrights may make written demand, upon the owner of the right of transmission in the United States, for the deposit of a copy or phonorecord of a specific transmission program. Such deposit may, at the option of the owner of the right of transmission in the United States, be accomplished by gift, by loan for purposes of reproduction, or by sale at a price not to exceed the cost of reproducing and supplying the copy or phonorecord. The regulations established under this clause shall provide reasonable periods of not less than three months for compliance with a demand, and shall allow for extensions of such periods and adjustments in the scope of the demand or the methods for fulfilling it, as reasonably warranted by the circumstances. Willful failure or refusal to comply with the conditions prescribed by such regulations shall subject the owner of the right of transmission in the United States to liability for an amount, not to exceed the cost of reproducing and supplying the copy or phonorecord in question, to be paid into a specially designated fund in the Library of Congress.

(3) Nothing in this subsection shall be construed to require the making or retention, for purposes of deposit, of any copy or phonorecord of an unpublished transmission program, the transmission of which occurs before the receipt of a specific written demand as provided by clause (2).

(4) No activity undertaken in compliance with regulations prescribed under clauses (1) or (2) of this subsection shall result in liability if intended solely to assist in the acquisition of copies or phonorecords under this subsection.

17 USC 408.

§ 408. **Copyright registration in general**

(a) REGISTRATION PERMISSIVE.—At any time during the subsistence of copyright in any published or unpublished work, the owner of copyright or of any exclusive right in the work may obtain registration of the copyright claim by delivering to the Copyright Office the deposit specified by this section, together with the application and fee specified by sections 409 and 708. Subject to the provisions of section 405(a), such registration is not a condition of copyright protection.

(b) DEPOSIT FOR COPYRIGHT REGISTRATION.—Except as provided by subsection (c), the material deposited for registration shall include—

(1) in the case of an unpublished work, one complete copy or phonorecord;

(2) in the case of a published work, two complete copies or phonorecords of the best edition;

(3) in the case of a work first published outside the United States, one complete copy or phonorecord as so published;

(4) in the case of a contribution to a collective work, one complete copy or phonorecord of the best edition of the collective work.

Copies or phonorecords deposited for the Library of Congress under section 407 may be used to satisfy the deposit provisions of this section, if they are accompanied by the prescribed application and fee, and by any additional identifying material that the Register may, by regulation, require. The Register shall also prescribe regulations establishing requirements under which copies or phonorecords acquired for the Library of Congress under subsection (e) of section 407, otherwise than by deposit, may be used to satisfy the deposit provisions of this section. Regulations.

(c) ADMINISTRATIVE CLASSIFICATION AND OPTIONAL DEPOSIT.—

(1) The Register of Copyrights is authorized to specify by regulation the administrative classes into which works are to be placed for purposes of deposit and registration, and the nature of the copies or phonorecords to be deposited in the various classes specified. The regulations may require or permit, for particular classes, the deposit of identifying material instead of copies or phonorecords, the deposit of only one copy or phonorecord where two would normally be required, or a single registration for a group of related works. This administrative classification of works has no significance with respect to the subject matter of copyright or the exclusive rights provided by this title.

(2) Without prejudice to the general authority provided under clause (1), the Register of Copyrights shall establish regulations specifically permitting a single registration for a group of works by the same individual author, all first published as contributions to periodicals, including newspapers, within a twelve-month period, on the basis of a single deposit, application, and registration fee, under all of the following conditions— Regulations.

(A) if each of the works as first published bore a separate copyright notice, and the name of the owner of copyright in the work, or an abbreviation by which the name can be recognized, or a generally known alternative designation of the owner was the same in each notice; and

(B) if the deposit consists of one copy of the entire issue of the periodical, or of the entire section in the case of a newspaper, in which each contribution was first published; and

(C) if the application identifies each work separately, including the periodical containing it and its date of first publication.

(3) As an alternative to separate renewal registrations under subsection (a) of section 304, a single renewal registration may be made for a group of works by the same individual author, all first published as contributions to periodicals, including newspapers, upon the filing of a single application and fee, under all of the following conditions:

(A) the renewal claimant or claimants, and the basis of claim or claims under section 304(a), is the same for each of the works; and

(B) the works were all copyrighted upon their first publication, either through separate copyright notice and registration or by virtue of a general copyright notice in the periodical issue as a whole; and

(C) the renewal application and fee are received not more than twenty-eight or less than twenty-seven years after the thirty-first day of December of the calendar year in which all of the works were first published; and

(D) the renewal application identifies each work separately, including the periodical containing it and its date of first publication.

(d) CORRECTIONS AND AMPLIFICATIONS.—The Register may also establish, by regulation, formal procedures for the filing of an application for supplementary registration, to correct an error in a copyright registration or to amplify the information given in a registration. Such application shall be accompanied by the fee provided by section 708, and shall clearly identify the registration to be corrected or amplified. The information contained in a supplementary registration augments but does not supersede that contained in the earlier registration.

(e) PUBLISHED EDITION OF PREVIOUSLY REGISTERED WORK.—Registration for the first published edition of a work previously registered in unpublished form may be made even though the work as published is substantially the same as the unpublished version.

17 USC 409.

§ 409. Application for copyright registration

The application for copyright registration shall be made on a form prescribed by the Register of Copyrights and shall include—

(1) the name and address of the copyright claimant;

(2) in the case of a work other than an anonymous or pseudonymous work, the name and nationality or domicile of the author or authors, and, if one or more of the authors is dead, the dates of their deaths;

(3) if the work is anonymous or pseudonymous, the nationality or domicile of the author or authors;

(4) in the case of a work made for hire, a statement to this effect;

(5) if the copyright claimant is not the author, a brief statement of how the claimant obtained ownership of the copyright;

(6) the title of the work, together with any previous or alternative titles under which the work can be identified;

(7) the year in which creation of the work was completed;

(8) if the work has been published, the date and nation of its first publication;

(9) in the case of a compilation or derivative work, an identification of any preexisting work or works that it is based on or incorporates, and a brief, general statement of the additional material covered by the copyright claim being registered;

(10) in the case of a published work containing material of which copies are required by section 601 to be manufactured in the United States, the names of the persons or organizations who performed the processes specified by subsection (c) of section 601 with respect to that material, and the places where those processes were performed; and

(11) any other information regarded by the Register of Copyrights as bearing upon the preparation or identification of the work or the existence, ownership, or duration of the copyright.

17 USC 410.

§ 410. Registration of claim and issuance of certificate

(a) When, after examination, the Register of Copyrights determines that, in accordance with the provisions of this title, the material deposited constitutes copyrightable subject matter and that the other legal and formal requirements of this title have been met, the Register shall register the claim and issue to the applicant a certificate of registration under the seal of the Copyright Office. The certificate shall contain the information given in the application, together with the number and effective date of the registration.

(b) In any case in which the Register of Copyrights determines that, in accordance with the provisions of this title, the material deposited does not constitute copyrightable subject matter or that the claim is invalid for any other reason, the Register shall refuse registration and shall notify the applicant in writing of the reasons for such refusal.

(c) In any judicial proceedings the certificate of a registration made before or within five years after first publication of the work shall constitute prima facie evidence of the validity of the copyright and of the facts stated in the certificate. The evidentiary weight to be accorded the certificate of a registration made thereafter shall be within the discretion of the court. *Prima facie evidence.*

(d) The effective date of a copyright registration is the day on which an application, deposit, and fee, which are later determined by the Register of Copyrights or by a court of competent jurisdiction to be acceptable for registration, have all been received in the Copyright Office. *Effective date.*

§ 411. Registration as prerequisite to infringement suit   17 USC 411.

(a) Subject to the provisions of subsection (b), no action for infringement of the copyright in any work shall be instituted until registration of the copyright claim has been made in accordance with this title. In any case, however, where the deposit, application, and fee required for registration have been delivered to the Copyright Office in proper form and registration has been refused, the applicant is entitled to institute an action for infringement if notice thereof, with a copy of the complaint, is served on the Register of Copyrights. The Register may, at his or her option, become a party to the action with respect to the issue of registrability of the copyright claim by entering an appearance within sixty days after such service, but the Register's failure to become a party shall not deprive the court of jurisdiction to determine that issue.

(b) In the case of a work consisting of sounds, images, or both, the first fixation of which is made simultaneously with its transmission, the copyright owner may, either before or after such fixation takes place, institute an action for infringement under section 501, fully subject to the remedies provided by sections 502 through 506 and sections 509 and 510, if, in accordance with requirements that the Register of Copyrights shall prescribe by regulation, the copyright owner—

(1) serves notice upon the infringer, not less than ten or more than thirty days before such fixation, identifying the work and the specific time and source of its first transmission, and declaring an intention to secure copyright in the work; and

(2) makes registration for the work within three months after its first transmission.

§ 412. Registration as prerequisite to certain remedies for infringement   17 USC 412.

In any action under this title, other than an action instituted under section 411(b), no award of statutory damages or of attorney's fees, as provided by sections 504 and 505, shall be made for—

(1) any infringement of copyright in an unpublished work commenced before the effective date of its registration; or

(2) any infringement of copyright commenced after first publication of the work and before the effective date of its registration, unless such registration is made within three months after the first publication of the work.

Chapter 5.—COPYRIGHT INFRINGEMENT AND REMEDIES

17 USC 501.

§ 501. Infringement of copyright

(a) Anyone who violates any of the exclusive rights of the copyright owner as provided by sections 106 through 118, or who imports copies or phonorecords into the United States in violation of section 602, is an infringer of the copyright.

(b) The legal or beneficial owner of an exclusive right under a copyright is entitled, subject to the requirements of sections 205(d) and 411, to institute an action for any infringement of that particular right committed while he or she is the owner of it. The court may require such owner to serve written notice of the action with a copy of the complaint upon any person shown, by the records of the Copyright Office or otherwise, to have or claim an interest in the copyright, and shall require that such notice be served upon any person whose interest is likely to be affected by a decision in the case. The court may require the joinder, and shall permit the intervention, of any person having or claiming an interest in the copyright.

(c) For any secondary transmission by a cable system that embodies a performance or a display of a work which is actionable as an act of infringement under subsection (c) of section 111, a television broadcast station holding a copyright or other license to transmit or perform the same version of that work shall, for purposes of subsection (b) of this section, be treated as a legal or beneficial owner if such secondary transmission occurs within the local service area of that television station.

(d) For any secondary transmission by a cable system that is actionable as an act of infringement pursuant to section 111(c)(3), the following shall also have standing to sue: (i) the primary transmitter whose transmission has been altered by the cable system; and (ii) any broadcast station within whose local service area the secondary transmission occurs.

17 USC 502.

§ 502. Remedies for infringement: Injunctions

(a) Any court having jurisdiction of a civil action arising under this title may, subject to the provisions of section 1498 of title 28, grant temporary and final injunctions on such terms as it may deem reasonable to prevent or restrain infringement of a copyright.

(b) Any such injunction may be served anywhere in the United States on the person enjoined; it shall be operative throughout the United States and shall be enforceable, by proceedings in contempt or otherwise, by any United States court having jurisdiction of that person. The clerk of the court granting the injunction shall, when requested by any other court in which enforcement of the injunction is sought, transmit promptly to the other court a certified copy of all the papers in the case on file in such clerk's office.

§ 503. Remedies for infringement: Impounding and disposition of infringing articles

17 USC 503.

(a) At any time while an action under this title is pending, the court may order the impounding, on such terms as it may deem reasonable, of all copies or phonorecords claimed to have been made or used in violation of the copyright owner's exclusive rights, and of all plates, molds, matrices, masters, tapes, film negatives, or other articles by means of which such copies or phonorecords may be reproduced.

(b) As part of a final judgment or decree, the court may order the destruction or other reasonable disposition of all copies or phonorecords found to have been made or used in violation of the copyright owner's exclusive rights, and of all plates, molds, matrices, masters, tapes, film negatives, or other articles by means of which such copies or phonorecords may be reproduced.

§ 504. Remedies for infringement: Damages and profits

17 USC 504.

(a) IN GENERAL.—Except as otherwise provided by this title, an infringer of copyright is liable for either—

(1) the copyright owner's actual damages and any additional profits of the infringer, as provided by subsection (b); or

(2) statutory damages, as provided by subsection (c).

(b) ACTUAL DAMAGES AND PROFITS.—The copyright owner is entitled to recover the actual damages suffered by him or her as a result of the infringement, and any profits of the infringer that are attributable to the infringement and are not taken into account in computing the actual damages. In establishing the infringer's profits, the copyright owner is required to present proof only of the infringer's gross revenue, and the infringer is required to prove his or her deductible expenses and the elements of profit attributable to factors other than the copyrighted work.

(c) STATUTORY DAMAGES.—

(1) Except as provided by clause (2) of this subsection, the copyright owner may elect, at any time before final judgment is rendered, to recover, instead of actual damages and profits, an award of statutory damages for all infringements involved in the action, with respect to any one work, for which any one infringer is liable individually, or for which any two or more infringers are liable jointly and severally, in a sum of not less than $250 or more than $10,000 as the court considers just. For the purposes of this subsection, all the parts of a compilation or derivative work constitute one work.

(2) In a case where the copyright owner sustains the burden of proving, and the court finds, that infringement was committed willfully, the court in its discretion may increase the award of statutory damages to a sum of not more than $50,000. In a case where the infringer sustains the burden of proving, and the court finds, that such infringer was not aware and had no reason to believe that his or her acts constituted an infringement of copyright, the court it its discretion may reduce the award of statutory damages to a sum of not less than $100. The court shall remit statutory damages in any case where an infringer believed and had reasonable grounds for believing that his or her use of the copyrighted work was a fair use under section 107, if the infringer was: (i) an employee or agent of a nonprofit educational institution, library, or archives acting within the scope of his or her employment who, or such institution, library, or archives itself, which infringed by reproducing the work in copies or phonorecords; or (ii) a public broadcasting entity which or a person who, as a regular part of the nonprofit activities of a public

broadcasting entity (as defined in subsection (g) of section 118) infringed by performing a published nondramatic literary work or by reproducing a transmission program embodying a performance of such a work.

17 USC 505.

§ 505. Remedies for infringement: Costs and attorney's fees

In any civil action under this title, the court in its discretion may allow the recovery of full costs by or against any party other than the United States or an officer thereof. Except as otherwise provided by this title, the court may also award a reasonable attorney's fee to the prevailing party as part of the costs.

17 USC 506.

§ 506. Criminal offenses

(a) CRIMINAL INFRINGEMENT.—Any person who infringes a copyright willfully and for purposes of commercial advantage or private financial gain shall be fined not more than $10,000 or imprisoned for not more than one year, or both: *Provided, however,* That any person who infringes willfully and for purposes of commercial advantage or private financial gain the copyright in a sound recording afforded by subsections (1), (2), or (3) of section 106 or the copyright in a motion picture afforded by subsections (1), (3), or (4) of section 106 shall be fined not more than $25,000 or imprisoned for not more than one year, or both, for the first such offense and shall be fined not more than $50,000 or imprisoned for not more than two years, or both, for any subsequent offense.

(b) FORFEITURE AND DESTRUCTION.—When any person is convicted of any violation of subsection (a), the court in its judgment of conviction shall, in addition to the penalty therein prescribed, order the forfeiture and destruction or other disposition of all infringing copies or phonorecords and all implements, devices, or equipment used in the manufacture of such infringing copies or phonorecords.

(c) FRAUDULENT COPYRIGHT NOTICE.—Any person who, with fraudulent intent, places on any article a notice of copyright or words of the same purport that such person knows to be false, or who, with fraudulent intent, publicly distributes or imports for public distribution any article bearing such notice or words that such person knows to be false, shall be fined not more than $2,500.

(d) FRAUDULENT REMOVAL OF COPYRIGHT NOTICE.—Any person who, with fraudulent intent, removes or alters any notice of copyright appearing on a copy of a copyrighted work shall be fined not more than $2,500.

(e) FALSE REPRESENTATION.—Any person who knowingly makes a false representation of a material fact in the application for copyright registration provided for by section 409, or in any written statement filed in connection with the application, shall be fined not more than $2,500.

17 USC 507.

§ 507. Limitations on actions

(a) CRIMINAL PROCEEDINGS.—No criminal proceeding shall be maintained under the provisions of this title unless it is commenced within three years after the cause of action arose.

(b) CIVIL ACTIONS.—No civil action shall be maintained under the provisions of this title unless it is commenced within three years after the claim accrued.

17 USC 508.

§ 508. Notification of filing and determination of actions

(a) Within one month after the filing of any action under this title, the clerks of the courts of the United States shall send written notification to the Register of Copyrights setting forth, as far as is shown by the papers filed in the court, the names and addresses of the parties and the title, author, and registration number of each work involved in the action. If any other copyrighted work is later included in the action by amendment, answer, or other pleading, the clerk shall also send a notification concerning it to the Register within one month after the pleading is filed.

(b) Within one month after any final order or judgment is issued in the case, the clerk of the court shall notify the Register of it, sending with the notification a copy of the order or judgment together with the written opinion, if any, of the court.

(c) Upon receiving the notifications specified in this section, the Register shall make them a part of the public records of the Copyright Office.

§ 509. Seizure and forfeiture

17 USC 509.

(a) All copies or phonorecords manufactured, reproduced, distributed, sold, or otherwise used, intended for use, or possessed with intent to use in violation of section 506(a), and all plates, molds, matrices, masters, tapes, film negatives, or other articles by means of which such copies or phonorecords may be reproduced, and all electronic, mechanical, or other devices for manufacturing, reproducing, or assembling such copies or phonorecords may be seized and forfeited to the United States.

(b) The applicable procedures relating to (i) the seizure, summary and judicial forfeiture, and condemnation of vessels, vehicles, merchandise, and baggage for violations of the customs laws contained in title 19, (ii) the disposition of such vessels, vehicles, merchandise, and baggage or the proceeds from the sale thereof, (iii) the remission or mitigation of such forfeiture, (iv) the compromise of claims, and (v) the award of compensation to informers in respect of such forfeitures, shall apply to seizures and forfeitures incurred, or alleged to have been incurred, under the provisions of this section, insofar as applicable and not inconsistent with the provisions of this section; except that such duties as are imposed upon any officer or employee of the Treasury Department or any other person with respect to the seizure and forfeiture of vessels, vehicles, merchandise; and baggage under the provisions of the customs laws contained in title 19 shall be performed with respect to seizure and forfeiture of all articles described in subsection (a) by such officers, agents, or other persons as may be authorized or designated for that purpose by the Attorney General.

19 USC 1 et seq.

§ 510. Remedies for alteration of programing by cable systems

17 USC 510.

(a) In any action filed pursuant to section 111(c)(3), the following remedies shall be available:

(1) Where an action is brought by a party identified in subsections (b) or (c) of section 501, the remedies provided by sections 502 through 505, and the remedy provided by subsection (b) of this section; and

(2) When an action is brought by a party identified in subsection (d) of section 501, the remedies provided by sections 502 and 505, together with any actual damages suffered by such party as a result of the infringement, and the remedy provided by subsection (b) of this section.

(b) In any action filed pursuant to section 111(c)(3), the court may decree that, for a period not to exceed thirty days, the cable system shall be deprived of the benefit of a compulsory license for one or more distant signals carried by such cable system.

239

Chapter 6.—MANUFACTURING REQUIREMENTS AND IMPORTATION

Sec.
601. Manufacture, importation, and public distribution of certain copies.
602. Infringing importation of copies or phonorecords.
603. Importation prohibitions: Enforcement and disposition of excluded articles.

17 USC 601.

§ 601. Manufacture, importation, and public distribution of certain copies

(a) Prior to July 1, 1982, and except as provided by subsection (b), the importation into or public distribution in the United States of copies of a work consisting preponderantly of nondramtic literary material that is in the English language and is protected under this title is prohibited unless the portions consisting of such material have been manufactured in the United States or Canada.

(b) The provisions of subsection (a) do not apply—

(1) where, on the date when importation is sought or public distribution in the United States is made, the author of any substantial part of such material is neither a national nor a domiciliary of the United States or, if such author is a national of the United States, he or she has been domiciled outside the United States for a continuous period of at least one year immediately preceding that date; in the case of a work made for hire, the exemption provided by this clause does not apply unless a substantial part of the work was prepared for an employer or other person who is not a national or domiciliary of the United States or a domestic corporation or enterprise;

(2) where the United States Customs Service is presented with an import statement issued under the seal of the Copyright Office, in which case a total of no more than two thousand copies of any one such work shall be allowed entry; the import statement shall be issued upon request to the copyright owner or to a person designated by such owner at the time of registration for the work under section 408 or at any time thereafter;

(3) where importation is sought under the authority or for the use, other than in schools, of the Government of the United States or of any State or political subdivision of a State;

(4) where importation, for use and not for sale, is sought—

(A) by any person with respect to no more than one copy of any work at any one time;

(B) by any person arriving from outside the United States, with respect to copies forming part of such person's personal baggage; or

(C) by an organization operated for scholarly, educational, or religious purposes and not for private gain, with respect to copies intended to form a part of its library;

(5) where the copies are reproduced in raised characters for the use of the blind; or

(6) where, in addition to copies imported under clauses (3) and (4) of this subsection, no more than two thousand copies of any one such work, which have not been manufactured in the United States or Canada, are publicly distributed in the United States; or

(7) where, on the date when importation is sought or public distribution in the United States is made—

(A) the author of any substantial part of such material is an individual and receives compensation for the transfer or license of the right to distribute the work in the United States; and

(B) the first publication of the work has previously taken place outside the United States under a transfer or license granted by such author to a transferee or licensee who was not a national or domiciliary of the United States or a domestic corporation or enterprise; and

(C) there has been no publication of an authorized edition of the work of which the copies were manufactured in the United States; and

(D) the copies were reproduced under a transfer or license granted by such author or by the transferee or licensee of the right of first publication as mentioned in subclause (B), and the transferee or the licensee of the right of reproduction was not a national or domiciliary of the United States or a domestic corporation or enterprise.

(c) The requirement of this section that copies be manufactured in the United States or Canada is satisfied if—

(1) in the case where the copies are printed directly from type that has been set, or directly from plates made from such type, the setting of the type and the making of the plates have been performed in the United States or Canada; or

(2) in the case where the making of plates by a lithographic or photoengraving process is a final or intermediate step preceding the printing of the copies, the making of the plates has been performed in the United States or Canada; and

(3) in any case, the printing or other final process of producing multiple copies and any binding of the copies have been performed in the United States or Canada.

(d) Importation or public distribution of copies in violation of this section does not invalidate protection for a work under this title. However, in any civil action or criminal proceeding for infringement of the exclusive rights to reproduce and distribute copies of the work, the infringer has a complete defense with respect to all of the nondramatic literary material comprised in the work and any other parts of the work in which the exclusive rights to reproduce and distribute copies are owned by the same person who owns such exclusive rights in the nondramatic literary material, if the infringer proves—

(1) that copies of the work have been imported into or publicly distributed in the United States in violation of this section by or with the authority of the owner of such exclusive rights; and

(2) that the infringing copies were manufactured in the United States or Canada in accordance with the provisions of subsection (c); and

(3) that the infringement was commenced before the effective date of registration for an authorized edition of the work, the copies of which have been manufactured in the United States or Canada in accordance with the provisions of subsection (c).

(e) In any action for infringement of the exclusive rights to reproduce and distribute copies of a work containing material required by this section to be manufactured in the United States or Canada, the copyright owner shall set forth in the complaint the names of the persons or organizations who performed the processes specified by subsection (c) with respect to that material, and the places where those processes were performed.

§ 602. Infringing importation of copies or phonorecords

17 USC 602.

(a) Importation into the United States, without the authority of the owner of copyright under this title, of copies or phonorecords of a work that have been acquired outside the United States is an infringement of the exclusive right to distribute copies or phonorecords under section 106, actionable under section 501. This subsection does not apply to—

(1) importation of copies or phonorecords under the authority or for the use of the Government of the United States or of any State or political subdivision of a State, but not including copies or phonorecords for use in schools, or copies of any audiovisual work imported for purposes other than archival use;

(2) importation, for the private use of the importer and not for distribution, by any person with respect to no more than one copy or phonorecord of any one work at any one time, or by any person arriving from outside the United States with respect to copies or phonorecords forming part of such person's personal baggage; or

(3) importation by or for an organization operated for scholarly, educational, or religious purposes and not for private gain, with respect to no more than one copy of an audiovisual work solely for its archival purposes, and no more than five copies or phonorecords of any other work for its library lending or archival purposes, unless the importation of such copies or phonorecords is part of an activity consisting of systematic reproduction or distribution, engaged in by such organization in violation of the provisions of section 108(g)(2).

(b) In a case where the making of the copies or phonorecords would have constituted an infringement of copyright if this title had been applicable, their importation is prohibited. In a case where the copies or phonorecords were lawfully made, the United States Customs Service has no authority to prevent their importation unless the provisions of section 601 are applicable. In either case, the Secretary of the Treasury is authorized to prescribe, by regulation, a procedure under which any person claiming an interest in the copyright in a particular work may, upon payment of a specified fee, be entitled to notification by the Customs Service of the importation of articles that appear to be copies or phonorecords of the work.

Regulations.

17 USC 603.

§ 603. Importation prohibitions: Enforcement and disposition of excluded articles

Regulations.

(a) The Secretary of the Treasury and the United States Postal Service shall separately or jointly make regulations for the enforcement of the provisions of this title prohibiting importation.

(b) These regulations may require, as a condition for the exclusion of articles under section 602—

(1) that the person seeking exclusion obtain a court order enjoining importation of the articles; or

Surety bond.

(2) that the person seeking exclusion furnish proof, of a specified nature and in accordance with prescribed procedures, that the copyright in which such person claims an interest is valid and that the importation would violate the prohibition in section 602; the person seeking exclusion may also be required to post a surety bond for any injury that may result if the detention or exclusion of the articles proves to be unjustified.

(c) Articles imported in violation of the importation prohibitions of this title are subject to seizure and forfeiture in the same manner as property imported in violation of the customs revenue laws. Forfeited articles shall be destroyed as directed by the Secretary of the Treasury or the court, as the case may be; however, the articles may be returned to the country of export whenever it is shown to the satisfaction of the Secretary of the Treasury that the importer had no reasonable grounds for believing that his or her acts constituted a violation of law.

Chapter 7.—COPYRIGHT OFFICE

§ 701. The Copyright Office: General responsibilities and organization

17 USC 701.

(a) All administrative functions and duties under this title, except as otherwise specified, are the responsibility of the Register of Copyrights as director of the Copyright Office of the Library of Congress. The Register of Copyrights, together with the subordinate officers and employees of the Copyright Office, shall be appointed by the Librarian of Congress, and shall act under the Librarian's general direction and supervision.

(b) The Register of Copyrights shall adopt a seal to be used on and after January 1, 1978, to authenticate all certified documents issued by the Copyright Office.

Seal.

(c) The Register of Copyrights shall make an annual report to the Librarian of Congress of the work and accomplishments of the Copyright Office during the previous fiscal year. The annual report of the Register of Copyrights shall be published separately and as a part of the annual report of the Librarian of Congress.

Report to Librarian of Congress.

(d) Except as provided by section 706(b) and the regulations issued thereunder, all actions taken by the Register of Copyrights under this title are subject to the provisions of the Administrative Procedure Act of June 11, 1946, as amended (c. 324, 60 Stat. 237, title 5, United States Code, Chapter 5, Subchapter II and Chapter 7).

5 USC 551, 701.

§ 702. Copyright Office regulations

17 USC 702.

The Register of Copyrights is authorized to establish regulations not inconsistent with law for the administration of the functions and duties made the responsibility of the Register under this title. All regulations established by the Register under this title are subject to the approval of the Librarian of Congress.

§ 703. Effective date of actions in Copyright Office

17 USC 703.

In any case in which time limits are prescribed under this title for the performance of an action in the Copyright Office, and in which the last day of the prescribed period falls on a Saturday, Sunday, holiday, or other nonbusiness day within the District of Columbia or the Federal Government, the action may be taken on the next succeeding business day, and is effective as of the date when the period expired.

§ 704. Retention and disposition of articles deposited in Copyright Office

17 USC 704.

(a) Upon their deposit in the Copyright Office under sections 407 and 408, all copies, phonorecords, and identifying material, including those deposited in connection with claims that have been refused registration, are the property of the United States Government.

(b) In the case of published works, all copies, phonorecords, and identifying material deposited are available to the Library of Congress for its collections, or for exchange or transfer to any other library. In the case of unpublished works, the Library is entitled,

Regulations.

243

under regulations that the Register of Copyrights shall prescribe, to select any deposits for its collections or for transfer to the National Archives of the United States or to a Federal records center, as defined in section 2901 of title 44.

(c) The Register of Copyrights is authorized, for specific or general categories of works, to make a facsimile reproduction of all or any part of the material deposited under section 408, and to make such reproduction a part of the Copyright Office records of the registration, before transferring such material to the Library of Congress as provided by subsection (b), or before destroying or otherwise disposing of such material as provided by subsection (d).

(d) Deposits not selected by the Library under subsection (b), or identifying portions or reproductions of them, shall be retained under the control of the Copyright Office, including retention in Government storage facilities, for the longest period considered practicable and desirable by the Register of Copyrights and the Librarian of Congress. After that period it is within the joint discretion of the Register and the Librarian to order their destruction or other disposition; but, in the case of unpublished works, no deposit shall be knowingly or intentionally destroyed or otherwise disposed of during its term of copyright unless a facsimile reproduction of the entire deposit has been made a part of the Copyright Office records as provided by subsection (c).

(e) The depositor of copies, phonorecords, or identifying material under section 408, or the copyright owner of record, may request retention, under the control of the Copyright Office, of one or more of such articles for the full term of copyright in the work. The Register of Copyrights shall prescribe, by regulation, the conditions under which such requests are to be made and granted, and shall fix the fee to be charged under section 708(a)(11) if the request is granted.

§ 705. Copyright Office records: Preparation, maintenance, public inspection, and searching

17 USC 705.

(a) The Register of Copyrights shall provide and keep in the Copyright Office records of all deposits, registrations, recordations, and other actions taken under this title, and shall prepare indexes of all such records.

(b) Such records and indexes, as well as the articles deposited in connection with completed copyright registrations and retained under the control of the Copyright Office, shall be open to public inspection.

Report.

(c) Upon request and payment of the fee specified by section 708, the Copyright Office shall make a search of its public records, indexes, and deposits, and shall furnish a report of the information they disclose with respect to any particular deposits, registrations, or recorded documents.

§ 706. Copies of Copyright Office records

17 USC 706.

(a) Copies may be made of any public records or indexes of the Copyright Office; additional certificates of copyright registration and copies of any public records or indexes may be furnished upon request and payment of the fees specified by section 708.

(b) Copies or reproductions of deposited articles retained under the control of the Copyright Office shall be authorized or furnished only under the conditions specified by the Copyright Office regulations.

§ 707. Copyright Office forms and publications

17 USC 707

(a) CATALOG OF COPYRIGHT ENTRIES.—The Register of Copyrights shall compile and publish at periodic intervals catalogs of all copyright registrations. These catalogs shall be divided into parts in accordance with the various classes of works, and the Register has discretion to determine, on the basis of practicability and usefulness, the form and frequency of publication of each particular part.

(b) OTHER PUBLICATIONS.—The Register shall furnish, free of charge upon request, application forms for copyright registration and general informational material in connection with the functions of the Copyright Office. The Register also has the authority to publish compilations of information, bibliographies, and other material he or she considers to be of value to the public.

(c) DISTRIBUTION OF PUBLICATIONS.—All publications of the Copyright Office shall be furnished to depository libraries as specified under section 1905 of title 44, and, aside from those furnished free of charge, shall be offered for sale to the public at prices based on the cost of reproduction and distribution.

§ 708. Copyright Office fees

17 USC 708.

(a) The following fees shall be paid to the Register of Copyrights:

(1) for the registration of a copyright claim or a supplementary registration under section 408, including the issuance of a certificate of registration, $10;

(2) for the registration of a claim to renewal of a subsisting copyright in its first term under section 304(a), including the issuance of a certificate of registration, $6;

(3) for the issuance of a receipt for a deposit under section 407, $2;

(4) for the recordation, as provided by section 205, of a transfer of copyright ownership or other document of six pages or less, covering no more than one title, $10; for each page over six and each title over one, 50 cents additional;

(5) for the filing, under section 115(b), of a notice of intention to make phonorecords, $6;

(6) for the recordation, under section 302(c), of a statement revealing the identity of an author of an anonymous or pseudonymous work, or for the recordation, under section 302(d), of a statement relating to the death of an author, $10 for a document of six pages or less, covering no more than one title; for each page over six and for each title over one, $1 additional;

(7) for the issuance, under section 601, of an import statement, $3;

(8) for the issuance, under section 706, of an additional certificate of registration, $4;

(9) for the issuance of any other certification, $4; the Register of Copyrights has discretion, on the basis of their cost, to fix the fees for preparing copies of Copyright Office records, whether they are to be certified or not;

(10) for the making and reporting of a search as provided by section 705, and for any related services, $10 for each hour or fraction of an hour consumed;

(11) for any other special services requiring a substantial amount of time or expense, such fees as the Register of Copyrights may fix on the basis of the cost of providing the service.

(b) The fees prescribed by or under this section are applicable to the United States Government and any of its agencies, employees, or officers, but the Register of Copyrights has discretion to waive the requirement of this subsection in occasional or isolated cases involving relatively small amounts.

Waiver.

(c) The Register of Copyrights shall deposit all fees in the Treasury of the United States in such manner as the Secretary of the Treasury directs. The Register may, in accordance with regulations that

Regulations.

he or she shall prescribe, refund any sum paid by mistake or in excess of the fee required by this section; however, before making a refund in any case involving a refusal to register a claim under section 410(b), the Register may deduct all or any part of the prescribed registration fee to cover the reasonable administrative costs of processing the claim.

17 USC 709.

§ 709. Delay in delivery caused by disruption of postal or other services

In any case in which the Register of Copyrights determines, on the basis of such evidence as the Register may by regulation require, that a deposit, application, fee, or any other material to be delivered to the Copyright Office by a particular date, would have been received in the Copyright Office in due time except for a general disruption or suspension of postal or other transportation or communications services, the actual receipt of such material in the Copyright Office within one month after the date on which the Register determines that the disruption or suspension of such services has terminated, shall be considered timely.

17 USC 710.

§ 710. Reproduction for use of the blind and physically handicapped: Voluntary licensing forms and procedures

Regulation.

The Register of Copyrights shall, after consultation with the Chief of the Division for the Blind and Physically Handicapped and other appropriate officials of the Library of Congress, establish by regulation standardized forms and procedures by which, at the time applications covering certain specified categories of nondramatic literary works are submitted for registration under section 408 of this title, the copyright owner may voluntarily grant to the Library of Congress a license to reproduce the copyrighted work by means of Braille or similar tactile symbols, or by fixation of a reading of the work in a phonorecord, or both, and to distribute the resulting copies or phonorecords solely for the use of the blind and physically handicapped and under limited conditions to be specified in the standardized forms.

Chapter 8.—COPYRIGHT ROYALTY TRIBUNAL

17 USC 801.

§ 801. Copyright Royalty Tribunal: Establishment and purpose

(a) There is hereby created an independent Copyright Royalty Tribunal in the legislative branch.

(b) Subject to the provisions of this chapter, the purposes of the Tribunal shall be—

> (1) to make determinations concerning the adjustment of reasonable copyright royalty rates as provided in sections 115 and 116, and to make determinations as to reasonable terms and rates of royalty payments as provided in section 118. The rates applicable under sections 115 and 116 shall be calculated to achieve the following objectives:
>
> > (A) To maximize the availability of creative works to the public;

246

(B) To afford the copyright owner a fair return for his creative work and the copyright user a fair income under existing economic conditions;

(C) To reflect the relative roles of the copyright owner and the copyright user in the product made available to the public with respect to relative creative contribution, technological contribution, capital investment, cost, risk, and contribution to the opening of new markets for creative expression and media for their communication;

(D) To minimize any disruptive impact on the structure of the industries involved and on generally prevailing industry practices.

(2) to make determinations concerning the adjustment of the copyright royalty rates in section 111 solely in accordance with the following provisions:

(A) The rates established by section 111(d)(2)(B) may be adjusted to reflect (i) national monetary inflation or deflation or (ii) changes in the average rates charged cable subscribers for the basic service of providing secondary transmissions to maintain the real constant dollar level of the royalty fee per subscriber which existed as of the date of enactment of this Act: *Provided,* That if the average rates charged cable system subscribers for the basic service of providing secondary transmissions are changed so that the average rates exceed national monetary inflation, no change in the rates established by section 111(d)(2)(B) shall be permitted: *And provided further,* That no increase in the royalty fee shall be permitted based on any reduction in the average number of distant signal equivalents per subscriber. The Commission may consider all factors relating to the maintenance of such level of payments including, as an extenuating factor, whether the cable industry has been restrained by subscriber rate regulating authorities from increasing the rates for the basic service of providing secondary transmissions.

(B) In the event that the rules and regulations of the Federal Communications Commission are amended at any time after April 15, 1976, to permit the carriage by cable systems of additional television broadcast signals beyond the local service area of the primary transmitters of such signals, the royalty rates established by section 111(d)(2)(B) may be adjusted to insure that the rates for the additional distant signal equivalents resulting from such carriage are reasonable in the light of the changes effected by the amendment to such rules and regulations. In determining the reasonableness of rates proposed following an amendment of Federal Communications Commission rules and regulations, the Copyright Royalty Tribunal shall consider, among other factors, the economic impact on copyright owners and users: *Provided,* That no adjustment in royalty rates shall be made under this subclause with respect to any distant signal equivalent or fraction thereof represented by (i) carriage of any signal permitted under the rules and regulations of the Federal Communications Commission in effect on April 15, 1976, or the carriage of a signal of the same type (that is, independent, network, or noncommercial educational) substituted for such permitted signal, or (ii) a television broadcast signal first carried after April 15, 1976, pursuant to an

247

individual waiver of the rules and regulations of the Federal Communications Commission, as such rules and regulations were in effect on April 15, 1976.

(C) In the event of any change in the rules and regulations of the Federal Communications Commission with respect to syndicated and sports program exclusivity after April 15, 1976, the rates established by section 111(d)(2)(B) may be adjusted to assure that such rates are reasonable in light of the changes to such rules and regulations, but any such adjustment shall apply only to the affected television broadcast signals carried on those systems affected by the change.

(D) The gross receipts limitations established by section 111(d)(2)(C) and (D) shall be adjusted to reflect national monetary inflation or deflation or changes in the average rates charged cable system subscribers for the basic service of providing secondary transmissions to maintain the real constant dollar value of the exemption provided by such section; and the royalty rate specified therein shall not be subject to adjustment; and

(3) to distribute royalty fees deposited with the Register of Copyrights under sections 111 and 116, and to determine, in cases where controversy exists, the distribution of such fees.

Notice.

(c) As soon as possible after the date of enactment of this Act, and no later than six months following such date, the President shall publish a notice announcing the initial appointments provided in section 802, and shall designate an order of seniority among the initially-appointed commissioners for purposes of section 802(b).

17 USC 802.

§ 802. Membership of the Tribunal

(a) The Tribunal shall be composed of five commissioners appointed by the President with the advice and consent of the Senate for a term of seven years each; of the first five members appointed, three shall be designated to serve for seven years from the date of the notice specified in section 801(c), and two shall be designated to serve for five years from such date, respectively. Commissioners shall be compensated at the highest rate now or hereafter prescribe for grade 18 of the General Schedule pay rates (5 U.S.C. 5332).

(b) Upon convening the commissioners shall elect a chairman from among the commissioners appointed for a full seven-year term. Such chairman shall serve for a term of one year. Thereafter, the most senior commissioner who has not previously served as chairman shall serve as chairman for a period of one year, except that, if all commissioners have served a full term as chairman, the most senior commissioner who has served the least number of terms as chairman shall be designated as chairman.

(c) Any vacancy in the Tribunal shall not affect its powers and shall be filled, for the unexpired term of the appointment, in the same manner as the original appointment was made.

17 USC 803.

§ 803. Procedures of the Tribunal

(a) The Tribunal shall adopt regulations, not inconsistent with law, governing its procedure and methods of operation. Except as otherwise provided in this chapter, the Tribunal shall be subject to the provisions of the Administrative Procedure Act of June 11, 1946, as amended (c. 324, 60 Stat. 237, title 5, United States Code, chapter 5, subchapter II and chapter 7).

5 USC 551, 701.
Publication in
Federal Register.

(b) Every final determination of the Tribunal shall be published in the Federal Register. It shall state in detail the criteria that the Tribunal determined to be applicable to the particular proceeding, the various facts that it found relevant to its determination in that proceeding, and the specific reasons for its determination.

§ 804. Institution and conclusion of proceedings

17 USC 804.

(a) With respect to proceedings under section 801(b)(1) concerning the adjustment of royalty rates as provided in sections 115 and 116, and with respect to proceedings under section 801(b)(2)(A) and (D)—

(1) on January 1, 1980, the Chairman of the Tribunal shall cause to be published in the Federal Register notice of commencement of proceedings under this chapter; and

(2) during the calendar years specified in the following schedule, any owner or user of a copyrighted work whose royalty rates are specified by this title, or by a rate established by the Tribunal, may file a petition with the Tribunal declaring that the petitioner requests an adjustment of the rate. The Tribunal shall make a determination as to whether the applicant has a significant interest in the royalty rate in which an adjustment is requested. If the Tribunal determines that the petitioner has a significant interest, the Chairman shall cause notice of this determination, with the reasons therefor, to be published in the Federal Register, together with notice of commencement of proceedings under this chapter.

(A) In proceedings under section 801(b)(2)(A) and (D), such petition may be filed during 1985 and in each subsequent fifth calendar year.

(B) In proceedings under section 801(b)(1) concerning the adjustment of royalty rates as provided in section 115, such petition may be filed in 1987 and in each subsequent tenth calendar year.

(C) In proceedings under section 801(b)(1) concerning the adjustment of royalty rates under section 116, such petition may be filed in 1990 and in each subsequent tenth calendar year.

(b) With respect to proceedings under subclause (B) or (C) of section 801(b)(2), following an event described in either of those subsections, any owner or user of a copyrighted work whose royalty rates are specified by section 111, or by a rate established by the Tribunal, may, within twelve months, file a petition with the Tribunal declaring that the petitioner requests an adjustment of the rate. In this event the Tribunal shall proceed as in subsection (a)(2), above. Any change in royalty rates made by the Tribunal pursuant to this subsection may be reconsidered in 1980, 1985, and each fifth calendar year thereafter, in accordance with the provisions in section 801(b)(2)(B) or (C), as the case may be.

(c) With respect to proceedings under section 801(b)(1), concerning the determination of reasonable terms and rates of royalty payments as provided in section 118, the Tribunal shall proceed when and as provided by that section.

(d) With respect to proceedings under section 801(b)(3), concerning the distribution of royalty fees in certain circumstances under sections 111 or 116, the Chairman of the Tribunal shall, upon determination by the Tribunal that a controversy exists concerning such distribution, cause to be published in the Federal Register notice of commencement of proceedings under this chapter.

(e) All proceedings under this chapter shall be initiated without delay following publication of the notice specified in this section, and the Tribunal shall render its final decision in any such proceeding within one year from the date of such publication.

17 USC 805.

§ 805. Staff of the Tribunal

(a) The Tribunal is authorized to appoint and fix the compensation of such employees as may be necessary to carry out the provisions of this chapter, and to prescribe their functions and duties.

5 USC 3109.

(b) The Tribunal may procure temporary and intermittent services to the same extent as is authorized by section 3109 of title 5.

17 USC 806.

§ 806. Administrative support of the Tribunal

(a) The Library of Congress shall provide the Tribunal with necessary administrative services, including those related to budgeting, accounting, financial reporting, travel, personnel, and procurement. The Tribunal shall pay the Library for such services, either in advance or by reimbursement from the funds of the Tribunal, at amounts to be agreed upon between the Librarian and the Tribunal.

(b) The Library of Congress is authorized to disburse funds for the Tribunal, under regulations prescribed jointly by the Librarian of Congress and the Tribunal and approved by the Comptroller General. Such regulations shall establish requirements and procedures under which every voucher certified for payment by the Library of Congress under this chapter shall be supported with a certification by a duly authorized officer or employee of the Tribunal, and shall prescribe the responsibilities and accountability of said officers and employees of the Tribunal with respect to such certifications.

17 USC 807.

§ 807. Deduction of costs of proceedings

Before any funds are distributed pursuant to a final decision in a proceeding involving distribution of royalty fees, the Tribunal shall assess the reasonable costs of such proceeding.

17 USC 808.

§ 808. Reports

In addition to its publication of the reports of all final determinations as provided in section 803(b), the Tribunal shall make an annual report to the President and the Congress concerning the Tribunal's work during the preceding fiscal year, including a detailed fiscal statement of account.

17 USC 809.

§ 809. Effective date of final determinations

Any final determination by the Tribunal under this chapter shall become effective thirty days following its publication in the Federal Register as provided in section 803(b), unless prior to that time an appeal has been filed pursuant to section 810, to vacate, modify, or correct such determination, and notice of such appeal has been served on all parties who appeared before the Tribunal in the proceeding in question. Where the proceeding involves the distribution of royalty fees under sections 111 or 116, the Tribunal shall, upon the expiration of such thirty-day period, distribute any royalty fees not subject to an appeal filed pursuant to section 810.

17 USC 810.

§ 810. Judicial review

Any final decision of the Tribunal in a proceeding under section 801(b) may be appealed to the United States Court of Appeals, within thirty days after its publication in the Federal Register by an aggrieved party. The judicial review of the decision shall be had, in

5 USC 701.

accordance with chapter 7 of title 5, on the basis of the record before the Tribunal. No court shall have jurisdiction to review a final decision of the Tribunal except as provided in this section.

TRANSITIONAL AND SUPPLEMENTARY PROVISIONS

17 USC note
prec. 101.

SEC. 102. This Act becomes effective on January 1, 1978, except as otherwise expressly provided by this Act, including provisions of the first section of this Act. The provisions of sections 118, 304(b), and chapter 8 of title 17, as amended by the first section of this Act, take effect upon enactment of this Act.

Sec. 103. This Act does not provide copyright protection for any work that goes into the public domain before January 1, 1978. The exclusive rights, as provided by section 106 of title 17 as amended by the first section of this Act, to reproduce a work in phonorecords and to distribute phonorecords of the work, do not extend to any nondramatic musical work copyrighted before July 1, 1909.

17 USC note prec. 101.

Sec. 104. All proclamations issued by the President under section 1(e) or 9(b) of title 17 as it existed on December 31, 1977, or under previous copyright statutes of the United States, shall continue in force until terminated, suspended, or revised by the President.

17 USC note prec. 101.

Sec. 105. (a) (1) Section 505 of title 44 is amended to read as follows:

44 USC 505.

"§ 505. Sale of duplicate plates

"The Public Printer shall sell, under regulations of the Joint Committee on Printing to persons who may apply, additional or duplicate stereotype or electrotype plates from which a Government publication is printed, at a price not to exceed the cost of composition, the metal, and making to the Government, plus 10 per centum, and the full amount of the price shall be paid when the order is filed.".

(2) The item relating to section 505 in the sectional analysis at the beginning of chapter 5 of title 44, is amended to read as follows:

"505. Sale of duplicate plates.".

(b) Section 2113 of title 44 is amended to read as follows:

"§ 2113. Limitation on liability

44 USC 2113.

"When letters and other intellectual productions (exclusive of patented material, published works under copyright protection, and unpublished works for which copyright registration has been made) come into the custody or possession of the Administrator of General Services, the United States or its agents are not liable for infringement of copyright or analogous rights arising out of use of the materials for display, inspection, research, reproduction, or other purposes.".

(c) In section 1498(b) of title 28, the phrase "section 101(b) of title 17" is amended to read "section 504(c) of title 17".

28 USC 1498.

(d) Section 543(a)(4) of the Internal Revenue Code of 1954, as amended, is amended by striking out "(other than by reason of section 2 or 6 thereof)".

26 USC 543.

(e) Section 3202(a) of title 39 is amended by striking out clause (5). Section 3206 of title 39 is amended by deleting the words "subsections (b) and (c)" and inserting "subsection (b)" in subsection (a), and by deleting subsection (c). Section 3206(d) is renumbered (c).

39 USC 3202, 3206.

(f) Subsection (a) of section 290(e) of title 15 is amended by deleting the phrase "section 8" and inserting in lieu thereof the phrase "section 105".

15 USC 290e.

(g) Section 131 of title 2 is amended by deleting the phrase "deposit to secure copyright," and inserting in lieu thereof the phrase "acquisition of material under the copyright law,".

2 USC 131.

Sec. 106. In any case where, before January 1, 1978, a person has lawfully made parts of instruments serving to reproduce mechanically a copyrighted work under the compulsory license provisions of section 1(e) of title 17 as it existed on December 31, 1977, such person may continue to make and distribute such parts embodying the same mechanical reproduction without obtaining a new compulsory license

17 USC 115 note.

under the terms of section 115 of title 17 as amended by the first section of this Act. However, such parts made on or after January 1, 1978, constitute phonorecords and are otherwise subject to the provisions of said section 115.

17 USC 304 note.

SEC. 107. In the case of any work in which an ad interim copyright is subsisting or is capable of being secured on December 31, 1977, under section 22 of title 17 as it existed on that date, copyright protection is hereby extended to endure for the term or terms provided by section 304 of title 17 as amended by the first section of this Act.

17 USC 401 note.

SEC. 108. The notice provisions of sections 401 through 403 of title 17 as amended by the first section of this Act apply to all copies or phonorecords publicly distributed on or after January 1, 1978. However, in the case of a work published before January 1, 1978, compliance with the notice provisions of title 17 either as it existed on December 31, 1977, or as amended by the first section of this Act, is adequate with respect to copies publicly distributed after December 31, 1977.

17 USC 410 note.

SEC. 109. The registration of claims to copyright for which the required deposit, application, and fee were received in the Copyright Office before January 1, 1978, and the recordation of assignments of copyright or other instruments received in the Copyright Office before January 1, 1978, shall be made in accordance with title 17 as it existed on December 31, 1977.

17 USC 407 note.

SEC. 110. The demand and penalty provisions of section 14 of title 17 as it existed on December 31, 1977, apply to any work in which copyright has been secured by publication with notice of copyright on or before that date, but any deposit and registration made after that date in response to a demand under that section shall be made in accordance with the provisions of title 17 as amended by the first section of this Act.

SEC. 111. Section 2318 of title 18 of the United States Code is amended to read as follows:

18 USC 2318.

"§ 2318. Transportation, sale or receipt of phonograph records bearing forged or counterfeit labels

"(a) Whoever knowingly and with fraudulent intent transports, causes to be transported, receives, sells, or offers for sale in interstate or foreign commerce any phonograph record, disk, wire, tape, film, or other article on which sounds are recorded, to which or upon which is stamped, pasted, or affixed any forged or counterfeited label, knowing the label to have been falsely made, forged, or counterfeited shall be fined not more than $10,000 or imprisoned for not more than one year, or both, for the first such offense and shall be fined not more than $25,000 or imprisoned for not more than two years, or both, for any subsequent offense.

"(b) When any person is convicted of any violation of subsection (a), the court in its judgment of conviction shall, in addition to the penalty therein prescribed, order the forfeiture and destruction or other disposition of all counterfeit labels and all articles to which counterfeit labels have been affixed or which were intended to have had such labels affixed.".

"(c) Except to the extent they are inconsistent with the provisions of this title, all provisions of section 509, title 17, United States Code, are applicable to violations of subsection (a).".

17 USC 501 note.

SEC. 112. All causes of action that arose under title 17 before January 1, 1978, shall be governed by title 17 as it existed when the cause of action arose.

SEC. 113. (a) The Librarian of Congress (hereinafter referred to as the "Librarian") shall establish and maintain in the Library of Congress a library to be known as the American Television and Radio Archives (hereinafter referred to as the "Archives"). The purpose of the Archives shall be to preserve a permanent record of the television and radio programs which are the heritage of the people of the United States and to provide access to such programs to historians and scholars without encouraging or causing copyright infringement.

American Television and Radio Archives Act. 2 USC 170.

(1) The Librarian, after consultation with interested organizations and individuals, shall determine and place in the Archives such copies and phonorecords of television and radio programs transmitted to the public in the United States and in other countries which are of present or potential public or cultural interest, historical significance, cognitive value, or otherwise worthy of preservation, including copies and phonorecords of published and unpublished transmission programs—

(A) acquired in accordance with sections 407 and 408 of title 17 as amended by the first section of this Act; and

(B) transferred from the existing collections of the Library of Congress; and

(C) given to or exchanged with the Archives by other libraries, archives, organizations, and individuals; and

(D) purchased from the owner thereof.

(2) The Librarian shall maintain and publish appropriate catalogs and indexes of the collections of the Archives, and shall make such collections available for study and research under the conditions prescribed under this section.

(b) Notwithstanding the provisions of section 106 of title 17 as amended by the first section of this Act, the Librarian is authorized with respect to a transmission program which consists of a regularly scheduled newscast or on-the-spot coverage of news events and, under standards and conditions that the Librarian shall prescribe by regulation—

(1) to reproduce a fixation of such a program, in the same or another tangible form, for the purposes of preservation or security or for distribution under the conditions of clause (3) of this subsection; and

(2) to compile, without abridgment or any other editing, portions of such fixations according to subject matter, and to reproduce such compilations for the purpose of clause (1) of this subsection; and

(3) to distribute a reproduction made under clause (1) or (2) of this subsection—

(A) by loan to a person engaged in research; and

(B) for deposit in a library or archives which meets the requirements of section 108(a) of title 17 as amended by the first section of this Act,

in either case for use only in research and not for further reproduction or performance.

(c) The Librarian or any employee of the Library who is acting under the authority of this section shall not be liable in any action for copyright infringement committed by any other person unless the Librarian or such employee knowingly participated in the act of infringement committed by such person. Nothing in this section shall be construed to excuse or limit liability under title 17 as amended by the first section of this Act for any act not authorized by that title or this section, or for any act performed by a person not authorized to act under that title or this section.

Citation of
section.
Appropriation
authorization.
17 USC note
prec. 101.
Severability.
17 USC note
prec. 101.

(d) This section may be cited as the "American Television and Radio Archives Act".

SEC. 114. There are hereby authorized to be appropriated such funds as may be necessary to carry out the purposes of this Act.

SEC. 115. If any provision of title 17, as amended by the first section of this Act, is declared unconstitutional, the validity of the remainder of this title is not affected.

Approved October 19, 1976.